FLOURISHING WITHIN LIMITS TO GROWTH

To my dear Ruta-Maria Kind regards

Decades of research and discussion have shown that human population growth and our increased consumption of natural resources cannot continue – there are limits to growth. This volume demonstrates how we might modify and revise our economic systems using nature as a model to sustain and flourish within these limits.

The book describes how nature uses three growth forms: biomass; information and networks, resulting in improved overall ecosystem functioning; and co-development. As biomass growth is limited by available resources, nature uses the two other growth forms to achieve higher resource use efficiency. Through a universal application of the three Rs – reduce, reuse, and recycle – nature shows us a way forward toward better solutions. However, our current approach, dominated by short-term economic thinking, inhibits full utilization of the three Rs and other successful approaches from nature.

Building on ecological principles, the authors present a global model and future scenario analysis that shows that implementation of the proposed changes will lead to a win–win situation. In other words, we can learn from nature how to develop a society that can flourish within the limits to growth with better conditions for prosperity and well-being.

Sven Erik Jørgensen is Professor of Environmental Chemistry at the University of Copenhagen, Denmark. He has received several awards, including the very prestigious Stockholm Water Prize.

Brian D. Fath is Professor in the Department of Biological Sciences, Towson University, Maryland, USA, and Research Scholar in the Advanced Systems Analysis Program at the International Institute for Applied Systems Analysis, Laxenburg, Austria.

Søren Nors Nielsen is Visiting Professor at the Section for Sustainable Transitions, Department of Planning, Aalborg University-Copenhagen, Denmark.

Federico M. Pulselli is Researcher in Environmental and Cultural Heritage Chemistry at the University of Siena, Italy.

Daniel A. Fiscus is Lecturer and Sustainability Liaison at Frostburg State University, Maryland, USA.

Simone Bastianoni is Professor of Environmental and Cultural Heritage Chemistry at the University of Siena, Italy.

"The Club of Sienna has provided a helpful review, exposition, and extension of the Club of Rome's systems modeling approach, demonstrating the increasing relevance of the 1972 book *The Limits to Growth* to problems that continue today. Especially recommended for environmental studies and economics courses."
— *Herman E. Daly, University of Maryland, USA*

"This book creates the intellectual spine for the Club of Siena, walking in the footsteps of the famous *Limits to Growth*, but turns away from the fears of collapse towards showing that staying within the limits can offer agreeable, pleasant, even wonderful living conditions. An inspiring read for those who believe in the need to change course."
— *Marina Fischer-Kowalski, Institute of Social Ecology, Vienna, Austria*

"A profound treatise of the fallacies of the growth paradigm. Plus good suggestions for flourishing within the limits. Good tax signals can make us more successful. Bravo!"
— *Ernst Ulrich von Weizsäcker, Co-President, The Club of Rome, Emmendingen, Germany*

FLOURISHING WITHIN LIMITS TO GROWTH

Following nature's way

Sven Erik Jørgensen, Brian D. Fath,
Søren Nors Nielsen, Federico M. Pulselli,
Daniel A. Fiscus, and Simone Bastianoni

Routledge
Taylor & Francis Group

LONDON AND NEW YORK

from Routledge

First published 2015
by Routledge
2 Park Square, Milton Park, Abingdon, Oxon OX14 4RN

and by Routledge
711 Third Avenue, New York, NY 10017

Routledge is an imprint of the Taylor & Francis Group, an informa business

British Library Cataloguing in Publication Data
A catalogue record for this book is available from the British Library

Library of Congress Cataloging-in-Publication Data
Jørgensen, Sven Erik, 1934–
 Flourishing within limits to growth : following nature's way / Sven Erik Jørgensen, Brian D.
Fath, Simone Bastianoni, Daniel A. Fiscus, Søren Nors Nielsen and Federico M. Pulselli.
  pages cm
 Includes bibliographical references and index.
 1. Sustainable development. 2. Conservation of natural resources. 3. Natural resources
management. 4. Nature—Effect of human beings on. 5. Consumption (Economics)
6. Population. I. Title.
 HC79.E5J665 2015
 338.9'27—dc23
 2015003745

ISBN: 978-1-138-84252-6 (hbk)
ISBN: 978-1-138-84253-3 (pbk)
ISBN: 978-1-315-73144-5 (ebk)

Typeset in Bembo
by Apex CoVantage, LLC

The publication of this book has been supported by the Velux Foundation.

CONTENTS

PREFACE

In April 2010, at a symposium in Siena about sustainability and how to use ecological models to assess sustainability, the results of the Club of Rome and the general use of global economic-ecological models were discussed. The general agreement was that the Club of Rome results were very important contributions to the ongoing discussion about the unsustainable global development, which – as shown by the *Limits to Growth* books – inevitably will lead to a collapse due to our overexploitation of the Earth. However, economic priorities dominate almost all political decisions and the direction of development. The very clear messages from the *Limits to Growth* books have had hardly any effect on global development since the first *Limits to Growth* book was published and widely debated in 1972. In Siena, we discussed why the books had such little impact to change the direction of development; we concluded that it was probably because politicians and economists could not reconcile a long-term reduction of the growth of population, production, use of resources, and pollution to more straight forward, concrete initiatives with preferably visible short-term agendas. The controlling growth-oriented paradigm has the advantage of status quo and can work effectively during early periods of development but eventually, as resources become limiting, should naturally give way to more qualitative development. This turn-the-corner transition from growth to development was not agreeable with the current mindsets and approaches of the 1970s. The reality of resource shocks, such as the oil shortages and the recent financial crises, have only made the message more urgent, but an appropriate response has not come from the politicians. Nature has coped with the same problems of balancing growth and development, and therefore it is sensible to ask how nature deals with this situation. By imitating nature, we could launch a workable plan to manage overexploitation. Of course, the benefits from such a plan must be recognized by politicians, economists, and the general public. We do not have political power, but we could develop a very clear, easily applied, and understood plan based on the principles that nature follows to achieve sustainable development without relying on overexploitation to fuel growth only-oriented policies. Our nature-inspired plan is tested on a global ecological-economic model similar to the models developed and applied by the *Limits to Growth* books. More importantly, we want to refocus the debate away from the fears that come with the concept of no growth toward the advantages of a system that focuses on qualitative development. The restrictions imposed by *Limits to Growth* do not entail stagnation and strife but rather give an opportunity for new priorities, greater equity, and higher well-being. Living within the limits can offer agreeable, pleasant, even thriving and wonderful living conditions. Therefore, the message of the Club of Siena, presented in this book, is the possibility and processes necessary on how to flourish within these limits.

The book consists of nine chapters. After an introduction and a presentation of the important *Limits to Growth* books in Chapters 1 and 2, Chapter 3 presents an overview of ecological principles describing the main drivers for nature, to the best of our understanding, to operate as a sustainable system. Nature avoids overexploitation and uses a development strategy that considers limits to growth: trees are not growing into the sky, resources are used sustainably, and depletion is avoided by complete recirculation. Chapter 4 translates these principles into rules that we can implement in society, while Chapter 5 tests these rules on a global model to be able to answer the crucial questions: Can it work? Can the principles of nature be used to solve our sustainability problems and to avoid a major collapse with all the disastrous consequences? Chapter 6 discusses the eternal problem: is it better to introduce nature's principles through a top-down or bottom-up approach; the chapter also gives successful examples on how nature's principles have been applied locally and regionally to solve specific environmental problems. The results of employing nature's principles in our society presented using a global model in Chapter 5 are very clear, but it would be beneficial to elucidate the results further to supplement the investigation with two other angles: to apply the widely used ecological footprint and to use a sustainability analysis based on work energy as an indicator, which have given workable results in a number of cases. Therefore, Chapters 7 and 8 are devoted to an interpretation of the model results in Chapter 5 using ecological footprints and a sustainability analysis based on work energy. The last chapter has the title "Can we overcome the obstacles?" The conclusion is that the three chapters with the global results – Chapters 5, 7, and 8 – present the action items in such a clear language that the politicians and economists ought to understand it, but, if not the case, then the population in all democratic countries will be able to understand the clear headlines and provoke a change. Ironically, the changes are not a question about sacrificing our well-being – on the contrary, it will ensure it because the society will reorganize in a structure that is fairer, offer more well-being, have more logic and realism in the sense that the limits are considered, be longer lasting, and increase equality.

The six authors have many colleagues and scientific friends and know many people who are interested in the focal theme of the book, and we have therefore invited everybody who can approve the main lines of the book (but not necessarily all the details) and its main messages to join the **Club of Siena**. Hopefully it could be a beginning to a movement of all that have acknowledged that a change close to what is formulated as the 12 recommendations in Chapter 9 is urgently needed. Millions have already accepted that changes are needed due to the limits to growth, but the Club of Siena idea is to make it concrete and easily applicable politically and economically to guide the development to cope with the limits. If you are interested in joining the Club of Siena, then please use the blog at www.clubofsiena.dk. We will include your name in our list of members that will be accessible on the blog, currently updated, and referred to in coming discussions. The blog is also open for exchange of opinions and ideas about the focus and the content of the book.

The publication has been supported by the Velux Foundation.

The authors are grateful for the support that will be applied to strengthen the dissemination of our message.

Sven Erik Jørgensen and Søren Nors Nielsen, *Copenhagen, January 2015*

Simone Bastianoni and Federico Pulselli, *Siena, January 2015*

Brian D. Fath, *Towson, January 2015*

Dan Fiscus, *Frostburg, January 2015*

1

INTRODUCTION

Natural principles of chemistry, mechanics and biology are not merely limits. They're invitations to work along with them.

—Jane Jacobs, *The Nature of Economies*, 2000, p. 12

1.1 Uncontrolled growth

The worst economic crisis since the 1930s started in 2008, and the industrialized countries have hardly recovered by 2014. The crisis was blamed on a combination of lax Wall Street oversight, short-term profit taking (essentially gambling), risky loans, a naïve belief in continuously increasing real estate prices (and policies to encourage this bubble), and an irresponsible use of state money in some Southern European countries, to name the major culprits. Yet, rarely in the mainstream media did one read about the problem in terms of a fundamentally flawed economic structure or a real debate to use the crash to implement new, economic approaches. One notable exception was Thomas Friedman, reporter and author, who wrote in 2009 in the *New York Times* that the crisis may show something very fundamental being more than just a temporary recession in the normal business cycle. The crisis, in his opinion, revealed that the basic economic growth model used as a compass for our decisions during the last 60 years has failed and the next warning may be a major collapse. He was not the first to propose this vision, but it is one that needs much further attention, as we explore in this book. This is in contrast to most economists and politicians who claim that the crisis is provisional and momentary, not structural. In this mainstream worldview, the medicine politicians in industrialized countries prescribed to recover the ailing economy was growth, more growth, and "back to normal growth," whatever that means. Not one world leader questioned the neoliberal, growth-oriented economy or proposed an alternative socioeconomic structure to avoid new crises or to meet the challenges of the future such as unemployment/underemployment, diminishing financial capital, human misery and alienation, loss of community and sense of place, resource shortages, climate change, and the general deterioration of nature and thereby the services that it provides to human societies. An apt description is given in the book *Enough is Enough* by Rob Dietz and Dan O'Neill (2013) (see Note 1). It is no secret that the dominant economic philosophy of modernity is *more* – more people and more production, more money and more consumption. Employers try to earn more income, business managers try to report more revenue on the balance sheet, and politicians try to ensure that the economy can provide steadily more goods and more services.

Physical growth cannot continue indefinitely because the Earth has only finite resources. Nature sets limits to growth. Natural laws that inexorably must be obeyed tell us that unlimited growth is impossible. Even the most conservative politician or economist has to admit that, but no structural changes to the economy or society are pursued and implemented. There were hopes in 2012 due to the Rio+20 Conference (United Nations Conference on Sustainable Development in Brazil on June 20–22, 2012) and the COP 18 (United Nations Framework Convention on Climate Change, 18th meeting of the Conference of the Parties held in Doha, Qatar, November 26 to December 7, 2012), but all hopes were crushed when the results of these global events were presented. Nations are more occupied with the ongoing financial crisis than with finding solutions to the far greater, long-term problems that we are facing in the coming decades: how do we stop our depredation of nature, which is the very basis for our life on Earth? Most discouraging is the lack of understanding regarding how the economic crises and environmental degradation are linked. The very solutions to the global environmental crisis will in fact set the course to a more sustainable economic system, such that one problem cannot be addressed in isolation. Rather than heed the advice of scientists and seek an approach that addresses environment, society, and economy as a complex, integrated whole, we focus on putting the economic machinery back the way that it was, knowing full well that similar crises will arise in the future. Thousands of pages have been written about the irrational, uncontrolled, and unintelligent misuse of our global resources, but any changes have been at the margins, tinkering with rates and efficiencies, not fundamentally addressing the systemic needs. Most economists and politicians are deaf or blind to the signals about them as well as the loud shouts for changes. A Nobel Symposium on Global Sustainability in Stockholm in May 2011 warned against the global predicament that we are facing, but politicians are not listening to natural scientists but rather let orthodox economists dominate the decision making. There seems to be a sound barrier between the world of economists and politicians on the one side and long-term reality and natural scientists on the other side. How do we break through the sound barrier?

Confronting crises and resource limitations is nothing new. In 1972, the Club of Rome published the well-known book *The Limits to Growth*, in which they used several global model scenarios to demonstrate that population growth and the growth of our consumption of natural resources, both renewable and non-renewable, cannot continue without precipitating a collapse – there *are* limits to growth. Business as usual in 1972 regarding the growth rates of human population, of the withdrawal of renewable and nonrenewable resources, and of pollution emissions would inevitably lead to a collapse. But the global population and politicians have not followed the prudent advice of the Club of Rome because the controlling factors of society are obviously tethered to a short-term perspective, not wise long-term planning. One reason for inaction was the scenarios were painted as too dire and unwelcoming, not motivational and attractive enough to steer the global population toward them. The idea of limits was derided as pessimistic and not relevant to our modern conditions – yes, maybe Malthus had to worry about natural resources when the population was directly dependent on land for a living, but today's economy is service-based, and economists insisted that perfect substitutability could solve any resource constraints. Therefore, little action was taken.

The world has experience with systems that on the surface appear completely different, notably socialism in the former Soviet Union and communism in China; however, both were governed and dominated by a growth paradigm. The Soviet Union failed for some of the same reasons that caused the global crisis in 2008: human selfishness, misuse of resources, and shortsightedness. We have to acknowledge, in Mahatma Gandhi's words, that "there is enough for everyone's need, but not for everyone's greed." Is being selfish, shortsighted, and therefore unfortunately also foolishly self-destructive embedded in our genes? Or are we like teenagers that never listen to parents' advice but instead only learn firsthand through their own experience? However, if we need a collapse before we perceive what we need to do, then it would be too late.

Perhaps being self-destructive is a characteristic of any technologically advanced society. Since the 1960s, we have built a chain of radio-telescopes that have been listening to radio signals that might emanate from other civilizations. Drake (Note 2) has calculated that if a technologically advanced society has a lifetime of 1,000 years, we should find 25 other societies in our galaxy with at least our level of technology. Of course, if a civilization's lifetime is more than 1,000 years, the probability is correspondingly higher – for instance, if the lifetime is 10,000 years, we should find 250 other technologically advanced societies on planets in our galaxy. We have now been listening to radio signals for about 50 years with no contact with other civilizations. It would be unfortunate to conclude that intelligent life is inevitably self-destructive, or expressed differently: intelligent life is self-destructive before it becomes sufficiently intelligent to understand how to cooperate meaningfully with each other and with nature. Maybe our species has the wrong name and should not be called *Homo sapiens* but *Homo not-yet-sapiens*. Drake's equation can, of course, be criticized for being too optimistic (Note 2), and other calculations indicate that there are maybe only two other technologically advanced planets if the lifetime for an advanced civilization is 10,000 years.

Similarly, China and the other emerging economies have not learned from the mistakes of North America, Europe, and Japan: that it pays better to integrate environmental considerations into all projects from the very beginning. This was the clear experience learned from the mistakes in the 1950s, '60s, and '70s by the industrialized countries. China wanted, however, economic growth as fast as possible during the last 20 years, but now the Chinese leaders acknowledge that the fast growth has generated many environmental problems that China must solve. Air quality is so poor in many major cities that people are opting to wear masks, and the overall livability of these areas is being questioned. Solutions to the problems are much more expensive now than if they were integrated step-by-step during all phases of the projects.

The Limits to Growth and other books have clearly defined the problems and made the consequences of not shifting direction very apparent. The messages they promote, however, have not changed the direction of global development very much – maybe slightly if we use our very positive "glasses," but very far from sufficiently. We are still directed toward a collapse. The present economic crisis is just a symptom of the disease: the idea of continuous, resource-based economic growth as the primary organizing factor for society. Another approach should be used as a compass for our development.

With this book, we would like to present a possible alternative pathway to avoid the threatening collapse based on changing the economy from an end goal in decision making to a means toward realizing sustainable communities. Primarily, this requires a reorientation from growth to development – from a quantitative concept to a qualitative one and from short-term to long-term considerations. We will be careful and mindful here to refer to quantitative change only as growth and qualitative change as development. When global annual car production increases, this is a quantitative growth, while the increasing efficiency of the produced vehicle motors constitutes development, for example. We will furthermore emphasize the need for systems thinking and holistic approaches and solutions. The economy provides roles in which individuals can productively contribute to the overall society. It is a fundamental and necessary aspect of our societies, but it should serve us as a useful tool. We should not be beholden to the economy but rather be its boss. The preconditions for a sustainable economy are clear: 1) it is a subsystem of the global ecology, 2) it has to reach for optima not maxima, and 3) it must be based on real physical-chemical-biological transactions, not on virtual or speculative exchanges. *Homo sapiens* are shortsighted but also ambitious to solve problems. How can we improve our quality of life, alleviate poverty, and provide meaningful employment to everyone willing? If one idea is not working, then we are open-minded to try to find another approach that is better. Humans strive for betterment and attempt to find solutions to urgent problems. We need to have goals and see the horizon. Therefore, development should not be stopped, but we can direct it from quantitative growth to qualitative development, which can continue in the face of physical limits. This shift is even a must, as constraints will render the present quantitative growth imperative unattainable and unsustainable. The constraints are clearly defined in the laws of nature. We know that, but how can we change the economy and the growth paradigm toward sustainable development? We could learn from nature, which has been constantly developing and sustaining for a period of almost four billion years. Catastrophes have massively destroyed nature from time to time, but nature recovers and finds new ways to develop under changing conditions. Which properties of nature have ensured this steady, sustainable, and persisting development? How has nature been able to utilize qualitative development when quantitative growth is no longer possible due to limits? We could imitate how nature has been able to bypass the problems of continuous growth. This book proposes to learn from nature how to change the direction of human development to solve the gigantic problems that we are facing. This entails not only the economic crisis, because it is just a symptom caused by our irrational and unintelligent economic system, but also the real and very serious problem that we are destroying the conditions for sustaining our life on Earth.

1.2 Different types of quantitative growth

Growth can occur more or less rapidly, which implies that we approach the limits to growth at different rates. Four types of growth are important for our understanding of the global problems that we are facing. The four types will be used several times in Chapters 2–9. Therefore, they are defined and presented here in the Introduction:

1) Zero growth occurs when the focal variable is constant. The state is not zero or dead but not increasing or decreasing because there is a balance between inputs and outputs. The rate of change, as given by the first derivative of the state variable, is zero. For instance, it would be ideal if we could stop carbon dioxide growth in the atmosphere. This would level the atmospheric greenhouse gas concentration and stabilize the climate. Under conditions for this to occur, our emissions to the atmosphere must be balanced by sequestration out of the atmosphere. Figure 1.1 illustrates no growth.

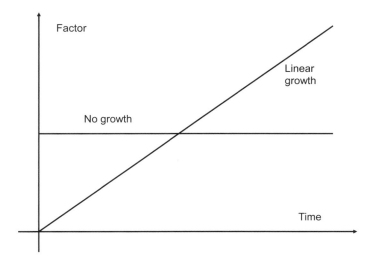

FIGURE 1.1 Illustration of a variable or factor without growth and a factor (variable) growing linearly.

2) Linear growth means that the considered variable is increasing (growing) with the same amount per unit of time. The growth (increase per unit of time) is therefore constant. The population of many towns has increased linearly over a certain phase of time. Figure 1.1 illustrates linear growth.

3) Exponential growth occurs when the growth of the variable increases at the same rate per unit of time. This type of growth corresponds to the growth of capital in an interest-bearing account as it compounds according to the interest and the interest on the interest, and so on. This is called first-order growth because the growth rate is directly proportional to the amount. Therefore, the acceleration (= increase in growth rate) is constant. A state variable with exponential growth experiences a constant doubling time – to go from two to four, from four to eight, or from eight to 16 and so on requires the same time. It is relentless and rewarding early, becoming instable and insidious late. If one of your ancestors would have deposited one cent in a bank with an annual interest rate of 5 percent 1,000 years ago, then today you would inherit 1,000 times all the capital in the world. Of course, this is impossible, meaning that exponential growth does not continue unabated. Our consumption of fossil fuel has increased exponentially, on average about 2.33 percent per year, for the last many years. Continuing such conditions going forward requires that the total consumption of fossil fuel doubles in about 30 years, and will be four times the present level 60 years from now, eight times the present level 90 years from now, and so on. Given the resource constraints imposed by nature, these doublings are unrealistic, so a lowering of the growth rate will be imminent. Therefore, without improved efficiency or implementation of sequestration technologies, the carbon dioxide emissions to the atmosphere will be twice as much 30 years from now, four times as much in 60 years, and so on. Figure 1.2 illustrates exponential growth. The British scholar Malthus claimed over 200 years ago that exponential growth of the population could not continue and it would lead to famine and disease and a collapse known as a Malthusian catastrophe.

4) Logistic growth starts as exponential growth but is regulated by a carrying capacity or a limit. The state variable increases with the same percentage per unit of time but at the same time is regulated (reduced) more and more as the value approaches the carrying capacity. Figure 1.2 compares exponential and logistic growth curves. The latter shows an s-shape. The amount of increase is greater and greater in the beginning and will then diminish due to regulation from the carrying capacity. Many factors in nature follow logistic growth. For instance, the size of an organism often grows according to logistic growth. A population exposed to new (and better) conditions follows logistic growth. When the regulation is not tight (due to time delays or indirect feedback), growth follows a path that exceeds the carrying capacity in a process known as overshoot. The system is then forced into decline either gradually or by collapse. Exceeding the carrying capacity may degrade the environment in such a way that the carrying capacity itself is lowered. Mathematical expressions for the four types of growth are presented in Box 1.1.

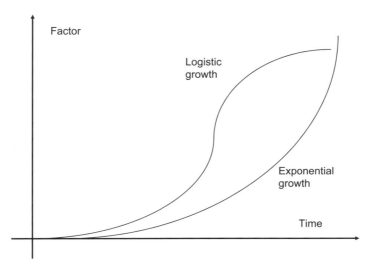

FIGURE 1.2 Exponential and logistic growth curves are illustrated by the graph.

Box 1.1 Four standard growth forms and the equations that describe them (for further details, see Note 3).

Assume we have a state variable such as number of fish in a lake at a certain time. Let us call that variable X to indicate the condition and the growth rate, and use K to notate the carrying capacity of the system. The state variable and rate of growth are governed by the following equations.

Growth form	State variable	Growth rate
Zero growth	Constant	0
Linear growth	Constant × time	Constant
Exponential growth	Constant × e^{time}	Constant × time
Logistic growth	$\dfrac{K}{1 + e^{(a - constant \times time)}}$	Constant × time × $(1 - X/K)$

These basic growth forms need to be understood in context with our economic and social systems as well. Exponential growth, for certain, cannot continue indefinitely, so a system that relies on borrowing and interest is inherently unsustainable. The conclusion is that we need to modify and revise the economic system and our economic goals. We need to understand there are better ways to achieve harmony between humans and nature and that we have to redefine the economy and even the meaning of the word growth. But most importantly, we recognize clearly now that constraints are not only negative. They challenge us to find innovative and transformative solutions. Therefore, the message in this book is steered not toward the limits but the possibilities within the limits. Nature has managed quite success-fully to construct and maintain complex, wonderful, diverse, creative systems in spite of the constraints. Therefore, just as in nature, our aim is to learn how we may flourish within the limits. The message of the Club of Siena is cast as an addition to the important message of the Club of Rome. The economic and environmental crises are two sides of the same coin. The problems causing both are the same and can only be eliminated by shifting to another economic structure.

1.3 The content of the book

Chapter 2 reviews the book, *The Limits to Growth*, and the six books that have been published to follow up on the original idea from 1972. The latest is the book by J. Randers, *2052*, which predicts world conditions in 2052, presuming humans follow different but very probable scenarios. A few other books focusing on the same theme are mentioned in this chapter. The crucial question is: will there be social and political will to shift direction? The books that we mention and discuss in this chapter show clearly that a collapse is waiting around the corner if we do not alter business as usual. In accordance with the books, we will have to radically slow down population growth, growth of industrial production, our consumption of resources, and our emissions of pollutants to the environment. The key problem is, however, that we know what to do, but we do not do it because humans are dominated in their decisions by the short-term economic benefits. The incredibly passive reactions by particular politicians to the limits to growth debate imply that the business-as-usual attitude is dominant. We address in this chapter why politi-cians have been passive and why practically nothing has changed, although the consequences of continuing the same procedure are made very clear in these books. We conclude that a change in the social-economic structure is needed to be able to control the economic growth better than we do today. We must dig deeper to understand why such clear messages as presented in the *Limits to Growth* books are not adopted politically and economically. It is obviously not sufficient to shout that the wolf is coming. Must we wait until the wolf has attacked before the population and the politicians awake? Must much of Florida be flooded before it is understood in the United States that global warming is threatening our life and it is associated with our over-reliance and exploitation of fossil fuels? Or, can we change some structural elements in our society that will facilitate our understanding of the prob-lems and shift development in another direction? In this context, we could learn from nature, which is the focus of Chapter 3. The unfolding of the problems as they have been presented by the key environmental books during the last 40 years will hopefully give an understanding of how serious the problems are and that inaction cannot be accepted. Chapters 3–6 delve into the structural changes we have to introduce in society to be able push the economy and policies in another direction so that the problems are considered much more seriously by decision makers in all fields.

Chapter 3 presents how nature deals with the problems of limited resources. We identify and discuss 14 very significant properties of ecosystems – the systems of nature. We articulate how ecosystems manage to avoid, to a large extent, the same obstacles as our societies. It is rooted in four billion years of experience and steady evolution within the 14 mentioned properties. Nature has, of course, experienced catastrophic events caused by external factors, but nature has been capable to recover after major catastrophes and to benefit from both quantitative growth, when the timing is right, and qualitative development. We should and could learn from nature how to change the social-economic structure and pathways to manage both quantitative growth and qualitative development.

Chapter 4 presents how we could adopt nature's 14 properties in our society. Specifically, we describe how our society could differ from today, particularly the "everyday" consequences of adopting these properties. A green society with a green economy would be heavily based on the simple, yet crucial, three Rs of resource management: reduce, reuse, and recycle. Reduction is the primary strategy, but, when not possible, finding reuse or then recycling will help our material flow balance in a limited world. The consequences of adopting nature's 14 properties are a changed economic structure based on the three Rs along with a massive investment in education, innovation, research, and better global cooperation among the countries and their people. It is particularly important in this context that the developed countries invest in better education in the developing countries, which will lead to a win–win situation. It is touched again and again in this chapter that economics cannot solve our problems because the economists simply do not have the answer to the problems. Their answer back to "normal" growth does not work in a world with limited resources.

Chapter 5 answers the crucial question: How will adopting nature's 14 properties change the future for humans? Can we cope with the gigantic problems that we otherwise are facing? We develop a model based on the original *The Limits to Growth* book and update it with our scenarios based on implementing nature's 14 properties. The model details are presented in the Appendix. Model scenario results are presented as graphs and tables in this chapter. These model scenarios give robust evidence that we could and should learn from nature to build a sustainable future. We should, however, examine the consequences of the implemented changes in more details and from different angles, which leads to the content of the next chapters.

Chapter 6 explores the view that part of our problem is improperly understanding the current human crisis and also seeing clearly that nature and living ecosystems provide pragmatic examples of how to solve the crisis. We need to revise our most basic ideas and mental models of life, environment, and the relationship between life and environment. Our current scientific paradigm of life science, and our current mainstream image of life in modern industrial culture, focuses on organisms and individuals as fundamental units of life (and fundamental units of economies, i.e., the rational individual). As long as this remains our dominant scientific model and single cultural image, we mainly study isolated population dynamics, and we get stuck grappling with seemingly irreconcilable choices between either using the environment for human needs or in saving the environment for itself. If we adopted a new paradigm of life and environment in which the two are integrated into a single, holistic life-environment system, then this apparent paradox goes away.

We present, and continue to develop, a holistic science paradigm that integrates three major subdisciplines of biology/ecology to provide a progressive view of life and nature, which we believe then provides better means to apply nature's lessons, successes, and role models to solve human–environment problems. Our proposed paradigm involves dual and complementary models of life, analogous to dual and complementary models of light in physics. We propose that organisms and individuals represent "discrete life" (similar to particles or photons of light), while communities, ecosystems, and the biosphere represent "sustained life" (similar to nonlocal and wave aspects of light). Examples of win–win relations are presented. Finally, in this chapter, we suggest applications, tests, and further work to explore how such a revised foundation for life-environment science can be applied to serve human needs.

Chapter 7 presents the concept of ecological footprint and uses this ecological approach to examine and compare the alternative developments tested in the global model in Chapter 5. The conclusions are similar to those in Chapter 6, but they are based on a different viewpoint that supports the overall conclusions from another angle. The chapter touches on and discusses briefly the balance between renewable and nonrenewable resource use. In this chapter, we examine the interrelations between ecological footprint, biocapacity, ecological economic measures, and gross national product (GNP).

Chapter 8 presents the application of work energy capacity as a measure for sustainability. The idea is that all activities require energy that can do work for us. It is possible to distinguish between energy that can do work and energy that cannot do work. Therefore, work energy must be available for future generations so they can choose activities that meet their own desires. We use work energy capacity as an indicator to show how one deviates from a sustainable pathway when society depends on fossil fuels, deforestation, overfishing, and the extensive use of nonrenewable resources. The focus is to compare the indicator expressed as work energy for the present development with the indicator that we can expect if the changes presented in Chapters 4–6 are followed. The alternative developments presented in Chapters 4–6 and their consequences for the Earth are discussed in this chapter. Evidence from real life of how this future might play out exists on a Danish island that largely relies on renewable energy. The chapter uses this case study to demonstrate that it *is* possible to change the direction of development radically and to flourish within the limits. The analysis is based on a carbon balance model for the island and uses work energy as a sustainability indicator. The conclusion from this case study is also – which is particularly important – that development has to be bottom-up, that is, from the people to the politicians and other leaders, not ordered top-down from the leaders to the people. It cannot be excluded that the needed drastic changes will be a democratic requirement of the population, rather than a vision of the politicians.

Chapter 9 summarizes the implementation of nature's properties as our guideline for development and new approaches in our societies. In the chapter, we discuss the political issues, the probable obstacles, and other difficulties the proposed changes to our societies inevitably will meet. This chapter confronts the obvious and important questions: Is it possible to implement the proposed changes in our societies? And, if yes, then how? Or, if not, then is collapse inevitable? Or is a collapse needed before we really can understand that a major shift is absolutely necessary? The answer can be seen as the conclusion of the previous eight chapters.

2
LIMITS TO GROWTH

Trees cannot grow into the sky.

2.1 The Club of Rome

The 1972 book *The Limits to Growth* was a report for the Club of Rome's project on the human predicament, under the leadership of MIT systems scientist Donella H. Meadows. The core of the project was to erect a world model that could be used to produce scenarios about global development given specified conditions. The global development is described by a number of state (or internal) variables in the model literature. They chose a parsimonious model with a few key state variables that could adequately represent the main conditions for the focal system – in this case the Earth. The 11 state variables selected were:

1. Nonrenewable resources
2. Service capital
3. Industrial capital
4. Agricultural capital
5. Population aged 0–14 years
6. Population aged 15–45 years
7. Population aged above 45 years
8. Pollution
9. Urban and industrial land
10. Arable land
11. Potential arable land.

The model results were influenced by the resource use assumptions in the various scenarios. For example: How do we regulate population growth or the rate of non-renewable resource use? How much do we develop industries, the service sectors, or agriculture? These interactions are named forcing functions or external variables in the modeling literature. They determine the conditions for growth and development. The relations between the state variables and forcing functions are described using known process-based relations and a number of statistical correlations.

The model gives an experimental laboratory that is used to explore various conditions that may or may not arise in the real system and to prognosticate future outcomes. The purpose of the world model is to answer questions about these various scenarios. For example, we can simulate the response of the state variables to differing conditions established by a chosen set of forcing functions, the selection of which is directly and strongly dependent on our policies. From these conditions, it is possible to estimate the course of global development.

The standard – business as usual – world model run assumes no major changes in the conditions. Under this scenario, in 2050, when the global population reaches its maximum, the most important state variables will show the following values:

1. Population will be 9–9.5 billion.
2. Pollution will be slightly less than today (year 2013); however, it would increase significantly if the initial resources would be larger than presumed in the model and we would use these resources at a higher rate, creating faster industrial production growth.
3. Available food per capita will decrease about 10% compared with the present level.
4. Industrial output per capita will be about 40% lower than today. The maximum value of this state variable occurs in 2013 in the simulation.
5. Resources would be slightly less than one half of today's value, which again is 40% of the value of the resources at year 1900, which was the starting year for the simulations.

In other words, the baseline model simulation points toward a resource crisis. One could conclude from this that the present socioeconomic system is headed toward collapse shortly after 2050. By then, there is a dramatic decrease in industrial output and significantly reduced resources, which would make it very difficult, if not impossible, to recover our industrial production.

The other scenarios presume various modifications to the baseline intended to stabilize the outcomes. One scenario presumes that population growth stops in 1975 and another that the industrial growth capital is stabilized at the 1985 level. Neither of these scenarios is realistic to use today for the calculations as they have already passed. Both scenarios and also scenarios based on increased economic allocation toward food production and services show, however, a very significant difference from the business-as-usual scenario. The resources in 2050 are three to six times higher for all these scenarios than by the business-as-usual scenario. Furthermore, pollution is much lower and food per capita much higher, while the industrial output per capita is higher. The depletion of the resources that causes the collapse shortly after the year 2050 in the business-as-usual scenario is prevented.

The message from this original *The Limits to Growth* model was very clear: we cannot continue business as usual but have to stop population growth, pollution increases, and our rapidly growing use of natural resources. If we do not change direction, then we will be confronted with a dramatic collapse in the conditions that provide a high quality of life, probably during the second half of the 21st century.

There was little to no reaction from politicians to the original Club of Rome message. The economists, when commenting at all on the project, heavily criticized it: the prognoses are unrealistic as they do not take into consideration society's inevitable technological progress or the future regulations, and so on. The Club of Rome project was nevertheless a first audacious attempt to make a world model, and it did not present prognoses *but* rather scenarios. The debate was sometimes dominated by unfair criticism of the book because it was not pretending to do more than ask the questions about how the main factors of our society will change if we do not change our development path. The model was able to explore whether or not the negative outcomes could be averted with better control of growth, particularly population and resource consumption. The results of the scenarios should provoke a change – it was the intention of the project.

The critical voices, notably economists and politicians, also used several assumptions that were cornucopian, at least on a long-term basis. They claimed that: 1) we have been able to increase agricultural production over the last decades, and nothing indicates that we cannot continue this into the future; 2) we are continuously finding new resources, and this will compensate for the growing demand of resources; 3) we have not yet exploited the enormous resources in the oceans; and so on. There was no discussion among the critical voices of some of the most basic laws of nature – thermodynamics and the conservation principles – that are inexorably valid for our life on Earth. The critics seem to believe that by denying their validity we can solve the problems, yet even they have to accept the laws of physics.

The message of *The Limits to Growth* was very clear but very inconvenient. It is almost impossible – or at least very, very difficult – to stop the growth because the dominant neoliberal capitalistic system presumes and even requires economic growth. Since the materialistic standard of living increased rapidly in North America, Europe, and Japan in the 1950s and 1960s, politicians feared that a reduction of the growth rate would prevent their reelection. The message was counter to the perceived conventional wisdom and status quo and had practically no effect on the growth rates.

Two years after *The Limits to Growth* came *Mankind at the Turning Point, The Second Report to The Club of Rome* by Mihajlo Mesarovic and Eduard Pestel. This book gave more details, such as accounting for variable development of the different continents. It took into consideration that industrial capital growth and industrial production occur primarily in the industrial countries, while the poorest countries have the highest population growth.

The book *Reshaping the International Order* (published in 1977), with Jan Tinberger as coordinator, proposed to create a new international order to address the global problems that were evident after the publication of *The Limits to Growth*. The book contains many good ideas on how to improve international organizations with the scope of making radical changes in the course of societal development. The book presents a coherent vision, but again the politicians did not launch the needed action. In this context, we should quote Nelson Mandela's saying: "A vision without action is just a dream and an action without vision is just to let the time pass, but a vision with action can turn the world." And this is what is needed: to turn the world.

2.2 Doomsday or collapse

The 1970s were dominated by a number of books focusing on similar themes as *The Limits to Growth* but without presenting a world model. In 1970, Gordon Rattray Taylor published a book titled *Doomsday*. The book considers, as does *The Limits to Growth*, population growth, increasing pollution, and growing resource consumption and also discusses the impacts on the Earth of some very large engineering projects, global warming, the possibilities of nuclear war, and how many anthropogenic activities radically change the balance of nature. The book uses the term "technological nightmare," meaning that the root of our crisis is technology, but technology can be used for human benefit or detriment. It is the economic and politic decisions that determine how technology should be applied. Innovative ideas cannot be stopped, but how they are used and implemented can be steered through political discourse. It is up to humans to make the best possible decisions on the directions of technological innovation.

Global climate change was not discussed publicly very much in the 1970s, but it was discussed scientifically, including a brief mention in G.R. Taylor's book. The first models running scenarios of increasing atmospheric carbon dioxide concentration and simulating the temperature rise were developed in the mid-1970s. The computers were not sufficiently powerful to make predictions about the global temperature distribution, but the models could estimate the rise in global average temperature and humidity. The models (see Note 4) could include practically all known relevant mechanisms, and the results were actually very close to the results of today's more complex models. They were based on a continuous exponential growth (2% per year) in fossil fuel use. The results of one of several models (Jørgensen and Mejer 1976) (see Note 4) are shown as an illustration of the global average models in Figure 2.1. The scenario is based on a 2% increase in fossil fuel use until year 2030. After 2030, the energy consumption continues to increase 2% per year, but at the same time renewable energy is introduced with a rate such that, by 2100, 50% of the energy is renewable energy. It is a modest shift to renewable energy – much less than needed if the problem of global warming is to be solved. This represents a scenario between business as usual and a nearly acceptable solution. Some of the model results of the scenario are quoted because they are very consistent with many up-to-date model results, published currently within IPCC reports (Intergovernmental Panel on Climate Change):

1. Year 2013, the carbon dioxide concentration in the atmosphere reaches 400 parts per million (ppm), and the global temperature is about 0.8°C higher than 40 years ago. These simulation results are very close to the observations today.

2. Year 2050, the carbon dioxide concentration is calculated to be 480 ppm, and the global temperature has increased 2.3°C since 1990 (which was not very different from the temperature in 1975–1990). The temperature in 1990 is often used as initial value for the global warming simulations. This means that in 2050 we can expect a temperature increase of 1.5°C compared with the temperature today (2013) based on the scenario.

3. Year 2100, the carbon dioxide concentration has reached 650 ppm, and the temperature is 4.2°C higher than in 1990 or 3.4°C higher than today.

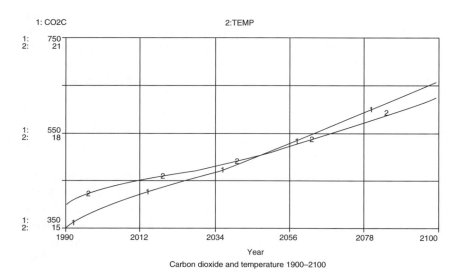

Carbon dioxide and temperature 1900–2100

FIGURE 2.1 The results of a simulation from 1990 to 2100 using the global average model mentioned in Note 4 from 1976. The simulation is based on an increase from year 1990 of the use of fossil fuel by 2% per year and a shift to renewable energy starting in year 2030 with a rate corresponding to one half of the energy demand based on fossil fuel in 2100 being covered by renewable energy. The carbon dioxide concentration is in ppm, and the temperature in degrees Celsius.

Oceanic sequestration of carbon dioxide is a slow process, and it takes decades for the carbon dioxide to reach a steady concentration in the bottom water. Therefore, to reduce the rise in temperature, we have to start phasing out the use of fossil fuels very soon, at the latest by 2020. If we start to reduce the use of fossil fuel in 2020 and have replaced it completely by alternative energy by 2060, then we will be able to limit the temperature rise during this century to 2.5–3.0°C. The two-degree increase, which was the goal five years ago, is most probably too late to reach now. The increase in atmospheric carbon dioxide concentration has continued and will continue at least during the next five to seven years, according to all available information from the two major users of fossil fuels, China and the United States.

One area of uncertainty in the climate change models is the reflectance of the Earth's surface. The model includes an albedo of 85% for ice surface and only 15% on an average land surface with vegetation. The rate of ice melting is, however, not known with a high certainty, and the models could therefore underestimate the rate and therefore underestimate the rate of global warming, too.

A global agreement about fossil fuel reduction seems, unfortunately, not around the corner. It costs a significant up-front investment to shift to alternative energy, but, ironically, it will cost more in damages due to hurricanes, flooding, climate refugees, and desertification not to make the investment. We have observed the consequences already in 2012, such as a drought in Australia and several states in the United States and the damages by Hurricane Sandy in New York and New Jersey. Major flooding caused havoc in China, the Philippines, and Thailand during 2013. The same year, the Philippines had 25 hurricanes, including the strongest ever measured on land, Haiyan, which killed more than 10,000 and made more than 500,000 homeless. In early 2014, England was suffering from the worst flooding in 250 years. It will be significantly worse when the temperature increases further; in 25 years, it will probably be close to two degrees warmer than today. Given the expected climate changes, if we do not do anything, then they will inevitably lead to massive societal disruptions, such as forced migration due to coastal inundation; food and water shortages; and unbearable costs caused by hurricanes, flooding, and desertification. The sea will rise at least one meter during this century; although the industrial countries can afford to build dikes or sea walls, developing countries such as Bangladesh cannot afford it, and vast areas will be flooded by the sea.

Unfortunately, the political decisions needed to find a solution are paralyzed between the necessary short-term costs and the long-term consequences. Furthermore, politicians are under pressure from the fossil fuel companies and cling to stories that conform to their fixed, pre-established conclusion regarding climate change. For example, it is common for climate denialists to refer to the specific, isolated points of uncertainty, yet they have no valid alternative scientific justification for the observations that do not include anthropogenic activities, primarily combustion of fossil fuels. It has been shown (Note 5) that some of the few scientists talking against the general consensus were funded by the oil industry. Today, there is no doubt at all that:

- experiments in laboratories clearly demonstrate that certain gases, namely carbon dioxide, methane, nitrous oxide, ozone, and fluorinated hydrocarbons, absorb infrared radiation and have a well-defined and determined greenhouse effect;
- monitoring and observations unambiguously show the rising level of greenhouse gases in the atmosphere;
- models published in the 1970s or later all show the actually observed carbon dioxide concentration and the corresponding temperature rise in 2012, respectively, 399 ppm and about 0.8°C;
- there has been a rise in sea levels;
- carbon absorption in the oceans has increased, leading to production of carbonic acid and a lowering of oceanic pH; and
- we have begun to see the consequences by more frequent hurricanes, drought, flooding, and more variable and extreme weather in general.

2.3 We need to think in systems

The book by Donella (Dana) Meadows, *Thinking in Systems, A Primer*, was published in 2008 (see Note 6). Dana had completed the book in 1993, but it was not published until seven years after she died unexpectedly in 2001. The book belongs to the series of *Limits to Growth* books. *The Limits to Growth* book in 1972 probably represents the first attempt to model the entire Earth as an economic-social-ecological system, using systems thinking in the conceptual framing and scenarios. *All* the central problems that humans are facing require systems thinking and cannot be solved separately, as they are strongly connected. Let us mention the most important ones:

1. Can we provide enough food for a growing population?
2. How will the climate change under various energy policies (discussed earlier)? How will the changes influence the conditions for human well-being?
3. How can we abate poverty in developing countries so their populations have a better life and reduce the number of economic refugees at the same time?
4. How can we offer *all* children (girls and boys) in the world a proper education?
5. We have – as will also be discussed in Chapters 4 and 5 – a number of possibilities to slow down human population growth, but how can we obtain the best effect of these initiatives?
6. Which are the most effective combinations of renewable energy alternatives, considering the limited economy we are facing?

We need a systems approach to answer these questions because the problems are rooted in many interacting, coherently organized components with associated processes. The components and the processes can, of course, be analyzed one by one, but this reductionist approach will not reveal the system properties because the system is more than just the sum of the elements (components and their processes).

The system has, as we say, emergent properties. A human being is, for instance, more than the sum of the body's $10^{14} = 100,000,000,000,000$ cells. Each cell has a very specific biochemistry and has metabolism and anabolism, activated by the genetic and environmental conditions. The cell properties cannot, however, explain that a human being can think, be emotional, feel pain, learn to read, and so on. These emergent properties are associated with a human being as a system.

Similarly, the global climate system has many interacting components, but to understand the system we need to overview the integration of the most important components and their processes and interactions. One approach to integrate these components and processes is by building models of the global climate system. It is how we could (maybe) answer questions 2 and 6 in the list. Similarly, the Club of Rome built a world model considering the 11 state variables (components) listed in the first section of this chapter. In the next chapter, we will present and discuss models of nature's systems, ecosystems. With ecosystem models in hand, we try, as we say, to see the forest for the trees. Most systems have processes that imply flows of energy, matter, and information. In the model-building phase, all three types of flows must be considered.

A systems approach is only possible by a simultaneous application of many disciplines. We need multidisciplinary and interdisciplinary research and policy making. In a book titled *Bankrupting Nature* by Anders Wijkman and Johan Rockström (Note 7), this is expressed in the following way: we cannot hope to solve major environmental problems such as climate change with today's fragmented and isolated scientific disciplines. Research needs to be organized on a much broader understanding of systems. An even greater problem is that despite improved understanding of how the planet works and what risks we are taking, we are not making any significant progress toward a more desirable, sustainable future. What we need is interdisciplinary science that focuses on solving problems. Fortunately, we are seeing more and more research emerging that really tries to integrate social sciences, humanities, and natural sciences. We simply have to recognize that at this crucial stage in human history, when major decisions must be made to change the course of world development, science is not really on track with systems-based solutions. We need an interdisciplinary revolution in our schools and universities to educate the coming candidates to be global problem solvers. Interdisciplinary science emerges, however, quite naturally from a focus on problem solving. The problems that we face are so complex that they require collaboration across disciplinary boundaries.

Unfortunately, systems approaches are not deeply adopted in two of the most powerful disciplines steering our socioeconomic development, namely economics and policy. Economists also make models, but orthodoxy puts the focus in most cases only on the flow of money – not the flows of information, matter, and energy. Some exceptions are the work by ecological economists or industrial ecologists who focus on material and energy flow analysis, among other things. Most economic model predictions are therefore too limited on one currency and without a direct anchoring to biophysical reality. The economic crisis starting in 2008 was a surprise for most economists. Public perception, whether optimistic or pessimistic, is very influential in economic development, as was clearly demonstrated after the start of the crisis. People in industrialized countries hesitated to spend money and are saving more, in contrast to the recommendations from politicians and economists. Economists do not typically consider these "mood" factors in their models. If they would do that, then they may have predicted the crisis in 2008 because the public, political, and business community optimism was much too high and the consumption subsequently unrealistically high. It would have been obvious that it could not continue and that the mood factors would change radically and maybe suddenly. Similarly, in 2013, populist pessimism added further drag on the economic crisis, which is not included in the economic models. In hard times such as recessions, people are reluctant to spend money, which slows a "normal" economic recovery, but which is actually beneficial environmentally as resource use is slowing down, too. Moreover, the economic models are often only looking forward a few years and do not consider the long-term effects our economy has on the resources and their impacts, notably, on climate. The role of resource constraints is not evident in many economic models, which is completely unrealistic. Consequently, it would be a clear advantage to try to build economic-ecological models as it actually has been done by the Club of Rome, but it is very difficult to persuade powerful economists to cooperate with ecologists and environmentalists. In spite of the common word origins, economy and ecology are two different perspectives that speak two different languages with different goals and time scales. Much more cooperation between these disciplines is needed such as international workshops, where economists and ecologists meet together to discuss, exchange, and even build models of global processes that include economic and ecological factors.

2.4 *Limits to Growth* is still not accepted politically

As the recommendations in *The Limits to Growth* were not followed and growth continued unabated, updates were needed to adjust the previous scenarios and to try to answer the question: what now? A 20-year update, from 1972–1992, was published in the book *Beyond the Limits*, which concluded, based on the global patterns, that humanity had already overshot the limits of the Earth's carrying (support) capacity. The book underlined the following unsustainable developmental trends:

• Rainforests were cut at an unsustainable rate – about 100,000 km² per year.
• Consequences of global warming for agricultural production was a major concern.
• Grain production could no longer keep up with population growth.

Stratospheric ozone depletion was also an issue in the 1980s, but for this problem a global agreement, which at least partially solved the problem, was set forth in the Montreal Protocol of 1987. This success, unfortunately, created an optimism that global agreements could be made for biodiversity and global warming, but no international breakthroughs have been achieved so far for these two very essential environmental problems. The Rio de Janeiro summit in 1992 brought attention to some environmental problems that we are facing, but little tangible action resulted. The Rio+10 Conference in Johannesburg, South Africa, produced even less. It was a very big disappointment for all environmentalists. There is an evident gap between talk and action (see Note 8 with reference to a recent report produced for the United Nations). The politicians excuse their lack of action with their focus on lowering unemployment. They seem not to understand that all actions that address the global long-term problems require a massive employment but, of course, also a reallocation of economic resources. Recently, President Obama expressed the general political message when he was asked about the absence of climate change policy in United States. He answered: "If we are going to ignore jobs and growth simply to address climate change, I don't think that anybody is going for that. I won't go for that." It is, however, a completely wrong judgment, as the transition to renewable energy will create many new jobs, but all politicians abuse this argument.

A second update book, *Limits to Growth: The 30-Year Update*, was published in 2002. It introduced ecological footprint as a measure of our impact on the Earth. According to the calculations presented in the book, the global carrying capacity was reached in 1979; in the year 2000, the ecological footprint of humanity, which gets larger day-by-day, exceeded the carrying capacity by 20%. Chapter 7 will present this measure of the human impact in more details and calculate the ecological footprints for the most important scenarios presented in Chapter 5. The 2002 book emphasizes that it does not present forecasts about what will happen in the future but simply presents a range of alternative scenarios on how the 21st century could unfold. It is further underlined that the data and the theories do not permit accurate predictions, and the same is the case for the scenarios that we present in Chapter 5. Nevertheless, the *Limits to Growth: The 30-Year Update* claims that we will experience global overshoots that inevitably will lead to collapse. A vivid first example of what we can expect is behind the 2008–2013 economic crisis, which was indeed a consequence of overshoot.

The 30-year update summarizes development from 1950 to 2000 by presenting the worldwide growth of selected human activities and products:

Human population increased 2 ×
Number of registered vehicles increased 10 ×
Oil consumption increased 7 ×
Rice production increased 4 ×
Wheat production increased 4 ×
Iron and steel production increased 4.5 ×
Aluminum production increased 15 ×

It is clear that the growth of these activities and products is so high that it is unrealistic to believe that they can continue to increase at the same rates between 2000 and 2050. Growth of the aforementioned activities must be curtailed and redirected because they create other unacceptable consequences such as water stress, lost biodiversity, increased pollution, and decreased ecosystem services. Humans depend on ecosystem services, which are largely taken for granted. Since the mid-1990s, we have discussed ecosystem services in ecology and environmental science and have made efforts to calculate their economic values to make it clearer for economists and politicians that it may be economically unwise to drain wetlands or clear forests to enlarge agricultural areas, for example. Let us list the most significant ecosystem services to obtain a better understanding of the concept:

1. Primary production and the creation of new biomass
2. Purification of water and air
3. Decomposition of organic matter that otherwise would deplete the oxygen in aquatic ecosystems
4. Decomposition of harmful toxic organic compounds
5. Mitigation of droughts and floods
6. Recycling of important elements
7. Moderation of extreme weather conditions
8. Storage of the genetic pool and maintenance of biodiversity
9. Pollination
10. Pest control
11. Aesthetic and recreational areas.

The Limits to Growth: The 30-Year Update presents several scenarios, as does *The Limits to Growth* (1972). The global model has been updated in a version named World 3 containing approximately the same state variables as the 1972 model, listed earlier. If the world society proceeds in the same manner as it has done the last hundred years, then the result will be that – not very different from the 1972 simulations – the population will increase to 9–9.5 billion in year 2050 and afterward decline to 4–5 billion in 2100. Industrial output, life expectancy, food per person, ecosystem service per person, and human welfare will all reach a maximum in 2012–2015 and then decline radically toward 2050. This implies that the ecological footprint reaches a maximum at the same time and declines as industrial output and food production decrease. Other scenarios based on a stable population and/ or a stable industrial output per person show that it is possible to stop decreasing human welfare, life expectancy, and food production per capita. However, as in the 1972 scenarios, we need to stabilize human population, the production of industrial goods, and the consumption of resources. The simulations show that if we do not achieve this stabilization, then nature and consequences of natural laws will, without mercy, and it will be very tough for people in the industrialized rich countries expecting comfortable business-as-usual conditions.

There are many reasons to take the scenarios presented in the *Limits to Growth* books seriously. In particular, note that Graham M. Turner from Commonwealth Scientific and Industrial Research Organization in Canberra has demonstrated that the observations of the actual development of the population, the use of resources, the pollution level, and food production from 1972–2012 actually are very close to the business-as-usual scenarios published in 1972.

Population growth cannot be stopped immediately due to the demographic realities. Today, there are many children and young people in developing countries; if we presume that all couples have two children, then the population will continue to grow until the year 2040. Under this scenario, it would stabilize at 7.5 billion, provided that we would start the two-children policy in 2002! It is not too late, but much more difficult today than it would have been if we had enacted changes 20 or 40 years ago.

In 2012, Jørgen Randers published the book *2052 – A Global Forecast for the Next Forty Years* as a report to the Club of Rome, commemorating the 40th anniversary of *The Limits to Growth*. The book goes one step further than *The Limits to Growth* and *The 30-Year Update*; it attempts to make a forecast on how the world would look in year 2052. Randers introduces a new paradigm that promotes a lower fixation on economic growth. Once income levels exceed a certain threshold, non-economic aspects of development become more important to human well-being. This is true for the majority of the population, but unfortunately there exists a tension between promoting satisfaction and a compulsive push for ever more. In addition, even rich nations have many poor citizens who have not reached the "certain threshold" yet. We will turn back to this problem in Chapters 4–6.

Randers proposes several possible solutions; for instance, the current economic paradigm has to be changed, and a relatively engaged citizenry who recognize the need for control of the liberalistic society, as it is known from the Scandinavian countries, seems to offer a less unsustainable development. His recommendations match in accordance with the suggestions that we will present in Chapters 4–6. His book presents scenarios for the period 2012–2052 but focuses on five different regions to obtain a more detailed view: the United States, China, the OECD minus the US, BRISE (covering Brazil, Russia, India, South Africa, and 10 emerging economies), and ROW (rest of the world). These revisions of the World 3 model provided more detailed energy and climate sectors.

Randers predicts that the transition will not occur before the disruptions are onset. He expresses it this way: the sustainability crowd will win in the end but not fast enough to avoid damage to the planet. They will win only after destruction caused by climate change, resource depletion, biodiversity loss, and growing inequity and disparity can easily be seen and felt. He points out that the challenge is not to solve the problems that we are facing, because we can do that, as we shall also discuss in Chapters 4–6, but to reach agreement to do so. The real challenge, Randers espouses, is to have people and capital owners accept making the short-term investments, roll up their sleeves, and do the heavy lifting to transition to a new economy. Here, we add to learn from nature how we should do the heavy lifting.

2.5 Sustainable development

The phrase "sustainable development" was launched into the environmental agenda in a publication of the International Institute for Applied Systems Analysis (Laxenburg, Austria) in 1986 in a volume edited by William Clark and R.E. Munn titled *Sustainable Development of the Biosphere.* The concept was given further notice and directive in the 1987 book *Our Common Future.* The book was a general summary of the United Nations Environment Programme, referred to as the Brundtland Commission Report. In the book, the authors laid out the now-authoritative definition of sustainable development as "development that meets the needs of the present generation without compromising the needs of future generations." The compromise with the business and economics communities was to focus on development and not growth. The phrase is vague enough that it was possible to get large-scale buy in for the concept. However, some tried to co-opt and alter the phrase to "sustainable growth," but this was exposed as the oxymoron that it is. Although sustainable development has been generally accepted politically, these words without action and restructuring have not caused the radical changes that are needed.

Note also that the Brundtland Commission definition is entirely human-centric. It includes no reference to environmental quality, biological integrity, ecosystem health, or biodiversity. We will touch on all four issues in Chapters 3–6. According to the Brundtland Report presented in *Our Common Future,* our environmental management plans should ensure *sustainable development,* which would imply the following:

1. *Renewable resources* are not used at a higher rate than the rate of renewal.
2. *Nonrenewable resources* should not be used at a higher rate than alternatives could be developed in due time before the resources are exhausted.
3. *The rates of pollution emissions* should be adjusted to the rate at which the ecosystems can decompose and adsorb the discharged pollutants.

Neumayer (2003) (Note 9) gives the following summarizing definition of sustainable development: it is a development that maintains the capacity to provide non-declining per capita utility for "infinity."

The sustainable development concept is therefore based upon the ethics and the considerations that:

1. Future generations should have the same basic possibilities for development as the present generation has had.
2. Development is strongly dependent on the available renewable and nonrenewable resources. For instance, without the relatively cheap sources of high quality energy that humanity has exploited the last two centuries, the rapid rise in the gross national product (GNP) per capita, which has characterized many countries, particularly the industrialized countries, would have been impossible.
3. Resources in general have been utilized at an increasing rate the last one hundred years, which, if the exploitation of the resources would continue with the same acceleration, would hinder future generations to have the same standard of living as we have enjoyed. Therefore, we should return the earth in approximately the same shape to our children as we received it from our parents.

In Chapter 8, we will discuss sustainable development and more generally sustainability and how to quantify the concept. Furthermore, the chapter will present a case study in which sustainability has been expressed as the work energy capacity. All activities require work energy, and therefore we should provide the coming generations with the same work energy capacity as we have had. Additionally, all resources can be expressed as work energy, including biodiversity and ecosystem services. Work energy capacity is used to assess the sustainability of a Danish Island, Samsø, which has shifted to renewable energy. Of course, work capacity is but one indicator of sustainability, but one that must be ensured. Therefore, it can be considered a necessary condition, but it may not be sufficient. Additional indicators may be required, as will also be discussed in Chapter 8.

Heather M. Farley and Zachary A. Smith have published a book with the title *Sustainability – It Is Everything, Is It Nothing?* They show in the book (Note 10) that many companies, nongovernmental organizations (NGOs), politicians, and economists embrace the concept of sustainability and thereby make the concept more diffuse. The word sustainable is nowadays used to characterize any action that considers social, economic, and environmental impacts – sometimes in combination. Sustainability of humanity is based on three pillars supporting social, economic, and environmental systems, but this multi-disciplinarity also facilitates the possibilities to abuse the concept, such as commercially by "greenwashing" products or processes. Farley and Smith give a clear definition of weak and strong sustainability. The former refers to a form of sustainability aimed at non-diminishing capital stock from generation to generation. This is the concept of substitutability that assumes available alternatives for all goods in the capital stock basket. Human actions can be characterized as weakly sustainable if the total per capita stock of capital does not change over time, even if some forms of capital are ultimately lost or eliminated. This implies that material capital can be replaced by other material capital or also by nonmaterial capital of equal desirability by the recipient. In contrast, strong sustainability requires maintenance of all types of capital independently (see Notes 9 and 10).

The book by Farley and Smith mentions the strategy proposed by the World Business Council for Sustainable Development (WBCSD) in 2010. It is very consistent with the proposals presented in Chapters 4 and 5 based on how nature is working (Chapter 3). WBCSD proposes the following strategy:

1. Increase investment in education, particularly for women
2. Internalize the costs of externalities
3. Increase agricultural production without increasing the amount of land
4. Halt deforestation and increase plant yields for planted forests
5. Decrease greenhouse gas emissions to one-half the present level
6. Provide universal access to low carbon mobility
7. Increase resource and material use efficiency by a factor of four to ten.

The book (see Note 10) introduces neo-sustainability to surpass the comprehensive discussion about what sustainability actually is covering. Neo-sustainability is the ability to sustain a system by improving its quality and operating within its limits. The concept of neo-sustainability is based on three rules:

1.   There are natural limits to growth (quantitative growth).
2.   The limits are dictated by the environment, and therefore all actions in any systems must adhere to the carrying capacity of the local natural systems.
3.   Because environmental, economic, and social systems are all nested systems, all actions must be based on system thinking and account for multilevel influences.

2.6 How to shift from quantitative growth to qualitative development?

The *Limits to Growth* books and numerous others have presented a clear message that we have to curtail growth in regards to human population, resources use, and consumption. We know what to do, but, unfortunately and unwisely, we cannot agree to implement the needed policies and practices. It would require short-term investments to achieve long-term advantages, investments that many perceive as sacrifices in the short term. We would obviously have to change the socioeconomic structure to make it beneficial to alter our direction toward qualitative development instead of quantitative growth. Our present growth-oriented paradigm, implemented in terms of a neoliberal, hyper-capitalistic system, is not working properly – the latest economic crisis has demonstrated that very clearly. Which changes are needed to achieve the needed shift? The question can be answered by learning from nature how to deal with limits to growth. Nature has survived about four billion years and, during that time, evolved using novel approaches for maintaining itself under the inexorable conditions of limited resources. In fact, one would say that nature not only survives in spite of these limitations but thrives and flourishes within them as evidenced by the complexity of ecosystems, biodiversity, and individual behaviors. The next chapter will focus on the properties of ecosystems to try to understand why and how nature is able to shift beneficially to qualitative development. How to adopt nature's properties to our economic and social systems is the topic of Chapter 4.

3

HOW NATURE FLOURISHES
WITHIN LIMITS

Mother Nature and Father Time know how to solve the emerging problems of nature.
—expression introduced by W. Mitsch, but modified here

3.1 Ecosystem theory

By studying nature and imitating ecological designs and processes, we can be inspired to solve many human problems. We can learn from nature how to achieve sustainability in a finite world. The properties of ecosystems can be summarized as 14 propositions, which will be presented in this chapter. They will be used as motivation to address the many very serious problems that we are facing; see Section 2.3. The state of the science in ecology has arrived at an ecosystem theory that can explain most ecological processes and transformations under changing environmental conditions (Note 11). The headings of the sections in this chapter are the 14 properties. We explain how these properties are working in nature and how our dominant economic and social system is working in contrast to nature. Our aim is to show how to apply and adopt nature's properties in our economic, environmental, and social management. In this manner, we benefit from mimicking nature's ways, which have led to complex and successful system development throughout four billion years of experience in sustainable development. A more complete and detailed implementation of the 14 properties in our society is presented in Chapter 4. The treatment discussed later is based on first principles of physics, chemistry, ecology, and systems science. Of all these, perhaps the most fundamental concepts that underpin all ecological and social process are the laws of the thermodynamics (Box 3.1). The first law is valuable for our understanding because it guarantees that strict accounting procedures can be implemented that ensure energy and mass balance. It also gives the most basic rationale for why we can't get something from nothing. The consequences of the second law are even more profound. In terms of efficiency, the second law expresses that the transformation from one energy form to another is always less than 100%. All activities require energy to do work, and a part of the work energy is inexorably lost as heat energy to the environment. Therefore, new work energy is continually required to keep the system working (i.e., functioning).

Box 3.1 The two fundamental laws of thermodynamics.

First law of thermodynamics: Total energy of an isolated system is constant. Energy is never created or destroyed.

Second law of thermodynamics: Work energy of an isolated system never increases. Another formulation is: all processes are irreversible because lost work energy cannot be recovered.

For reference, see Note 12.

3.2 Ecosystems conserve matter and energy and use growth regulations

Nature must obey the conservation laws: both matter and energy are conserved. Matter and energy can, however, be transformed. The elements can be combined into numerous chemical compounds, but the amount of each element will remain the same. Energy can be transformed from one energy form to other energy forms. For instance, a hydroelectric power plant converts potential energy to electrical energy, while a fossil fuel-based thermoelectric power plant converts chemical energy to electricity. Chloroplast organelles in plants convert energy of solar radiation to chemical energy in biomass.

Although there are 91 naturally occurring elements of the periodic table, life on Earth – plants, animals, and microorganisms – utilize only about 20 of them in their biochemical processes. It is well known that the scarcest element relative to the needs will determine how much living matter a natural system can support. For instance, phosphorus is often, but not always, the limiting element for plants in lakes. This means that the overall plant biomass is regulated by the amount of available phosphorus. Practically all lake plants contain 0.4–2.0% phosphorus; when phosphorus is scarce, the concentration will be near the lower range, and when phosphorus is abundant, the concentration in the plants will be closer to 2%. If phosphorus is the limiting element, then the plant growth will stop when the plant biomass has reached close to 250 (100/0.4) times the amount of phosphorus. Plant growth will approach this limit following logistic growth (the *s*-shaped growth, see Figure 1.2). In this way, environmental constraints reduce the growth rate to adjust to the amount of the limiting elements.

Humans (or at least economists) seem to believe that the conservation principles are not valid for them. Our rate of use of several elements increases, though these elements may be limiting for our activities in 20, 40, or 100 years. We reuse and recycle only very modestly in contrast to nature, which has a complete recirculation of needed elements. We do not abate the growth rate but rather consume as if all resources were infinite. If we do not understand it now, then we will be forced to realize it later down the road when the resources are scarce. The first law of thermodynamics is sometimes expressed in everyday language as "there is no free lunch." Perhaps ironically, this is a common mantra for economists regarding economic transactions, but it is not considered by economists when applied to ecosystem services that are taken as free goods. Adding ecological factors more directly to the accounting of land, labor, and capital may help realize recirculation of all essential elements, which allows the system to shift from physical growth to development.

3.3 There are no trashcans in nature

Since matter is conserved, all important elements for living matter as already underlined are recycled in nature. Phosphorus, nitrogen, carbon, sulfur, hydrogen, oxygen, and calcium, to mention the most important elements, all participate in global biogeochemical cycles in which the elements pass from biosphere to lithosphere or hydrosphere or atmosphere and back to biosphere again through active, life-initiated processes. In this manner, the elements are used again and again in nature's way of recycling. When, for instance, microorganisms utilize dead organic matter as an energy source, the carbon energy bonds are utilized and released into the atmosphere as carbon dioxide and water vapor, and the nutrients are both incorporated by the microorganism and dispersed into the soil matrix. From the soil, they can be recovered by the plants and utilized for new growth.

Figure 3.1 illustrates how nitrogen recycles in a typical aquatic ecosystem. A number of processes work in concert to form a functioning, whole system that recycles the important element, nitrogen.

Nature recycles water by evapotranspiration (from both aquatic and terrestrial areas) → atmospheric humidity → clouds → precipitation → evapotranspiration, and so on. One complete cycle for all the water takes on average 2,000–3,000 years. This means that one liter of water contains recycled water, which, to put it graphically, contains an average of about 1,000 molecules that were in the bladder of Julius Caesar 2,000 years ago!

Nature deals with the constraints imposed through the conservation principles by an extensive use of recycling. Recycling is recognized as important in human society to avoid needing to continuously find, extract, and process virgin materials. In fact, when dealing with waste generation, we consider a three-stage approach commonly referred to as the three Rs: reduce, reuse, and recycle. While all three have a role to play, these are taken successively from most to least benign in regards to generating waste. Take beer bottling as an example. The first stage, to reduce

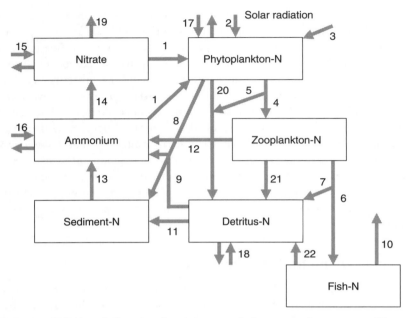

FIGURE 3.1 Conceptual diagram of a nitrogen cycle in an aquatic ecosystem. The processes working together to make the recycling possible are: 1) uptake of nitrate and ammonium by algae; 2) photosynthesis; 3) nitrogen fixation; 4) grazing with loss of undigested matter; 5), 6), and 7) are predation and loss of undigested matter; 8) settling of algae to the bottom of the aquatic ecosystem; 9) mineralization (microorganisms utilize the dead organic matter as an energy source and thereby the organic matter decomposed to inorganic matter); 10) fishery; 11) settling of detritus; 12) excretion of ammonia (NH_3) from zooplankton; 13) release of nitrogen compounds from the sediment; 14) nitrification; 15), 16), 17), and 18) are inputs/outputs from the environment; 19) denitrification (nitrate is converted to free nitrogen gas, which will be transferred to the atmosphere; and 20), 21), and 22) mortality of phytoplankton, zooplankton, and fish. See Jørgensen and Fath (2011) (for reference, see Note 11).

waste generation before it occurs, could occur by using larger containers or kegs to reduce the total number of beer bottles needed. We must also consider reduction in terms of absolute decrease of production. In some cases, the activity itself may be in line for reduction, but we would not make that case for beer! Assuming a certain number of beer bottles are produced and used, then the next best alternative would be to reuse them. This occurs if they are designed as returnable. Reusable bottles are common in Europe and had been decades ago in the United States, until lobbying by soft drink industries eliminated that option – another case where short-term profits outweighed doing the right thing. The bottles may be refilled numerous times before breakage occurs (studies indicate about 20 times), thereby reusing greatly lowers the need for new bottles. Lastly, when reduction and reuse are not available options, the materials can be recycled. In the case of glass bottles, they can be recast into new bottles again and again. However, the reality is that so much glass is currently produced that there are not enough markets to recycle it all back to glass; therefore, much recycled glass gets used as filler in road construction or other end-of-life applications. These simple resource strategies help us in order to manage with limited resources and the conservation laws, but we do not use the three Rs sufficiently to avoid depletion of important resources in the future. We should implement the three Rs much more fully into our economy through by-product synergies and industrial ecology. If these strategies are well integrated into community and commercial processes, then material reduction and reuse become the convenient and default options.

3.4 All processes result in degradation of work energy to energy that cannot do work

We have to distinguish clearly between two classes or qualities of energy: 1) energy that is useful because it can do work and 2) energy that is heat at a temperature comparable to that of the environment and it cannot do work. The latter form has energy in an absolute sense but cannot do work because there is no temperature gradient to extract further work. Work energy has many forms: chemical energy in fossil fuel, potential mechanical energy in water in a hydropower plant, electrical work energy, radiant work energy, and so on. For any process or function to occur, we must operate with energy that can do work. This energy can be used to construct roads and buildings, pump water, heat homes, refrigerate food, and make our life more comfortable in many ways. Heat released to the environment is only appreciated by the sparrows. It is the inexorable, fundamental second law of thermodynamics (Box 3.1) that guarantees *all* activities are associated with a loss of work energy to heat energy at the temperature of the environment. Energy is conserved, but all conversions of energy are in one direction: from higher to lower quality of energy – from energy that can do work to energy that cannot do work. This implies that the price for *all* activities is the loss of some work energy resulting in the inevitable conclusion that all processes are irreversible. Processes in a closed system cannot be reversed because the lost work energy is converted to heat energy at the temperature of the environment, making it unable to do further work in that environment.

Energy is conserved as depicted in Section 3.2. When we are talking about energy efficiency, we mean the amount of work energy that we obtain as a result of an energy transfer. A typical power plant using fossil fuel has a work energy efficiency of 40%, which means that the work energy produced as electricity is only 40% of the work energy used in the form of the chemical work energy in the fossil fuel. If the waste heat is utilized effectively, then it is possible to reach 70% efficiency at the very best.

The conversion efficiency of solar energy to chemical energy within plant biomass, the result of photosynthesis, is not very high, probably because it is not necessary as solar energy is rarely an ultimate limiting factor for ecosystems. Figure 3.2 shows a typical average distribution of the solar work energy. Ecosystems have an enormous energy source in solar radiation relative to their lifespans. However, solar radiation also drives the hydrological cycle, which is of crucial significance as water often is the limiting factor for plant growth.

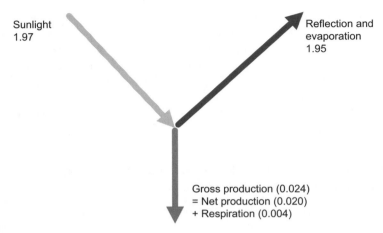

Sunlight
1.97

Reflection and evaporation
1.95

Gross production (0.024)
= Net production (0.020)
+ Respiration (0.004)

FIGURE 3.2 Fate of solar energy incident upon the perennial grass-herb vegetation of an old field community in Michigan. All values in GJ m^{-2} y^{-1}. About 99% of the solar radiation is reflected or used for evaporation. Only slightly more than 1% is used for plant production, of which one-sixth is applied for respiration (maintenance of the plants), which is the transfer of work energy as heat at the temperature of the environment. The loss of work energy as heat energy during respiration is the price that ecosystems pay for their activities, according to the second law of thermodynamics.

Furthermore, as we will discuss later in this chapter, ecosystems are able to improve their work energy efficiency by developing an effective network of organisms and by increasing information that regulates ecological processes. An interactive network ensures recycling of matter; see, for instance, Figure 3.1, which shows a network of components in an aquatic ecosystem. In this manner, chemical work energy in organic matter unutilized by one component in the network is utilized by another; see Figure 3.3.

Figure 3.4 shows a network (Note 13) with quantified storage (the rectangles) and flow (the arrows) values, with units, for instance, of MJ/ha for the components and MJ/(ha × year) for the flows. The flows exiting the system are the loss of work energy due to respiration. The figure demonstrates how work energy is recycled in spite of the respiration losses. as in Figure 3.2 caption. Due to the recycling in the network the 5 MJ ha^{-1} y^{-1} is generating flows of 11.4 MJ ha^{-1} y^{-1} inside the network and the total system through flow is therefore now 5 + 11.4 MJ ha^{-1} y^{-1} = 16.4 MJ ha^{-1} y^{-1} or 16.4/5 = 3.28 times more than the inflow. The work energy storage is 16.4 MJ ha^{-1} according to one year retention time. So, the result of the network is that flows and storages of work energy are increased a factor 3.28 times the inflow to the network.

All activities entail energy transformations that are irreversible and accompanied by a loss of work energy or energy quality: The second law always applies. So, as it is not possible to change this fundamental law, we have to learn to live with the law in our everyday life. It is expressed in the everyday proverb – "Do not cry over spilled milk" – because you cannot change the past, only the future.

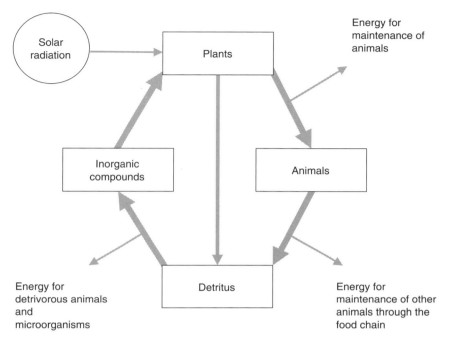

FIGURE 3.3 An ecosystem can be depicted as a biochemical reactor. The input of energy comes from solar radiation. The energy and biologically important elements cycle from organism to organism, supporting the overall ecosystem function.

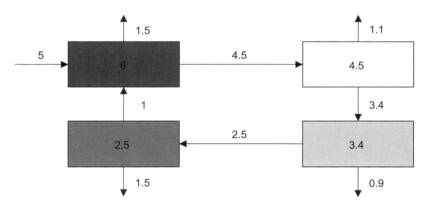

FIGURES 3.4 The work energy of the four components of the network is expressed as MJ ha^{-1} and the flows as MJ ha^{-1} y^{-1}. Notice that the input of work energy 5 MJ ha^{-1} y^{-1} is regenerating flows of totally 11.4 MJ ha^{-1} y^{-1} inside the network. The total system through flow is therefore $5 + 11.4 = 16.4$ MJ ha^{-1} y^{-1}. The work energy storage in the network is 16.4 MJ ha^{-1} corresponding to one year retention time of the work energy. If more connections are added to the network more flow inside the network and more work energy storage would be generated.

3.5 All organisms use the same biochemical processes to a large extent

As stated earlier, living systems use only around 20 of the 91 naturally occurring elements (see the references in Note 11). As a result of evolution, organisms use almost the same biochemical processes. This similarity is a design feature for compatibility and also puts a premium on those necessary elements, thereby making it more likely and more essential that these essential elements are recycled. Nature has devised pathways and processes to recycle the elements to continue overall biomass growth. Humans also rely on chemical elements that may be recycled, such as iron and most other metals that have numerous, different uses. But recycling in our society is far from sufficient, while it approaches 100% in ecosystems. Enhanced recycling of the scarcest elements compared with our use has even not started – only the economy seems to be determining the modest recycling that takes place today.

3.6 Ecosystems are open systems

The Earth is a system open to energy and receives an average irradiance from the sun of approximately 1400 W/m^2, which is used to power all life. The exchange of matter between the Earth and the space is very modest. The Earth loses a minor amount of hydrogen and receives a very minor amount of mass from meteorites. Overall, the vast majority of all matter we are left with arrived during the formation of the solar system.

The transformation of work energy to heat energy guarantees that work energy must be spent to maintain an ecosystem. The respiration corresponds to the maintenance work energy that is lost as heat energy at the environmental temperature – and it cannot do work; see Figures 3.3–3.4. Therefore, ecosystems *must* be open to an inflow of work energy (from the sunlight or thermal vents). Similarly, our society is open, and we require continued inputs of work energy to maintain our complex socioeconomic systems. Consider, for instance, using work energy to maintain the infrastructure of buildings and operations within. The difference between nature and our society is the source of that energy. Whereas ecosystems use renewable energy – the sun – we use mainly nonrenewable fossil fuels as the energy source. In addition to their finite supplies, fossil fuels emit air pollution such as sulfur dioxide (acid rain), nitrous oxide (acid rain and smog), and carbon dioxide (climate change). Therefore, our primary resource that supplies work energy is not sustainable in contrast to nature's provision of work energy.

3.7 Ecosystems grow and develop by using surplus energy to move further away from thermodynamic equilibrium

Look around you in nature on a spring day; the plants are growing almost from hour-to-hour, the flowers come into blossom, and animal offspring are abundant. Nature is full of activities because the solar radiation exceeds the work energy needed for maintenance and the surplus work energy is used for growth. Biological growth means that work energy is accumulated in the plants, the microorganisms, and the animals as biomass, as information, and as more complex (and effective) networks. In this context, growth means that work energy is accumulating in the ecosystems. At thermodynamic equilibrium, the work energy is zero — there is no structure, no life, and no gradients. Everything is homogenous, dull, and static.

The role of work energy accumulation is not very different for human society. If more work energy can be provided, then we use the surplus work energy to construct roads, build houses, invent new products, and so on. The roads, the houses, and the industries represent an accumulation of work energy (which have commensurate maintenance costs). The society is growing. Again, the main thermodynamic difference between nature and our society is the energy source. Nature relies entirely on renewable solar radiation, while society uses mainly fossil fuels.

3.8 Ecosystems apply three forms of growth and development

Nature uses three forms of growth and development: 1) biomass growth, 2) growth and development of the network linking the ecosystem components, and 3) information growth and development. All three growth and development forms contribute to increasing work energy, but we stress that network and information provide qualitative changes to underline that these result in higher efficiencies that do not require more resources in the form of solar radiation and matter. Biomass growth has clear limitations, as has been discussed. When the element present in the lowest concentration compared with the needs of the organisms in the ecosystem is completely used, biomass growth will stop. However, over time and selection, the ecological network becomes larger, more intricate, and more effective, while the amount of information embodied in the organisms continues to increase. So, nature is able to continue its growth and development in spite of the limitation of the biomass growth and that presented by a finite energy source. Both network and information growth and development can continue with practically no limits. In addition, these two qualitative forms are, as mentioned earlier, able to improve the overall ecosystem function in terms of energetics and behavior. We show (Note 13) that a more developed network can recycle the elements and utilize available work energy better than a less developed network. One way to characterize an organism's information is by the genome because this is utilized to build enzymes that catalyze subsequent biochemical processes. The greater the genomic information, the greater the capability for feedback processes to regulate organismal functions. Network and information growth and development result in an ecosystem that is better adapted to use the available resources effectively and still gain more work energy capacity. Nature's use of the three growth and development forms is a win–win situation: efficiency is increased, the resources are used better, and the ecosystems are still gaining more work energy capacity. Nature has four billion years of evolution and adaptation in which increased network complexity and information increases allows it to effectively and efficiently flourish within the limits.

Human society also uses the three growth and development forms, but information and network strategies are used to an extent far less than in ecosystems. We overexploit our resources because of a complex and historical fabric of incentives that do not adequately account for the finite aspects of the resources. We could use more information and networking to obtain a much better utilization of the resources. It would require investments and therefore less short-term profit (but more long-term revenue!), and therefore it is unfortunately and unwisely not realized. We seem not to care sufficiently for the coming generations, leaving diminishingly accessible resources for them. As we will discuss in the next three chapters, better networking and gaining more information are the keys to turn – as nature has done – to a win–win situation. We seem, however, to have chosen a win now and lose later situation. We should learn from nature how to obtain a more effective working system by an extensive and well-balanced use of all three growth and development forms.

3.9 Ecosystems select the pathways that yield the highest work energy of the system

Ecosystems support vast inter- and intra-species diversity. Darwin's theory tells us that the organisms with the properties that are best adjusted to the prevailing environmental conditions will be selected to survive and populate the area. Species that survive, grow, and develop have greater opportunity to increase biomass and information. From earlier, we see that biomass and information can be measured as work energy. We can translate Darwin into energy terms: the components and their processes that give ecosystems the most work energy will be selected. Numerous observations support this theory (Note 14). The more work energy an ecosystem has, the more resistance and resilience it has toward impacts or changes, and the more sustainable it becomes (see the references in Note 11).

Human society is not at all developing as consequently as nature toward higher work energy. The construction of infrastructure and buildings increases the work capacity of the society, but it is accomplished using nonrenewable resources including fossil fuels, emitting pollution and degrading nature resulting in a considerable decrease of work energy (see Chapter 8). Human society emphasizes the importance of information, although more effort could be invested in increased information, innovation, and education, as will be discussed in Chapters 4 and 5. The cooperative human network can also be improved considerably, whereby development of the entire global population could be toward more work energy and sustainability. It will also be discussed in more details in Chapters 4 and 5.

Furthermore, biological components in ecosystems are not overexploiting the resources. A lion kills only one zebra, which is sufficient for the pride to be satisfied in that instance in time – also because it is hard work (energetically costly) to kill a zebra. It is not possible for the lion to accumulate dead zebra, which would spoil, or to trade the extra zebra for currencies that do not spoil for use at a later time. The lion and zebra must live in the present. Humans have developed ways to store resource flows by harvesting all the "zebra"; capital can be accumulated in a currency that does not spoil (it may lose value due to inflation, but that is a different matter). In this manner, humans continue to accumulate money beyond their needs, which is used to further exploit limited resources. The structure of our society today makes this possible, and a shift is therefore needed for a better cooperation among humans and a fairer distribution of the work energy, which would enable society to flourish, mainly by increasing the network integration and level of information.

3.10 Ecosystems are organized hierarchically

A cell may contain one billion molecules, and an organism contains from one to about 10,000 billion cells. Hundreds or thousands of organisms form a population, and an ecosystem may support life for hundreds or thousands of populations. Ten or maybe 1,000 ecosystems make up a landscape, and a region may encompass many landscapes. The entire life-bearing part of the Earth is denoted the ecosphere. All the parts and processes in one level are integrated to make a sound and healthy system on the next level. A system is both a whole at one level made up of smaller scales as well as part of a larger system at a higher scale. There is an interplay and feedback of control over lower levels and support up to higher levels. For instance, organisms control their cells by exchanging biochemical components among the cells and provide the cells with the needed energy originated from animal biomass and ultimately solar radiation. The cells are working together to make a healthy organism, which, due to its holistic properties, is able to control the cells, but also to give positive, regulative feedback to the cells to the benefit of the cells and the organisms. The hierarchical organization is very beneficial because it is easy to solve a malfunction problem by replacing a lower level part, similarly to fixing a broken car by using spare parts. Furthermore, disturbances are damped through the hierarchical levels, which means that the higher levels that are more important are disturbed less by perturbations on the lower levels (Note 15). The vulnerability is thereby also damped throughout the hierarchical levels.

Human society applies also hierarchical organization, but it is more casual. Cells would function closely together to ensure a healthy organism, but the citizens in a town or country are integrated but not closely enough to ensure that a town or a country may be a healthy and nice environment for its citizens. There are always additional ways that a joint effort could create a good environment for the citizens and their children, maybe best described by John F. Kennedy who said: "Ask not what your country can do for you – ask what you can do for your country." Dysfunction occurs not only when people fail to work together, but also when higher levels in the society, such as a central administration, try to promote control rather than cooperation. A central administration sometimes admits that they set up control to meet the objectives defined by the central administration – not to optimize the overall efficiency. Lower levels often have to fill out forms to satisfy the central administration with information that may be needed, but the central administration does not consider the trouble and the time required by the lower levels. Integration and awareness that leads to cooperation in society could be much better and it could create a win–win situation for everybody, but humans fail to embrace the importance of better integration. We will turn to this theme in the section focusing on how network interactions are beneficial for the entire system.

3.11 Ecosystems have a high diversity in all levels of the hierarchy

The diversity in nature is enormous. The number of different biochemical components in cells and the number of different cells is astronomical (see references in Note 15). The number of different organisms is in the millions. Nature supports and preserves the high diversity by offering an enormous variation of conditions for life. Research has shown that the high diversity in nature makes the ecosystems less vulnerable and more sustainable because diversity helps to adsorb and dampen disturbances and meet new and often unknown perturbations. The enormous diversity of nature implies that we have access to a richness of chemical, biochemical, and biological solutions. It is therefore crucial that we protect the diversity of nature to maintain this richness for future generations.

The diversity in society is high, too, but far less than the astronomically high diversity of nature. In fact, due to globalization, the society's diversity is decreasing rapidly. In the past, local solutions for the prevailing conditions were implemented. Now, all societies copy what has worked (and not worked) in the Western capitalistic countries. There is not much room for high diversity. Human society could probably work with fewer rules, but it would require better cooperation and a higher information level of its inhabitants.

3.12 Ecosystems resist (destructive) changes

The high content of work energy, the high level of information, the system parts working together in effective networks, and the high diversity within ecosystems makes them less vulnerable and more sustainable and gives them a high resistance toward changes. Nature is continuously exposed to natural changes and even sometimes to catastrophes, but it has an ability to both resist the changes, to a certain extent, and also to recover after major destructive catastrophes. The volcanic eruption of Mount St. Helens in Washington State in 1980 completely destroyed many ecosystems – lakes, rivers, and wetlands – but 10 years later, they were largely recovered.

It would therefore be beneficial for humans to adopt similar characteristics that give ecosystems high resistance toward destructive changes. Clearly, society would be far less vulnerable if we would be less dependent on the limited resources and not steer the society as if the resources were unlimited. A major collapse will probably happen when we come closer to the limits to growth – probably later in this century. We experienced major economic difficulties when the oil prices increased.

Imagine what is going to happen when we are close to the limits for four or five or even more very essential resources and the prices skyrocket for copper, nickel, crude oil, and aluminum at the same time. The 2008–2013 crisis is minor compared with what we will experience in such a case.

3.13 Ecosystems work together in networks that improve the resource use efficiency

Figures 3.1, 3.3, and 3.4 illustrate how components in ecological networks are interconnected in ways in which the outcome is a higher efficiency in the use of resources and the energy and matter are recycled. We show (Note 13) how other benefits emerge from the network organization. Furthermore, it can be shown that the linkages in these networks give greater mutualistic interactions and fewer competitive ones. It is also possible to show that the direct effect of a transfer of work energy or matter is often smaller than the effect of the work energy, matter, and information coming from all the indirect flows along extended paths due to cycling. Finally, it should be mentioned that the control of the entire network becomes very distributed (more democratic one could say) due to the interactive recycling of the network. These network benefits are a result of the emergent properties of the ecosystem.

The emergence of cooperative relationships due to the network interactions has a great advantage for all the components of the network. Human societies have detected this advantage. Industries can co-locate and create functional by-product synergies such that the waste (material or energetic) from one industry is used as raw material in another industry. In Chapter 4, we will present a conceptual diagram of the Danish town Kalundborg, where the industries are cooperating in a network and, as a result, receive raw materials at low costs or they get rid of waste at a reduced cost. Using waste heat from power plants for domestic space house heating is another illustrative example.

3.14 Ecosystems contain an enormous amount of information

Each organism's genome contains an enormous amount of information, which is used to regulate the biological activities. The genome determines the amino acid sequence – the building blocks of proteins – that makes the enzymes (proteins that catalyze processes) fitted to promote and control specific and important biological processes. The human genome determines the sequence of one billion amino acids, and there are 20 possible different amino acids for each of these one billion amino acids. This means that each of our 10,000 billion cells carries the information of what corresponds to the number of letters in a book of 500 million pages. Information contains work energy, as Boltzmann showed more than 100 years ago. The work energy capacity of living biomass in material terms is about 18.7 kJ per gram of biomass, while living mammals contain about 2,127 times as much work energy due to the information content (Box 3.2).

Box 3.2 Boltzmann.

Boltzmann (1905) gives the following relationship between work energy, W, and thermodynamic information:

$$W = RT \ln(M)$$

where T is the absolute temperature and M is the number of possible states among which the information has been selected. R is 8.34 J/mole K or 8.34 kJ 10^{-8}/g, if an average molecular weight of 100,000 is presumed. Humans have 3.2 billion amino bases in the genome, and there are four possible amino bases. Not only the selection of the amino bases but also the sequence of the amino bases are decisive for the information determining the life processes in each cell, and humans have about 10 trillion cells. The information embodied in other living organisms is less than in humans but still enormous.

For reference, see Note 16.

Information is an important tool to improve the efficiencies of biological processes. It is therefore very beneficial for ecosystems to increase information and play on the possibility to increase information. For example, parental care for offspring as particularly witnessed in mammals and birds is based on information capacity, which gives higher efficiency due to a higher probability of offspring survival. A network with more components is often more effective, but a more complex network also means more information. All in all, nature prudently applies information to develop better and better solutions for its survival. Nature increases information by developing new and better fitted genomes as well as by an increased transfer of information among organisms. Information transfers are communicated through various types of signals that can be perceived by all the senses, which allow the recirculating of information similar to the recycling of matter and work energy.

Our societies are indeed also using information as a factor to develop better solutions. Education and research are important means in modern society to increase information and to provide a better life for its citizens. Our use of education and research could, however, be enhanced considerably to increase significantly the level of information. Just consider that one-third of the global population cannot read and write. Many children in developing countries do not go to school. In some Islamic countries, girls have no access to school. We can again learn from nature that we should greatly enhance the information level.

It should be mentioned in this context how telecommunications and particularly the introduction of the Internet have facilitated information transfer, which is a prerequisite for a wider distribution of information. We need both more information and a better distribution of the existing information. There is no doubt that the development of the Internet and the World Wide Web have made major contributions to a wider distribution of information, which probably will be significant – together will several other factors – for our possibilities to reach global sustainable development in the future. The development of the Internet and World Wide Web is actually an illustrative example on how cooperation and exchange of information can lead to improved solutions and how a development rides on the shoulders of information of another development.

3.15 Ecosystems have emergent system properties

All complex adaptive systems exhibit emergent properties – a system is more than the sum of its part – because the integration of the systems' parts to a working unit inevitably gives the systems additional and often very beneficial properties. Just consider that a human being consists of 10,000 billion cells. Many properties cannot be explained by this number of cells but only by the integrated functional coupling of the cells to make up a thinking, speaking, feeling, walking, sentient being. The emergent properties of nature and ecosystems are the properties that we have presented in Sections 3.2–3.14. The integration of these properties promotes ecosystems that are less vulnerable and more resistant to destructive changes – more diverse, more flexible, more adaptable, and more effective, with better integration among the parts – and contain and administer more work energy.

In the last two sections of this chapter, we will summarize where ecosystems and human societies are similar and where they are (very) different. Clearly, in our effort to learn from nature, we should focus particularly on the differences between the two types of systems.

3.16 Similarities between ecosystems and human societies

One important starting point is the universality of the laws of thermodynamics, which are valid for both systems. Therefore, both natural and human systems:

1. Have to respect that mass and energy are conserved
2. Have only irreversible processes
3. Will have processes and activities where work energy inexorably is lost as heat energy that cannot do further work
4. Are open and need an input of work energy
5. Apply multiple use of resources
6. Need work energy for maintenance
7. Are organized hierarchically
8. Have high diversity
9. Have components working in interactive networks
10. Have high information levels.

The similarities between the two types of systems should make it relatively easy for humans to learn from nature, adopt some of the properties that are characteristic for nature, and increase some of the qualities that nature possesses to a higher extent than our societies.

3.17 Main differences between ecosystems and human societies

The main differences between natural and human systems, which can explain ecosystem sustainability, are:

1. Ecosystems recycle all necessary resources in contrast to human systems that only reuse and recycle very modestly compared to the overall potential.
2. Ecosystems receive more work energy than needed for maintenance and store the surplus in biomass and increased organizational complexity. Human societies do the same to a certain extent, but the energy source is primarily from fossil fuels, which are limited and create pollution problems.
3. Ecosystems use the three forms of growth and development (biomass, network, and information) to continue flourishing, while human societies rely largely on increased quantities of natural resources beyond the limits and underutilize networks and information.
4. Ecosystems and human societies both have many possibilities to use the (surplus) work energy. The difference is that ecosystems mainly use it toward increased storage (work energy accumulation), whereas human societies use it to extract the most profit. One approach builds gradients, the other exploits them.
5. Tightly coupled integration is far better in ecosystems than in society both within and across hierarchical levels.
6. Ecosystems are both resistant and resilient to major changes.
7. Ecosystems have a greater overall diversity compared with the social and cultural diversity of society.
8. Ecosystem networks are organized in ways that promote the emergence of whole-system positive relations.
9. Information in ecosystems (particularly in an organism's genome) is much higher than the information content in our society.
10. Ecosystems have very advantageous emergent properties. Human societies also have emergent properties but could gain more advantages by imitating nature and incorporating the properties mentioned in points 1–9.

In summary, we can learn the following lessons from nature to come closer to sustainable development:

A. Use the three Rs (reduce, reuse, and recycle) much more extensively. Nature recycles all essential elements and also does not overuse the available resources. Our society has to play on all three Rs to improve circulation and avoid depletion of essential resources.
B. Use solar radiation – which is for all practical purposes unlimited – directly or indirectly, as the sole energy source.
C. Focus on flourishing rather than growing by changing from quantitative growth that requires natural resources to qualitative development that uses network organization and information to remain vigorous and dynamic.
D. Change the objective toward building and maintaining greater work energy capital rather than exploiting of the gradients for short-term economic return.

Economic profit should reflect how much work energy is built, not how much is extracted.

E. Improve integration on and between all hierarchical levels. Emphasis in this context is on cooperation, not on control. The focus is on developing a synergistic network system in a cooperative society with a spectrum of holistic, emergent properties.

F. Appreciate diversity and understand that it gives society a wider array of resistance and buffers to destructive changes.

G. Promote and value opportunities to increase information. This requires an extensive investment in education, research, and innovation, which will have long-term benefits by making society much more effective.

H. Human society is strongly dependent on ecosystem services (Table 3.1). We utilize many of them for free, not considering the cost of these services in our accounting. It is important to maintain nature's work capacity against damages caused by our activities if we want to continue to receive the benefits of ecosystem services.

Adoption of these eight lessons within human societies will address the problems identified in *The Limits to Growth* presented in Chapter 2 and can contribute to global sustainable development. But up to now, the emphasis on quantitative growth has continued unchanged in spite of all the warnings. Therefore, the crucial question is: how can we change society to integrate these eight lessons to install a more natural development of our societies? In the next chapter, we present how society's structure could be changed to make this integration possible.

TABLE 3.1 Ecosystem services reported in terms of the annual work energy increase for a number of ecosystems. Both the work energy of the biomass increase and the biomass increase with the addition of the information have been found.

Ecosystem type	MJ/m^2 year (biomass)	GJ/ha year (biomass and information)
Desert	0.9	2,070
Open sea	3.5	2,380
Coastal zones	7.0	4,830
Coral reefs, estuaries	80	96,000
Lakes, rivers	11	9,350
Coniferous forests	15.4	53,900
Deciduous forests	26.4	100,000
Temperate rainforests	39.6	150,000
Tropical rainforests	80	300,000
Tundra	2.6	7,280
Croplands	20.0	42,000
Grasslands	7.2	18,000
Wetlands	18	45,000

For reference, see Note 17.

4

HOW TO ADOPT NATURE'S PROPERTIES IN OUR SOCIETY

I would rather fight for what seems to be politically impossible than for what is physically impossible.
        —Ecological economist Herman Daly on why he fights for a green economy

4.1 Introduction

Limits to Growth and other concurring books (see the discussion in Chapter 2) have demonstrated that growth has limits whether it is population, use of natural resources, production, or our occupation on the landscape, giving correspondingly less areas for nature. The message is clear: on a long-term basis, humans are forced to change society in a sustainable direction, but the later we transition in this inevitable direction, the more painful the changes will be. Major changes from the current course are needed to avoid a major collapse. We are, however, not listening to the message. We continue our overexploitation of the Earth as if it has unlimited resources and areas available for us. Past experience indicates we prioritize short-term planning and we continue insouciantly an economic growth strategy. The economic crisis that started in 2008 was a warning about how wrong and destructive the unbalanced economic strategy is. But all politicians want now is to solve the problems of the crisis by returning to how things were before, with new growth. They have not understood that the unhealthy, economic growth strategy is the root of the crisis. Many economists claim that the neoliberal economic system requires growth, but as it is physically impossible to continue growth indefinitely, it can therefore be concluded that it is the economic system that is inappropriate for the current conditions. Continuous growth is a physically impossible *fata morgana*. What we need is to refocus away from quantitative growth requiring natural resources and to integrate the eight lessons that nature has taught us in our strategy for a new development based on qualitative development. In this chapter, we will take the eight lessons one by one and indicate how they could be integrated and implemented in our society to create a completely new development strategy. Warnings are obviously insufficient because business as usual is still the dominant strategy in spite of the numerous, serious, and scientifically-based warnings. We need to dig deeper and *change* the economic structure from a neoliberal, shortsighted, selfish structure to a balanced, sustainable, cooperative structure. And, we first of all need people to realize that this needed shift will result in improved and more fair opportunities for everybody, particularly on a long-term basis.

The neoliberal economy is based on a transparent market, free competition, and free transfer of money and products. The idea is that, under such economic conditions, the consumer will get all the needed products at a reasonable (low) price, and the producer will obtain a suitable and reasonable profit. Under these circumstances, global wealth will continue to grow. Neoliberalism underlines that the market must have no interference, and an invisible hand will make the necessary regulations to the benefit of everybody. This ideal economy does not exist, however, because the financial market and many of its products do their very best to avoid full transparency. Consider in this context the credit default swaps developed as a new financial product, or consider the real estate market and its fluctuating prices. In principle, the idea is that a free and functioning market serves the community, providing goods and services at low prices, but the economic development that has occurred favors markets to supersede all other considerations, in essence controlling the population. The economic crisis has shown that the market and the financial sector are out of line with the intended function. Yet, the financial sector is growing faster than the production economy. Why? Because profit in the financial sector is much higher than it is in the production sector. Why? Because politicians have allowed financial sector leaders to increase their profits enormously. Moreover, the virtual money is about twenty times as much as the real money. New rules in Europe – introduced recently – will improve control in the financial sector but are still probably far from sufficient. If the sector's profits have been in accordance with its results (equal to the benefit for society), then this would have been understandable, but there are numerous examples of high profits in spite of very negative results. Incredible, but unfortunately true. The financial sector should serve the population to facilitate the needed financial transactions, but the last years have shown us that profit and often personal profit is the main goal of the sector. An important factor behind the recent economic crisis is financial speculation and gambling. Until 1999, banks in the United States were not allowed to participate in financial speculations. This rule must be reintroduced if we want a stable financial market.

Economists are not able to give us the needed strategies and advice about how to handle the economic crises. Follow any economic problem over one month or so, for instance the recovery of the real estate market, and observe how different economists have different solutions and different predictions. There is a saying that the number of different opinions is equal to the number of economists. Only a very few economists predicted the recent crisis. Alan Greenspan, with one of the most high-profile economic jobs in the world, chief of the American Central Bank, rejected in 2004 the warning about an imminent subprime crisis; and Ben Bernanke, the new chief of the American Central Bank, described the American economy in 2007 – shortly before the crisis started – as healthy and stated that the real estate prices would continue to increase, although (he speculated) at a lower rate.

Politicians in industrialized countries promote solving the present economic problems by encouraging people to go further into debt (credit cards, mortgages, loans, etc.) because they want to solve the crisis with more growth, but the people know better. There is no need for higher consumption among a major part of the rich countries. Many people in the developed countries do not feel the need for more materialistic goods. They have realized that money cannot buy happiness. Mathematically, one can show that happiness or satisfaction versus wealth, income, or materialistic goods follows a Michaelis-Menten graph (see Figure 4.1), and 75–90% of the population in most industrialized countries have reached or almost reached the "saturation level." Research published by the Worldwatch Institute showed that the shape of Figure 4.1 is valid on the basis of statistics from a number of countries (Note 18). The result is that people are saving to have money to buffer against a new crisis because we never know when it is coming, as seen by the uniform surprise among economists and politicians whenever a crisis emerges.

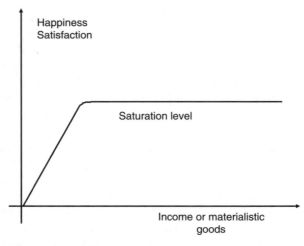

FIGURE 4.1 Happiness or satisfaction as a function of income or the amount of materialistic goods shows that, at a certain income or wealth, there is no further happiness to gain by more wealth. Once the saturation level has been achieved, factors other than income determine further increases in happiness.

The political and economic goals for most countries are increasing wealth and growing gross national product (GNP) per capita, but it looks like this is out of phase with the desire of at least a significant part of the population in industrialized countries. The economy should not be driven only by the part of the population that feels the need for the newest goods or focuses on status symbols. There is an urgent need for political-social-economic goals other than wealth and higher GNP per capita, such as adopting a measure that addresses sustainability while meeting the 10 most basic needs (see the references in Note 18): sufficient food, healthy food, shelter, sanitation, easy access to water, access to cultural events, wide social acceptance, access to communication, access to information, access to information about changes, and access to good education.

The changes that are needed will require political and individual decisions. Considering that some of these nature-inspired changes have been partially tested with promising results and that there is a beginning movement toward a shift in a sustainable direction, there is maybe some hope for a transformation. In addition, the structural changes proposed in this chapter should be relatively easy to implement, making public acceptance manageable. The changes will even be able to play partially on our short-term views. It is the hope of the Club of Siena's members that we can convince the readers that what we are proposing is a win–win strategy, as will be discussed in more detail in Chapters 5 and 6.

The neoliberal economists claim that changing society toward a green economy will be too expensive and that it will reduce the economic growth significantly – although it is what we have to do anyhow. The same economists recommended that the United States should use enormous funds to save the financial sector from collapse, which in 2009 amounted to $7,700 billion or an amount corresponding to 50% of the annual GNP (see Note 18). If this amount of money would have been spent on a shift to green economy, then we would have been on the right track toward a sustainable society. Instead, the $7,700 billion were spent to repair a nonsustainable system, which at the most can work on a short-term basis.

When the failures of the present economic system have to be repaired, the economists can easily find the needed capital, but when it is a question of a shift toward a sustainable society, then the cupboards are bare.

4.2 We need to reduce, reuse, and recycle

The short-term profit incentive driving our neoliberal economy is very far from being sustainable because it does not consider the rate of natural resource exploitation that it requires nor does it internalize the long-term consequences. It presumes that we can bypass the thermodynamic laws because it is based on infinite resources, but of course it is impossible to violate nature's most basic laws. If we try to build a perpetual motion machine, then we will fail. We cannot and should not exert efforts working against nature, but we should work with nature by accepting the most basic natural laws.

The depletion of natural resources can only be prevented by promoting the three Rs: reduce, reuse, and recycle, but how do we do that when short-term profit is the driving motivation in the economy? The answer is to convince politicians that fiscal incentives (carbon tax, resource depletion accounting, payment for ecosystem services, what we often call a Pigovian tax, etc.) are urgently needed to replace the income tax. The idea is that these fiscal incentives would encourage even the most neoliberal economists or capitalists to use the three Rs on a short-term basis. There will likely be a fight against the introduction of such measures, but the weight of evidence of their necessity cannot be ignored. The resulting economy is sometimes denoted as a circular economy because the resources circle and the economy follows the resources. Today, without incentives such as Pigovian taxes, the recycling rate is far too low. Only 20 metals are recycled at a rate above 50%, and 34 elements are recycled below 1% (Note 19). Even in an ideal circular economy with closed material recycling, the economy is still an open system requiring a continuous, clean energy flux.

Figure 4.2 illustrates the possibilities. Industries, farmers, and individual citizens will apply recycling and reuse directly, to the extent it is profitable, by reduction of waste treatment. The profit, P, of the production is the sales price minus the costs of raw materials including energy, minus the costs of production, and minus also the costs of treating the waste according with the environmental laws:

$$P = S - RM - C - W$$

where S is the sales price, RM the cost of raw material + energy needed for the production, C the production costs, and W the costs of treating (discharging) the waste. Businesses and industries try to optimize profit, P.

Reducing energy and material inputs is often profitable, particularly when the raw materials and energy costs inevitably will increase. To reduce often requires an investment, such as more insulation to reduce the loss of work energy as heat

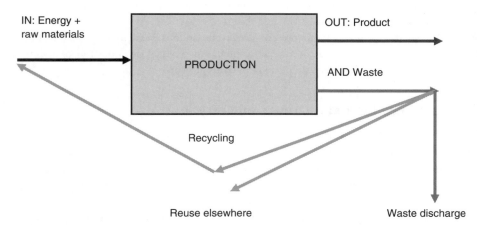

FIGURE 4.2 A production almost always has waste in addition to the product. The waste may be discharged to the environment, reused somewhere else, or recycled, which would save raw material and perhaps energy.

to the environment, which will save work energy. The question is whether the reduced costs due to the reduced use of raw material and energy can pay for the capital (interest) needed to realize the reduction. In many cases, it is very profitable to invest in reducing the consumption of raw materials and energy (or rather work energy), even with the present prices. It is inexplicable and frustrating that investments in "reduction" have not been greater in developed economies, particularly in the United States, because it is straightforward that it is profitable.

Reuse is profitable if the income by reuse sale plus the costs of treating the waste exceed the costs of making the reuse possible:

$$U - O + W \geq 0$$

where U is the income by reuse sale and O is the cost of making the reuse possible.

Recycling is profitable if the value of the recycled raw material plus the waste treatment exceed the cost of recycling:

$$RC - CC + W \geq 0$$

where RC is the value of the recycled raw material, CC is the cost of recycling, and W is as above the costs of discharging the waste. In some cases, it may be sensible to add the value of obtaining a green corporate image.

Generally, the costs of discharging waste have increased considerably during the last decades, sometimes due to the introduction of the "polluter pays principle." Therefore, we have seen an increased interest by industry and agriculture to recycle or reuse. There is, however, still the tendency for states, regional administrations, and communities to try to attract industries by reducing waste treatment costs. This is not acceptable because the costs will then have to be covered directly or indirectly by the regional and local community.

Nonrenewable and partially renewable raw materials are, or are going to be, the limiting factor in our production during this century. In addition, we have seen that as the GNP increases, the environment is gradually deteriorating due to increased waste discharge. Recycling and reuse would improve the situation. These approaches require local labor keeping jobs and money within the community. We could enhance the application of recycling and reuse considerably by increasing the costs of raw materials and of waste discharge by introduction of an ecologically focused Pigovian tax on raw materials and waste discharge, as shown in Figure 4.3. If we add a tax PT1 on raw materials and on nonrenewable energy sources and on waste discharge PT2, then the aforementioned equations would change.

Reduction of the consumption of raw material and energy becomes more attractive because now the interest of the investment needed to realize the reduction just has to be lower than the costs of saved raw materials and energy with addition of PT1.

Reuse is now profitable if the income by reuse sale plus the costs of treating the waste plus the cost of PT2 exceeds the cost of making the reuse possible:

$$U - O + W + PT2 \geq 0$$

Recycling becomes profitable if the value of the recycled raw material plus the waste treatment plus the tax exceed the cost of recycling:

$$RC - CC + W + PT1 + PT2 \geq 0$$

Clearly, reduce, reuse and recycle can easily be made more attractive by a suitable, appropriate resource tax PT1 and PT2. The Pigovian tax could be revenue neutral by reduction in other taxes such as income tax. That may even reduce the costs of reuse and recycling due to reduced labor costs, and thereby it becomes even more attractive to recycle and reuse. The motivation for introducing Pigovian taxes is therefore very strong. In this context, the use of a deposit for bottles and cans should be mentioned as it is an economic motivation to enhance reuse and recycling.

It is possible to find numerous examples of the positive effect of such a tax policy or of the "polluter pays principle." For instance, all industries in the Scandinavian countries have reduced their relative water consumption considerably during the last decades due to a high cost for discharge of wastewater. Particularly, breweries have been successfully able to reduce their water consumption.

Countries within Europe and all over the world, except the oil countries (including Russia, Saudi Arabia, Venezuela, and Nigeria) and the United States, have introduced a significant tax on gasoline. The result is that the gasoline consumption per km is considerably lower in these countries than in the United States and the few other countries where there is not a corresponding tax on gasoline. The Scandinavian countries have, for a long time, had a tax on oil and electricity, and the result is that the energy consumption per capita is less than half the energy consumption in the United States, although the United States and the Scandinavian

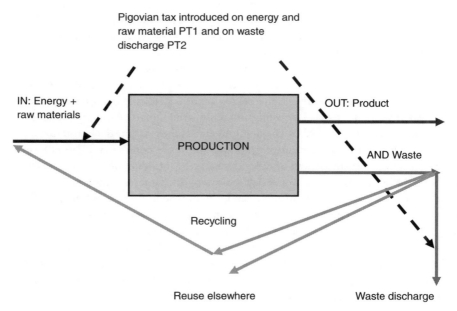

FIGURE 4.3 A production process has wastes in addition to the product. The total global amount of raw materials, particularly if the raw materials are nonrenewable, is limited. Therefore, the introduction of tax on raw material and energy (PT1) and/or on waste discharge (PT2) will enhance the motivation to recycle and reuse.

countries have approximately the same gross national income per capita. Clearly the introduction of Pigovian tax is an effective policy tool to motivate a reduction of natural resource consumption.

It is, however, necessary to introduce a tax on *all* raw materials and on *all* discharges of waste to provoke a major transformation in global resource consumption. Lately, many European countries have discussed the possibilities to decrease income tax because it may suppress employment. The effect on employment and sustainability would even be more pronounced by a transfer of tax from income tax to Pigovian tax. Most governments are, however, conservative and hesitate to make changes. The reduction of income tax and the increase of other taxes can be made gradually over a period of 10–15 years to avoid these changes imposing significant net income changes for a part of the population, which may be the result of very major changes of the tax structure. When it becomes more attractive to reduce, reuse, or recycle, industrial cooperative networks will inevitably be formed to reduce the costs (see also Section 4.6).

A number of important industries have understood the message and have changed the design of their product to facilitate reuse and recycling. Almost all parts of a scrapped car produced by Volkswagen can be recycled. It is easy to separate plastics, electronics, different kinds of metals, and so on. The Danish pump producer Grundfos has similarly designed their pumps to make it easy to separate the parts for reuse or recycling when pumps are scrapped. In these cases, the changed design was introduced mainly to give the enterprises a green image. Introduction of a Pigovian tax will inevitably inspire many more producers to introduce design changes that facilitate recycling.

4.3 We urgently need a transition from fossil fuels to renewable energy sources

Although the amount of coal is sufficient for our energy demand for the coming 200–300 years, crude oil and natural gas resources will only last 60–80 years at current rates of depletion. The high-quality fossil fuels that are cheap to extract are dwindling. Due to a decrease in easy-to-reach resources as well as the growing demand for crude oil and natural gases from the emergent economies, the price of these two convenient, and traditionally inexpensive, fossil fuels will increase dramatically during the next two decades. This will force the world to turn to energy sources that are more costly to produce. More important than the absolute amount of fuel in the ground is the energetic cost it takes to extract this. The concept – energy returned on energy invested (EROI; see Note 20) – calculates the energy obtained per unit of energy that is used to provide it. Table 4.1 shows EROI for various energy forms. If the EROI is less than 5.0, then it is probably not possible to maintain a functioning industrial society. Notice that the energy extracted from tar sands is at the edge of what is required for driving the industrial society. The costs of climate change, other air pollution problems, and the costs of storage of renewable energy sources are not included in the calculations of EROI.

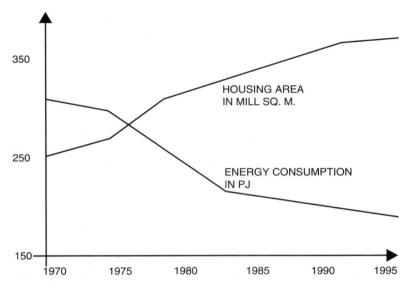

FIGURE 4.4 The Danish energy consumption for room heating and the housing area in Mill. Sq. M. are shown from 1970–2000. The energy consumption has decreased from about 314 PJ in 1970 to about 188 PJ in year 2000, while the housing area simultaneously has increased 50%.

Coal seems to have a beneficial EROI, but the use of coal does not solve the problem of global warming because coal use means even more carbon dioxide per unit of energy than crude oil or natural gas. Moreover, coal mining kills thousands of coal miners per year either because of mine accidents or lung diseases (black lung). Estimates are that 100,000 coal miners were killed during the 20th century in the United States, and, although coal mining is safer today, more than 1,000 miners are killed per year by mine accidents in China, where coal is the dominant energy source. Over 4,000 new cases of black lung disease are reported in the United States each year, and 10,000 new cases are recorded in China. If the costs of solving all the problems associated with coal use are added to the price of electricity produced in coal-fired power plants, then coal will probably not be able to compete with natural gas or wind energy.

Finally, it should be mentioned that coal causes much more air pollution than crude oil and natural gas due to the distribution of fine ash particles that contain heavy metals, including the very toxic element 80, mercury. The air pollution from modern coal-fired power plants can be reduced considerably, but coal-fired kilns are also used for heating individual houses. Therefore, the only solution is to shift to renewable energy sources based directly or indirectly on solar energy. It will make humans independent from fossil fuel resources and address the global warming problem on the long-term basis. The atmosphere of the Earth receives 1,400 watts of solar energy per square meter. The work energy of the solar radiation reaching the surface is more than 10,000 times the work energy consumed by humans. This

TABLE 4.1 Global production and EROI (the ratio energy returned on energy invested). See Note 20. Notice that the costs of climate change, air pollution, energy storage, and other indirect costs such as health problems and mining death risks are not included.

Energy source	GWh/day	EROI
A. Liquid fuel		
Conventional crude oil	116,000	16
Ethanol from sugar cane	560	9
Biodiesel from soy	160	5.5
Tar sand	2,700	5.0
Ethanol from corn	1,300	1.4
B. Electric power		
Hydropower	10,000	40
Wind turbines	830	20
Coal	24,000	18
Natural gas	13,000	7

enormous amount of energy is used to drive the biosphere, but it would hardly be affected if we would cover all our energy consumption by renewable solar energy. We will not lack energy – it is a question of using the right energy sources and using them prudently.

This is, however, not only a question about other energy sources but also of reducing the present energy consumption, which is possible by numerous methods. Most countries could probably easily save 20% of the energy consumption by using waste heat from power plants or waste incineration plants. All economic calculations have shown that the investment needed for more effective energy use would provide a high profit with an interest rate far above the present low market interest rate in the industrialized countries (from a radio discussion among energy experts in 2013). It is surprising that the United States is not taking greater advantage of this profitable investment than is the case. Due to the introduction of an energy tax in Denmark and due to the requirements of proper insulation according to the building standards, Denmark has been able to use less and less energy for room heating while increasing housing area (see Figure 4.4). Recently, U.S. President Obama launched a $1 billion program to abate climate change. The program does not focus sufficiently on renewable energy use and on reducing work energy use, which would attack the problem at its root. Instead, the provisions focus to a high extent on meeting the consequences of the climate changes, such as how to manage for drought and flooding. However, the program also includes measures to emit fewer greenhouse gases by increasing energy efficiency and using carbon sequestration. Overall, the program is insufficient because the changing climate problem can only be addressed by a major shift from fossil fuels to other energy sources.

Nonetheless, it is a small step in the right direction that can be later expanded to include the entire spectrum of possible solutions.

Recently, alternative energy plans for Denmark were presented covering the coming 25 years (Note 21). The present business-as-usual Danish energy policy, which is probably one of the most energy effective in the world, was compared with several other plans. The best plan is based on diverse energy sources: mini-power stations using the waste heat for room heating, solar panels, wind energy, geothermal energy, heat pumps, hydrogen production, and fuel cells. The analysis has shown that it pays to use a diversity of energy sources and let these sources "play together" in a complex network that facilitates the transfer from one energy source to another. It would be possible for Denmark to save €15 billion over the next 25 years and at the same time reduce crude oil consumption by 40% and carbon dioxide emissions by 42%. The loss of work energy would be correspondingly reduced about 40%. It is not surprising that a complex problem – a reliable supply of energy for transport, heating, and electricity in a complex modern society – requires a complex solution where multiple energy sources are used simultaneously and play together to find an optimum solution. One remaining issue to be resolved with renewable energy such as wind is the intermittency and corresponding storage. This has, however, been considered in the aforementioned energy plan, which presumes implementing a smart grid that directs the electricity to the consumer to use it most beneficially and effectively.

While Denmark is still able to reduce fossil fuel use by 40%, many other countries that have not already taken steps would probably be able to save 50% or more. Furthermore, Denmark's plan is largely based on present technology. Wind energy is able to compete today with fossil fuels for electricity production. The high cost of crude oil has driven it from the electricity production market in Denmark and elsewhere. Table 4.2 shows the cost of electricity produced by various technologies, according to the Danish Energy Ministry July 2014 (Note 22). The capital costs are based on 4% interest. The cost may, however, vary considerably from country to country.

TABLE 4.2 Cost of producing electricity in Denmark by various technologies ($/Mwh).

Technology	Capital costs	Fuel costs	Maintenance costs	Total costs
Wind, land based	41.0	0	11.0	52
Wind, offshore	75.5	0	25.5	101
Coal★	39.5	28.0	19.0	86.5
Natural Gas★	19.5	69.5	14.5	93.5
Bio fuel★	38.0	32.5	34.0	104.5
Natural gas	17.0	81.0	4.5	102.5
Solar PV	123.0	0	48.5	171.5

★ The waste heat is utilized for heating.

The costs in Table 4.2 are based on July 2014 prices under the assumption of new power plant construction to produce electricity from 2016–2035. The costs are therefore based on the newest technology. Land-based wind energy is able to offer the most affordable supply of electricity due to decreasing costs during the last decades. Currently, the conversion of solar radiation directly to electricity is expensive, about \$180/MWh, but it can be foreseen that the cost will decrease, as it has been the case with all new technologies, when they have had sufficient development time. In the coming decade, it will be attractive to find a wider use of solar technology, particularly in more remote places where the cost of installation of cables would be very expensive.

The uses of sea wave energy or tidal energy have not been considered yet because no promising results have been obtained. It is important that the industrialized countries invest massively in further research in alternative energy sources. In light of the advancements and achievements so far, further gains are expected, but supply-side solutions are not the only approach.

The Danish energy plans discussed so far have not considered the use of nuclear energy, which has many attractive properties. The nuclear waste problem has, however, not yet been resolved satisfactorily. The risk of nuclear energy is probably overestimated in people's imagination due to the Chernobyl and Fukushima accidents. There have been 33 nuclear power incidents and accidents the last 60 years, but the number of deaths per GWh is much higher for coal energy due to frequent coal mine accidents. It would therefore be beneficial if massive research would be allocated toward the nuclear waste problem because it would open a wider use of nuclear power as an alternative to fossil fuels. These considerations are concerned with fission energy, but it is not possible today to predict if we will be able to control fusion energy in the future. Fusion energy is, under all circumstances, at least 40 years ahead.

Introducing a Pigovian tax can play a very significant role in our effort to reduce energy consumption and particularly fossil fuel consumption. It is therefore – as also touched on previously – not understandable that the United States continues to be dependent on more or less unstable governments in the Middle East, when it would be sensible to reduce the fossil fuel consumption by introducing carbon taxes. This is very unfortunate for the global abatement of the greenhouse effect as the United States and China together contribute about 50% of the global carbon dioxide emissions.

Recently, the United States has started to recover shale gas and oil. The key to use these resources is through the process of hydraulic fracturing, also known as fracking or hydrofracking – a common shale gas extraction process. Fracking has emerged as a contentious issue in many communities due to numerous environmental problems. It is too early to conclude whether they will be properly solved or not. The use of shale gas has reduced the carbon dioxide emission per kWh by about 30% because shale gas is replacing coal for electricity production. Simultaneously, it has made the United States less dependent on imported oil. Since natural gas also emits carbon dioxide, the shift from coal to shale gas reduces, but does not solve, the problem of greenhouse gas emissions.

The carbon dioxide emissions per GNI (gross national income) decreases almost exponentially by increasing GNI. The developing countries have to cover their energy consumption corresponding to the basic needs, which is similar in rich and poor countries. In addition, it is expensive to introduce effective industries, and most developed countries generally have more efficient industries as well as a large share of the economy from less consumptive service industries. The United States and Canada, however, have significantly higher carbon dioxide emissions in kg per GNI than the European countries, most probably due to the much lower use of energy tax in North America (see Table 4.3).

It has been widely discussed if it is beneficial from an economic point of view to abate global warming by investing in renewable energy. It has been estimated that an investment of $1,500–2,500 billion (Note 23) is needed in the United States to increase the share of renewable energy from its current rate of 8–10% to 80–85% by 2050. This corresponds roughly to the annual military budget, or the United States could cut 3% of the military budget over the next 33 years and thereby divert enough money to invest in a transition to about 85% renewable energy. As the work energy use of the United States is about 25% of the global work energy consumption, a total global investment of about $10,000 billion is probably needed to realize the transition from fossil fuel to renewable energy sources: wind energy, biomass energy, photovoltaic energy, solar heat energy, geothermal energy, and hydropower, to mention the most important possibilities. How much would it cost if we accept a 3–4°C increase of the global temperature with the other consequences of even more frequent and stronger hurricanes, tornadoes, and other extreme weather conditions? This is even harder to estimate, but let us try. It has been estimated that the Hurricanes Katrina and Sandy each caused damages close to $50 billion. If we presume that the frequency of such extreme events could be at least three times per year, when the temperature would increase further (the present recorded increase has only been 0.8°C), then the annual costs in 40 years of the extreme weather events could easily be $50 billion × 3 = $150 billion for the United States. This is a low estimate because we have only counted the very extreme weather events of two hurricanes, while there was other damage caused by weather episodes. The

TABLE 4.3 Emission of carbon dioxide in 2011 per $1,000 gross national income (GNI).

Country	kg CO_2/$1,000
United States	0.66
Canada	0.86
EU	0.38
Russia	4.5
China	3.1
South Korea	0.9
Denmark	0.29

total cost for the next 40 years would be the average of $50 billion and $150 billion (annual costs in 40 years) times 40 or at least $100 \times 40 = \$4,000$ billion – considerably more than needed for the investment in renewable energy sources. Globally, the estimation of the costs of extreme weather events would probably be at least four times as much, considering that the United States has more capital to lose than most other countries. Therefore, the overall the cost is more than $16,000 billion or considerably more than the costs of shifting to renewable energy, which we above estimated to be globally $10,000 billion. So, abating global warming makes economic sense. The applied frequency of extreme weather events in our calculations seems reasonable (but probably on the optimistic side) when we consider that the last couple of years there were reported droughts in the Midwest of the United States and in Australia along with avalanches, flooding, and landslides in China and India, to name a few. These economic estimations have a high uncertainty, but there are ancillary benefits as well. Phasing out fossil fuels is a win–win situation because our transition to sustainable energy sources, reduce greenhouse gas emissions, and reserve fossil fuels as raw material for the petrochemical industry. The benefits of these changes would be more transparent if the price of the fossil fuels would consider the harmful consequences of its use.

However, many countries make the opposite conclusion on the basis of their economic calculations. They use an interest rate of 5–6% for renewable energy investment, which is far too high for the currently valid interest market, or they do not consider the benefits gained by introducing renewable energy because sometimes they are too far in the future to be accounted for under current accounting procedures. This is the eternal conflict between short-term and long-term considerations.

It is expected, as already mentioned, that renewable energy will be cheaper and cheaper and more and more effective as the development of energy technology continues. This is the case historically with a number of technological developments. The portable computer today is 10 times cheaper and 100 times more powerful than the portable computer you could buy 25 years ago. The digital camera is 10 times cheaper and 10 times more powerful today than 15 years ago. The TV we could buy 55 years ago had a 17-inch screen without color, and the price corresponded to three months' average salary in Western Europe. Today, you can buy a 42-inch screen TV in color (the screen area has increased by a factor of almost 10) for five to eight days' average salary in Western Europe. Technological developments will inevitably make renewable energy cheaper, particularly when produced at economies of scale. This is in contrast to the expected oil prices 10 or 20 years from now, when scarcity will inevitably increase prices. Fossil fuel is currently supported indirectly and directly by $409 billion per year (Note 23), which is wasted on the energy sources of the last century, while the money could be used to accelerate 21st-century renewable energy options.

Action is urgently needed now because every day about 70 million tons of carbon dioxide are emitted to the atmosphere. We need to decrease global carbon dioxide emissions. However, the transition period will take many years, during which time there will be an increase in the concentration of carbon dioxide in the atmosphere. For every day we hesitate to reduce the emissions at an acceptable and significant rate, the problem is growing. As a consequence, an even faster rate of reduction will be needed to avoid the destructive consequences of climate change. The goal to keep the global temperature increase below 2°C is almost impossible to reach today, and climate negotiators are discussing acceptance of a 2.5°C or even 3°C increase, which inevitably will bring more changes and generate more hurricanes, more flooding, more drought, and more extreme weather events. In this context, it should be remembered that the 2°C is a political target − not based on climate science − but it seems to be a reasonable target considering the realistic possibilities of nature to adapt to temperature changes.

It cannot be excluded that 1,000 ppm of carbon dioxide will be reached in the beginning of the next century (Note 24, and consistent with the discussion in the reference of Note 1) with the present rate of increase of 2 ppm per year, which is only expected to accelerate in the short term. The effects of such changes will be enormous, especially on ecosystems, the cryosphere, and sea level (Note 25), with potentially catastrophic impacts on human society (Note 24).

4.4 Shift from quantitative growth to qualitative development

We cannot continue to support population growth, production growth, consumption growth, and growth of natural resource use according to the basic, natural laws of mass and energy conservation. If we do not obey the basic, natural laws, then nature will kick back on us; the result will inevitably be that our society will collapse. It does not mean that we have to stop development but that we have to shift from quantitative growth to qualitative development, as nature does, when the quantitative growth becomes limited due to resource constraints.

There are numerous possibilities to develop society toward higher quality: better hospitals, better childcare, better schools, better universities, better food choices, better elder care, better transportation options, better communication systems, better environmental protection, and so on. These improvements will require more hands than natural resources, but it is not a problem as many countries are suffering from high unemployment. As we hardly can consume more (it is at least valid for 75–90% of the population in the industrialized countries), we could also work less and have more leisure time or at least make working hours more flexible. Another possibility is to produce more durable products, which can be used for many years instead of the products today based on planned obsolescence (physically, stylistically, or technologically). It would reduce the need for quantitative growth and simultaneously enhance qualitative development.

Qualitative development means that we focus more on environmental protection and conservation, including reduction of greenhouse gases. Unfortunately, the present economic crisis has been used as an excuse for not investing in a more green development, as pointed out by the Nobel Peace Prize winner Mohan Munashinghe from Sri Lanka. He cannot comprehend that we were immediately, when the crisis was hurting most, willing to use billions of dollars on saving the banks, while we are much less generous when we have to invest money in saving the planet.

Quality also means that development becomes more equitable. Currently, at least 20% of the global population lives in extreme poverty, which means that they have less than $1.25 to spend per day. The World Bank has acknowledged lately that inequality adds friction to development – both quantitatively and qualitatively. Furthermore, it is threatening the well-being not only of economy but also of our democratic societies because democracy is based on equality. The World Bank also claims that economic growth is the essential ingredient for sustained poverty reduction, but this is in contradiction with the statistical facts that between 1990 and 2001 for every $100, only 60 cents – or 0.6% – went to people below the $1.25 per-day-line (see Notes 1 and 26). In addition, the growth economy is failing to achieve social goals and provide lasting solutions to the problems of unemployment and poverty, while it is widely acknowledged that fair distribution will alleviate social problems as violence, crime, and drug abuse. Equality seems to be able to mend at least some social problems, whereas growth has been unable to fix the urgent social problems that the modern societies are facing, including the inequality itself. The conventional wisdom that states, "A rising tide lifts all the boats," is simply not working. The facts are that "the rising tide is lifting the yachts and swamping the rowboats" (see Note 23). The income gap between the richest 20% and the poorest 20% is about 3–4 in the Scandinavian countries but 8.5 in the United States (see Note 26), while in the United States there are more than 50 times more prisoners per capita than in the Scandinavian countries. The index of health is similarly increasing with the equality (see Note 26).

Thomas Piketty has provided a detailed examination of inequality development, and his comprehensive analysis shows that inequality has increased significantly during the last two to three decades. The *Financial Times* has published an article that questions the reliability of Piketty's conclusions, but several economic professors and Nobel Prize laureates have strongly supported Piketty's results.

Table 4.4 is based on numerical indications from Piketty's recent book, *Capital of the Twenty-First Century* (Note 27). He claims that inequality is multidimensional because there is a remarkable difference between the inequality in labor income, in capital ownership, and in total income. He is furthermore of the opinion that the observed and also expected decreasing growth rate in the industrialized countries inevitably will lead to increased inequality, and he tries to predict the inequality in the United States in 2030. His predictions are included in Table 4.4. The distribution is presented as approximately observed in four classes of inequality:

- Low (represented by the Scandinavian countries from 1970–1990)
- Medium (represented by the Western European countries in 2010)
- High (represented by Western European countries in 1910 before the First World War and by the United States in 2010)
- Very high (representing the United States in 2030, according to predictions).

The distribution is given for four population groups: the highest 1%, the highest 10%, the lowest 50%, and the 40% in the middle. The distribution is expressed as percentages of total income or capital ownership of the society. The GINI coefficient is indicated in the table as well. The numbers in the table give anxiety for social riot in the countries with most the inequality, particularly if the inequality continues to increase.

TABLE 4.4A Distribution of the labor income in four classes of inequality, expressed as a percentage of the total income of the society (see Note 27).

Income group	Classes of inequality			
	Low	Middle	High	Very high
1% highest	5%	7%	12%	17%
10% highest	20%	25%	35%	45%
50% least	35%	30%	25%	20%
40% middle	45%	45%	40%	35%
GINI coeff.	0.16	0.26	0.36	0.46

TABLE 4.4B Distribution of the capital ownership in four classes of inequality, expressed as a percentage of total capital of the society.

Income group	Classes of inequality			
	Low	Middle	High	Very high
1% highest	20%	25%	35%	50%
10% highest	50%	60%	70%	90%
50% least	10%	5%	5%	5%
40% middle	40%	35%	25%	5%
GINI coeff.	0.51	0.67	0.71	0.81

TABLE 4.4C Distribution of the total income in four classes of inequality, expressed as a percentage of total income of the society.

Income group	Classes of inequality			
	Low	Middle	High	Very high
1% highest	7%	10%	20%	25%
10% highest	25%	35%	50%	60%
50% least	30%	25%	20%	15%
40% middle	45%	40%	30%	25%
GINI coeff.	0.26	0.36	0.49	0.58

The French Mystery, recently published by the two statisticians Hervé Le Bras and Emmanuel Todd, is a technical volume full of statistics about France and the French population. It is almost a best-seller in France. The authors show that France has shifted from growth to development. While economists have derided the lower growth rates, development has occurred on other fronts. The statistics for the last 30 years show that the average educational level has increased, the health of the population has increased, the equality of the sexes has increased, and the differences between the high and low income level have decreased. Is it that important that the gross domestic product (GDP) increases? Is it that important that we consume more and more? Are other aspects of our everyday life not more important than continuously increasing consumption, when we have reached almost the saturation level? It is time in the richest countries that we recognize the limits to growth and emphasize much more qualitative development that can increase the quality of our everyday life.

4.5 Changing the scope of economic growth from increase of GDP to social and natural capital

A possible explanation of the present economic crisis could be a decoupling between parts of the financial sector from the system – society – it should serve. The financial sector thought that it could profit from a decoupling, but the profit was only short term and not sustainable, as the outcome of the crisis has shown. As emphasized in the introduction, the financial sector is not managed properly. Speculation and gambling is allowed in a sector that has an important societal task: to facilitate economic transactions. Therefore, a tax on particularly high frequency of financial transactions due to gambling and speculation could damp these unhealthy financial activities. A Tobin tax on financial transactions (0.1% and 0.001% on derivatives) will be introduced in several European countries, and new rules for profits for leaders in the financial sectors will be introduced in Europe, too. The previous American rules that the banks are not allowed to speculate in the financial sector should be reintroduced. It would be beneficial to direct the money away from financial transactions, speculations, and gambling to the production of useful goods for the population, such as better products lasting longer, better medicine, more efficient cars, and so on. The money used in the production sector rather than in the financial sector could more directly increase the work energy capital. Ecosystems, as we have seen in Chapter 3, develop in ways to gain as much work energy capital as possible, which is giving the ecosystems more resistance toward external impacts. It is therefore important to direct the growth and development in the direction of increased work energy capital in the society and maintenance of the work energy capital in nature. The financial sector should, in this context, be directed toward the economy of the production and service sector and be a much more servile part of society. During the financial crisis, the financial sector ignored the society because the profit of the financial sector became more important than to provide society with needed capital. The financial sector should be integrated with society and participate in providing solid system properties for society, similarly to the ecosystem. Furthermore, it poses a big problem to the economic functionality that some states are acting as tax havens (Luxembourg, Switzerland, Andorra, the Bahamas, and the Channel Islands, to name a few) and act as parasites on the other states.

In conclusion, strong regulations of the financial sector are needed to reduce the unreasonable profit and the possibilities to gamble and make speculative money transfers that have characterized this sector for several decades. Additionally, the financial sector needs to realize its role in society as a facilitator of productive activities so that all sectors blend as a cooperative and synergistically working system with a high level of sustainability. In this manner, the overall work energy capital will increase. These changes of the financial sector will probably require creative legislation, which is an open challenge for the politicians.

If the financial sector would have worked fully and unconditionally with society, then it could have benefitted from the higher utilization efficiency that characterizes systems compared with single components or processes. Society would also have benefitted from an open and unconditional cooperation with the financial sector. It would have been a win–win situation.

4.6 Improving cooperation using the synergistic effect of networks

It has been shown in Chapter 3 how network interactions lead to beneficial and cooperative outcomes that make it possible to improve efficiency of matter and energy in ecosystems. Similar network structures and interactions can be adapted by society and applied on many levels simultaneously. As mentioned in Section 4.5, it is important in this context that the financial sector is not only detached from the rest of society but also that all sectors are contributing accordingly to society. Cooperation between two or more levels of the hierarchy – as occurs in nature – is also important for achieving high utilization efficiency. It is, however, important that two or more hierarchical levels are cooperating, not the higher level controlling the lower levels, as it is sometimes the case in management hierarchy. Control – instead of cooperation – always gives occasion to an increased bureaucracy, which wastes human and material resources.

Cooperation emanating from network interactions offers a series of benefits. Therefore, it is important for society to adopt this approach on many levels and in many contexts. For example, it yields better resource use efficiency, which means that increasing cooperation will entail more quantitative growth by a slower depletion of the resources. A few possibilities mentioned later show these benefits clearly.

Industrial symbiosis, a network of coupled processes similar to those found in ecosystems, has been tested in the Danish town Kalundborg. The network consisting of flows of energy, matter, and information is shown in Figure 4.5. The heart of the system is the Asnæs Power Station (APS). It is the largest power plant in Denmark. One half of the plant is fueled by coal and the other half by a new fuel called orimulsion, a bituminous product produced from Venezuelan tar sands. The use of orimulsion was introduced in 1998 and reduced carbon dioxide emissions by 18% compared with the use of 100% coal. However, due to the sulfur content of Venezuelan tar, sulfur dioxide scrubbers were necessary, which resulted in a higher production of gypsum. The work energy efficiency (chemical work energy in the fossil fuel used) has increased to almost 80% by using energy that is otherwise wasted. APS has reduced the fraction of available energy directly discharged by about 80%. Since 1981, the municipality of Kalundborg has eliminated the use of 3,500 oil-fired residential furnaces by distributing heat from the power plant through a network of well-insulated underground pipes. The home owners have paid for the pipeline but receive cheap, reliable heat in return. The power plant also supplies cooling water that is warmed seven to eight degrees to an on-site fish farm producing about 200 tons of trout per year. In addition, APS also delivers process steam to its neighbors Novo Nordisk (a pharmaceutical and biotechnological industry) and Statoil (an oil refinery). APS produces 70,000 tons of ash that is sold for road building and cement production.

In 1993, APS installed a sulfur dioxide scrubber that produces calcium sulfate or industrial gypsum. Gypsum is the primary ingredient of wallboard, and APS is the primary supplier of gypsum to the wallboard factory Gyproc. Refinery gas, which used to be a waste product, is now sold after desulfurization as natural gas to be used in the town or elsewhere. The desulfurization process produces liquid sulfur that is used to produce a liquid fertilizer, ammonium thiosulfate.

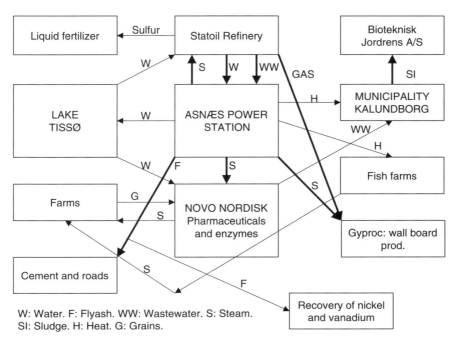

FIGURE 4.5 The industrial symbiosis at Kalundborg, Denmark. The flows of energy and matter make up an "ecological" network that yields a high overall efficiency work energy.

Novo Nordisk is a world leader in the production of insulin and enzymes. The plant employs 1,000 people. The products are produced by fermentation processes. Based upon agricultural crops, valuable products are produced by microorganisms. The waste is a nutrient-rich sludge that can be used by the nearby farmers as animal feed (the yeast sludge) or fertilizers (the microorganisms sludge). More than 3,000 tons of the two types of sludge are produced daily. The yeast sludge is sold, and the microorganisms sludge is given away due to the firm's concern for disposal security. Distribution of the sludge was the least costly way to comply with environmental regulations.

A new partner, A/S Bioteknisk Jordrens (means Biotechnical Soil Purification), joined the industrial symbiosis in 1999. The company uses municipal sludge as a nutrient in a bioremediation process to decompose pollution by toxic substances in contaminated soil.

It is clear from this review of the industrial ecological network in Kalundborg that there is enormous work energy-saving potential in designing an integrated network that promotes by-product synergies. In this context, it could also be mentioned that Nordiske Affaldsbørs (Nordic Waste Exchange) maintains an Internet page with information about industrial wastes produced in the Nordic countries of Finland, Iceland, Norway, Sweden, and Denmark. The idea is that what may be waste for one industry could be used as a raw material for another industry. For instance, used solvent in the pharmaceutical industry may be applicable for production of paint or dyestuff. It is very important to see such opportunities if we want to reduce the loss of work energy or raw materials waste to the environment.

Mimicking nature's use of integrated networks to achieve symbiosis has also been applied in agriculture. The calculations of work energy for various agricultural systems have revealed that the more an agricultural system imitates nature – high diversity, many interactive components, many feedback loops, and recycling of matter and energy – the higher work energy capacity the system has. Biological diversity in agriculture provides buffer capacity and resilience, while monocultures increase vulnerability.

The structure of modern industrial agriculture has been heavily discussed during the last several decades. Organic farming focuses on maintaining healthy soils so plants can flourish and be productive without the need to synthetic subsidies (pesticides, artificial fertilizers, etc.). It solves most of the pollution problems associated with industrial agriculture; organic farming in practice often means that a greater diversity of agricultural products are produced at the same farm with less resources, but not necessarily less profit.

Industrial agriculture is in crisis. It has imitated the linear structure of industries: mass production of one or at most a few products with minimum labor (labor is an expensive input) and large amount of material inputs. While the consumer products have been sold in an increasing amount, the industrialized countries have the need for food of higher quality but not for more food due to a very low population growth. The result of the industrialization of agriculture has been an overproduction of agricultural products. Modern industrial agriculture is furthermore heavily subsidized because it has not been possible for farmers to have the same increase in standard of living as the rest of the population. Farmers have tried to produce more and more to increase their income, but as the size of the market for agricultural products is almost unchanged in the industrialized countries and the export possibilities limited, this strategy has failed and only resulted in higher and higher over-production. The result is that an average farm in Europe or North America today receives annually approximately $35,000 in economic support. When it is considered that agriculture at the same time is a massive polluter, mainly of non-point pollution, it is clear that structural changes are urgently needed in North America and Europe to stop this negative spiral.

Implementations in agriculture of the eight principles of sustainability mentioned in Section 3.17 have been examined in practice (see Note 28) at die Hermannsdorfer Landwerkstätte in Glonn (abbreviated LHL), close to Munich, Germany, and the results are presented later. The practical application of the principles is of major interest in this context.

LHL was founded in 1986 based on sustainability principles. The characteristics of the farm and calculation of the total energy and work energy of this agricultural system is presented later (see also Note 28). Figure 4.6 shows a conceptual diagram of the material and energy flows of this integrated agricultural system. LHL is an illustrative example of the use of sustainability principles in farming, but many more examples can be found.

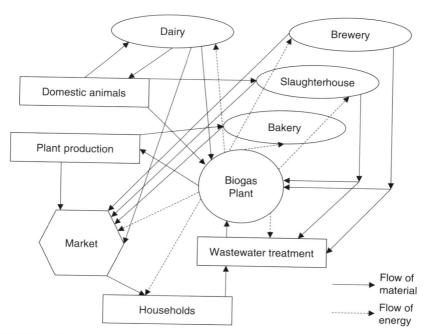

FIGURE 4.6 The material flows (full line arrows) and energy flows (dashed lines arrows) at LHL. The figure illustrates that LHL forms a symbiotic ecological network that facilitates the possibilities to obtain high efficiencies for the use of material and direct work energy, that is, it yields a high overall work energy efficiency.

The characteristics of LHL can be summarized in the following points (cited from the references in Note 28):

1. The principles of organic farming are applied.
2. All distribution is local, ensuring that waste of energy for transportation and conservation is avoided, and all products are tasteful and fresh when delivered to the customers.
3. The local network of skilled workers, customers, and others is utilized. Modern technology (provided non-locally) is utilized but only if it has clear advantages. The various production units are linked in a symbiotic ecological network, which facilitates the possibilities to obtain a high efficiency of material and work energy use; see Figure 4.6. The selection of products and their quality is a result of a dialog between LHL and the consumers.
4. A diversity of animal and vegetable products is produced.
5. LHL encompasses a slaughterhouse, bakery, dairy, brewery, and restaurant.
6. LHL works with nature, not against nature, because it uses nitrogen fixation, hedgerows, and a natural mosaic of the landscape.
7. The energy supply is based on biogas, wind energy, and solar energy. The water supply is, to a high extent, covered by collecting rainwater, and the wastewater is treated by constructed wetlands and reused to a high extent.

Ecological management of farms, as illustrated by LHL, requires more comprehensive and complicated control. For example, it is possible to reduce fertilizer use by developing a fertilizer model that considers all the possible forms of nitrogen and phosphorus and how and with which rate the forms are transformed to each other (Note 29). Figure 4.7 shows such a model for nitrogen.

If the available ammonium and nitrate is sufficient to obtain a close to optimum growth, then there is no reason to fertilize the soil further. Currently, new ammonium and nitrate are formed by the transformation processes; if these rates are known, it is possible to calculate when and whether the soil needs more ammonium and nitrate and for how long will there be a sufficient concentration of ammonium and nitrate for the cultivated crop.

It is also possible to improve weed control by considering (Note 30):

1. The normal emergence of different weeds types is known for the considered fields.
2. Expected crop yield losses due to the weed density based upon recent and anticipated weather conditions.
3. The development of different weed types that are followed by a rough quantification of the amount of weed of different types.

The LHL agricultural system has been compared with a normal Western European, heavily subsidized agricultural system (abbreviated LDK). The work energy of the inputs and the products have been found by the usually applied equations for work energy capacity (see references in Notes 17 and 28). The work energy

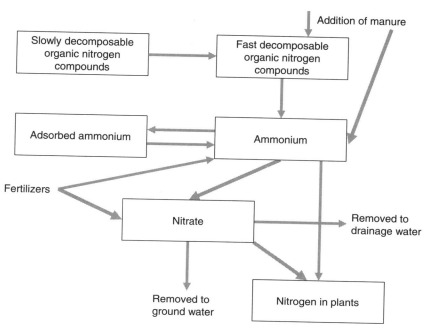

FIGURE 4.7 The model shows the nitrogen cycle in agricultural soil. It is possible to optimize the addition of manure and/or fertilizers by the model. It is not necessary to add more manure and/or fertilizer than the corresponding amount of ammonium and nitrate that is sufficient for uptake by plants. Nitrogen shall not be limiting, but there is no reason that the nitrogen is more abundant than needed. That would only increase the loss of nitrogen to the environment (drainage water and groundwater).

efficiency has been calculated as work energy of products divided by work energy of inputs (not considering the inputs from solar energy). The results are shown in Table 4.5. The table also contains information about the percentage of animal production because the production of animal products is – not surprisingly – more work-energy expensive than plant products. LDK has a slightly higher animal production than LHL but far from sufficient to explain the enormous difference in work energy efficiencies.

The difference in work energy efficiency between LHL (and probably many other organic farms following the principles of sustainability) and LDK (almost a factor of nine!) is explained by the use of artificial fertilizers, pesticides, import of

TABLE 4.5 Work Efficiency for LHL and LDK.

Factor	LHL	LDK
Work energy efficiency	2.64	0.3
% animal products	29.2	33.6

animal food, use of groundwater, and a significant transportation of the products for LDK. Transportation accounts for 46% of the total work energy consumption by LDK, while the need for transportation by LHL only is 7% and 16% of the resources are applied for transportation by LDK. The difference in the need for transportation between LDK and LHL explains partly the surprisingly high difference in work energy efficiencies between the two types of agriculture.

We conclude on the basis of this analysis that introducing systems analysis and ecosystem considerations in agriculture can lead to a more sustainable agriculture. What is more important is that it is possible to develop sustainable agriculture if we use network considerations, illustrated by Figure 4.6.

4.7 Appreciating diversity and understanding that it gives society resistance toward disruptive changes

Nature promotes diversity, while human-designed systems (governments, corporations, or organizations) tend to favor efficiency at the expense of redundancy, resulting in a homogenous society with the lowest possible diversity. The diversity that meets resistance is mostly cultural and religious. Religions are generally very intolerant to other religions; because religion still plays a very significant role in many societies, it is not surprising that religions as well as cultural habits and customs are the barrier for a more open society where there is room for as many different opinions as possible, with the goal being to find better approaches through new ideas. Diversity would lead to higher creativity and a more solid resistance toward disruptive changes because the changes would always be met by some opposition in part of the population.

The large gradient in the standard of living in different countries prevents more open societies. For instance, the large difference between African and European countries stimulates illegal emigration and economic refugees. An ideal open society can probably not be realized before the countries are more equal. It could be a result of a new global order, as will be discussed in Section 4.11 and in the next two chapters. It should, however, be mentioned in this context that it would probably be a more cost-effective solution for Europe and North America to support economies of the poorest developing countries to be self-sufficient and thereby reduce the needs for emigration. In addition, it is generally accepted that when income reaches a certain level, adding more income fails to buy more happiness. According to the book *Enough is Enough* by Rob Dietz and Dan O'Neill (2013) (Note 26), a graph of life satisfaction versus GNP per capita (Figure 4.1 illustrates the shape of the graph) for a number of countries shows a clear saturation at about $25,000 per year per person. But, it is presumed that higher pay serves as an incentive for hard work and innovation. If this were the case, then more patents per capita would be issued in countries with larger income gaps, but it is not the case. It is the satisfaction by being creative that drives people to be innovative. People perform best when they have the freedom to direct their own work and it has meaning and purpose.

4.8 More resources are needed for research, innovation, and education

During the last almost 100 years, we have been witnesses to enormous technological developments that are rooted in significantly increased scientific and technological research. These developments have occurred with a simultaneous increase in education. Unfortunately, the benefits of this increased research have not been distributed equally as the industrialized countries have taken their share, while the developing world has hardly experienced an increased quality of life.

There is no doubt that intensification of scientific and technological research can address many of the holistic problems that humans are facing: renewable energy sources, vaccines for diseases, a cure for cancer, food and water for all global citizens, sustainable development, and so on. Multidisciplinary and interdisciplinary research should be promoted to focus on these holistic, system-oriented problems.

In addition, we are confronted with the need for research in a number of reductionist problems:

* new specific medicine for a number of diseases;
* new energy technologies for all applications;
* batteries that have more capacity for storage of electrical work energy, which will make it very attractive to shift to electrical cars;
* medicine to replace the antibiotics; the resistance to the present antibiotics for infectious bacteria is increasing rapidly due to overconsumption, particularly in agriculture;
* better, more reliable, and faster distribution of information (an improved version of the Internet);
* better knowledge about the environmental consequences of many applied chemical compounds; in industrialized countries, we use about 100,000 different chemicals but only know the consequences for only about 5,000 or 5%;
* many more studies of the consequences of using genetically modified organisms;
* better irrigation systems;
* more energy-friendly transportation systems;
* better understanding of urban design and human well-being;
* connections between environmental pollutants and human health;
* food production systems that ensure healthier and higher quality food;
* and so on.

Many important research topics could facilitate addressing many global problems, including resource access and poverty in the developing countries. There is enough to keep scientists busy for centuries, so there is a lot of room for a qualitative development through research and innovation. Notice that increases in education, innovation, and research represent qualitative growth (a development), which will lead to a more effective use of the resources on line with development of cooperation (see Section 4.6). A slower depletion of the resources will furthermore entail enhanced possibilities for quantitative growth corresponding to the additionally available resources.

One crucial problem is that many politicians in the democratic countries generally are focusing on reelection rather than looking for solving long-term problems. Research costs money now but reaps benefits – very significant benefits – in maybe five, eight, 10, or 20 years. It can be shown that the countries (among the industrialized ones) that are investing most in research and education also are the countries with the fastest increasing economies and often with the best quality of life for the population. A growing economy, however, is, in itself, not necessarily a good measure of sustainability. But given the present competition among countries, it presently may be a good measure to encourage a massive investment in research and education. It is incomprehensible that most countries have not realized this tight relationship between research and education and a successful economy. The EU countries should, in accordance with the so-called Lisbon Treaty, use 3% of GNP for research in 2010. Only Finland has followed the recommendation and, as a result, has increased its GNP significantly the last few years. The countries that have felt the consequences of the economic crisis most – Greece, Italy, Spain, and Portugal – are also the countries that have invested the least during the past 10–15 years in research and education. The EU countries that have been able to meet the crisis with a minimum of privations are the countries that have invested the most in research and education during the previous 10–15 years: the Netherlands, Germany, and the Scandinavian countries have all used more than 2% of GNP for research. The best recommendations to the EU countries (and other countries as well) would be to make clear the global problems of today and invest massively in the solution of these problems:

1. Utilization of renewable energy
2. Global climate change: how to mitigate and adapt most effectively
3. Recycling of nonrenewable resources
4. AIDS
5. Cancer
6. Ebola
7. How to reduce the inequality among countries and among individuals
8. Transfer and utilization of information
9. Better and sustainable utilization of gene (bio) technology but only for the applications that ensure that the environment is not harmed
10. How to incorporate greater ecological-based management
11. A prudent utilization of nanotechnology because it will require very little resources compared with the effect
12. How to solve the poverty problem in the developing world
13. Sufficient and sustainable food production; see also Section 4.10, which mentions the most important problems of today.

Investment in education is needed in parallel to investment in research and innovation. Modern society requires a well-educated population, and the solutions of the urgent global problems will not be possible without a good education for everybody. The inequality is generally rooted very much in a difference in education level. It is not only on the academic levels that good education is required; on the contrary, the prerequisite for all progress is that the entire population – engaged in all forms of employment and activities – has a good education that fits the needs of the jobs and the individual requirements for an interesting and challenging job. Moreover, to be a citizen in a democratic country requires a good educational level because the society is very complex. A right to vote is also a duty to understand the main socioeconomic and political mechanisms.

Unfortunately, as the developing countries have struggled to meet basic needs, they have not invested as much in education, which only exacerbates the deep gap between the industrialized nations and the developing countries. Recently, China has developed quickly, which has indeed been rooted in a clever and massive investment in research, innovation, and education. The best support that industrialized countries can give to the developing countries is economic support toward a much better educational system. It is a major disadvantage in many developing countries that good primary schools for children – not to talk about a higher education – are very expensive, while in many industrialized countries the school is free and of a good standard. As will be discussed in the coming two chapters, it is very important that the educational systems in the developing countries are strengthened radically. The industrialized countries need to invest in the education in the developing countries, and it will lead to a win–win result because the developing countries will be developed, which will imply that they will reduce their population growth (see Chapter 5), improve their living conditions, increase their demand for the services and productions of the industrialized countries, and make it far less attractive to emigrate more or less illegally to the industrialized countries, which is a major burden for these countries.

4.9 Human society is strongly dependent on ecosystem services

Humans, and the socioeconomic systems we create and maintain, are ultimately reliant on nature, but in our everyday life we are removed from direct observation of this fact. Our food and goods come from shops, our water from a tap in our homes, heat and energy at the flip of a switch, and power to transport ourselves by lightly pressing a gas pedal, and so on. Yet, each of these end-use services originated, ultimately, from the environment. The natural ecosystems provide for us:

- regulating services that clean the air and water and moderate the climate
- all our provisioning resources: wood, food (crops, livestock, seafood), plants, genetic materials, fur, chemical compounds)
- a plethora of recreational possibilities
- solid, liquid, and gaseous energy forms that perform heating, cooling, and transportation work
- aesthetic values.

The list is almost endless.

In our everyday life, we take the services provided by nature for given. Nonetheless, we have a responsibility to preserve the ecosystems and protect them against damages and disruptions. Unfortunately, we have unwisely not worried very much about the conditions of ecosystems. We have, due to the enormous impact of our activities utilizing the landscape, extracting resources, and returning waste products, degraded vast areas of natural ecosystems and thereby prevented these ecosystems from providing us with their services.

The value of ecosystem services is very high. Prevention of disruption by protecting and managing them avoids having to find expensive methods to replace the services offered free of charge by nature. For example, if we drain wetlands – nature's water filtration areas – we must install expensive technological methods in order to provide the necessary flow of clean water.

Ecosystem services can be expressed by the work energy that the ecosystem provides per year because all activities – including ecosystem services – require work energy. Table 4.6 lists the value based on the work energy provided by different ecosystems (see Table 3.1 and Note 17). The value in the table is calculated from the cost of electricity: the production of 1 kWh costs about 3.6 euro cents or 5 U.S. cents. It means that 1GJ costs 10 euro or about $14 in U.S. currency. The table also lists the value of the actual used services, calculated according to Note 31. The actual used services have also a high value for the ecosystems that we are using intensively: rivers, lakes, coastal zones, coral reefs, and wetlands.

Lately, there has been a growing interest to assess values of ecosystem services, and it is the hope that this economic assessment will open the eyes of politicians

TABLE 4.6 Value of annual ecosystem services.

Ecosystem	kEURO/ha year (based on Table 3.1)	$/ha year (according to Note 31)
Desert	20.7	?
Open sea	23.8	252
Coastal zones	48.3	4,052
Coral reefs, estuaries	960	14,460
Lakes, rivers	93.5	8,500
Coniferous forests	539	969
Deciduous forests	1,000	969
Temperate forests	1,500	?
Tropical rainforests	3,000	2,007
Tundra	72.8	?
Croplands	420	92
Grasslands	180	232
Wetlands	450	14,785

and economists to the urgent need for nature conservation when economic terms are applied to convince them. Destruction of nature is not only an ecological issue but also is extremely unwise from an economic point of view. A green policy is, in spite of that, not supported very much politically. The idea seems to be: let us take what we can free of charge, when we can. Who knows what the future will bring. A very primitive approach but nevertheless what we apparently must be thinking. Particularly, during the last years when the economic crisis has been the focus, short-term economic growth has been on the agenda and not the needed green, environmental policy that would provide a far better economy on a long-term basis.

4.10 Global agricultural policy

In a resource limited world, it is important to use the available resources efficiently and wisely. Human population is increasing by 70 million per year, meaning we must find food for 70 million more people every year. This is on top of the already more than 800 million people that currently do not have sufficient food and suffer from malnutrition (Note 20). The immediate solution to this problem would be to cultivate more land; but land is a very limited natural resource. With agricultural production, if we cannot continue to increase the area of arable and cultivated land, then we need to extract more crops per hectare but in an environmentally benign way. One way is through better water use efficiency and agricultural management (Note 32). It helps if we distinguish between blue

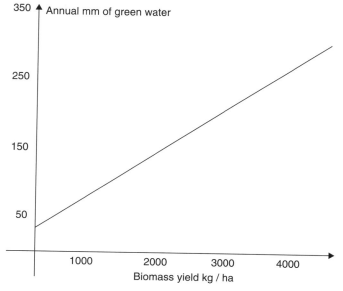

FIGURE 4.8 Yield increases proportional to the water availability provided that water is the limiting factor. Falkenmark and Rockström (2004) (see also Note 32).

and green water. Annual continental precipitation is about 120,000 km³ water of which roughly one-third (40,000 km³) flows directly to the sea. This is called blue water in contrast to green water that is returned to the atmosphere by evapotranspiration.

It is possible to get "more crop per drop," as it is expressed by Falkenmark and Rockström (2004) (see Note 32). Clearly, more water makes it possible to get a higher yield; see Figure 4.8. Notice, however, that there is no biomass yield below 30 mm of green water. Therefore, when water is limiting, it is more water economic to use the water intensively on a smaller area than to expand the area cultivated. This productivity of the green water in kilograms per hectare and per mm green water is increasing with increasing yield (Figure 4.9). A higher efficiency of the water use leads to higher yield. This assumes no other factors (for instance nutrients) are limiting that would reduce productivity, as shown in Figure 4.10.

Evaporation from bare soil is most pronounced just after sowing, and the amount of water required is relatively small. Therefore, a more effective use of the water would try to use it later (see about water harvesting later) and by covering the soil with straw, for example, to reduce the evaporation.

From a water-productivity perspective, the goal is to increase the proportion of productive transpiration flow relative to total evapotranspiration. The evaporation losses in the early season can be achieved by intercropping, rapid development of a canopy, cover, mulching, and improved foliage. What is called vapor shift – the point that productive transpiration replaces soil evaporation – is obtained by increasing shading from a denser canopy cover. Multi-cropping and permaculture

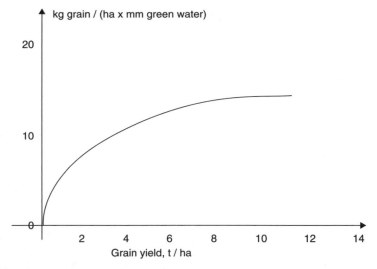

FIGURE 4.9 The plot gives an approximate productivity expressed as kg /(ha × mm green water). Or expressed differently, a higher yield has a more effective use of the green water. The approximate plot is based upon information in Pandey et al. (2000) and the discussion in Falkenmark and Rockström (2004) (see also Note 32).

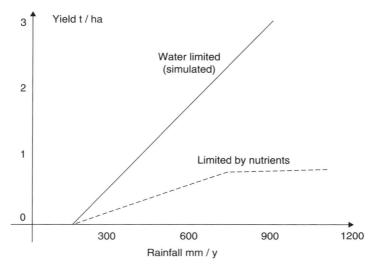

FIGURE 4.10 The difference in yield (t/ha) by increasing water availability with and without nutrient limitation.

are additional techniques that use vegetative diversity to divert more water from blue to green.

Water harvesting is a management practice in which runoff is collected and used for productive purposes. It includes the collection and storage of run-off water, such as in small dams upstream for irrigation uses or water supplies downstream. A number of additional methods that make up the "more crop per drop" approach and far more details than it is possible to include in this context are discussed in Note 32.

Nowhere is the challenge of increasing the food production as large as in the savanna regions, where four interacting processes coincide: 1) rapid population growth, 2) poverty and low purchasing power, 3) poor access to land, and 4) low performing land and agriculture management. The present yield in the savanna region can be increased through better agricultural management and particularly by better utilization of the available water. It should be possible to reduce the water demand by 1500 km^3/y by using "more crop per drop" approaches. We need (see Note 32) a second green revolution with the following goals and conditions:

1. be achieved under highly diverse conditions in terms of soil and water
2. be adoptable by the resources of poor farmers
3. be environmentally sustainable.

This requires a strong focus on agricultural research and development as well as more broadly in the systems that manage agriculture and society (see also Section 4.8), considering the points 1–3. The long-term goals are to more than double the farm yields over the coming 25 years without using more land.

A more effective use of irrigation, along with an increase of irrigation where it still is possible, would contribute another 800 km³/y; but we probably still need to find 3,000 km³/y to be able to produce food for the growing population that, according to some scenarios, may peak around year 2050 at 9 billion. Notice, however, that the 2,300 km³/y that we have found so far are not based on the assumption that we have to cultivate more land. On the contrary, Note 32 references anticipate that we are using the same area of agricultural land as today but using it more effectively. This approach implies no decrease in the natural land of the Earth, and the increased density of trees and plants can even be considered an increase of natural growth.

There are additional possibilities to improve the utilization of water. It is recommended to measure the most important water flows in a drainage area as a function of the precipitation and the seasonal variations. It is called water harvesting; and a further optimization is possible by having a clear image of all the important flows and their dependence on the season (time) and the precipitation. The application of such an improved water harvest strategy requires a complete and rather detailed water flow model of the entire drainage area. It will require many observations and measurements and a comprehensive modeling effort, but, for drainage areas where water is the limiting factor, it would be very beneficial in most cases to develop such a water flow model of the drainage area.

Another initiative would be to consider water as an economic good. It may be necessary to adjust the price given the context, instead of an economic price under all circumstances. The price should give full recovery while considering water as a global right and also safeguarding ecological requirements. On the other hand, increasing prices decreases water consumption; unnecessary or luxury uses of water consumption are reduced considerably. See also the discussion on environmental tax incentives in Section 4.2. Moreover, when water is considered an economic good, it becomes more beneficial to make a second use or reuse of water, for instance use of gray water (water from kitchens and bathrooms but not from toilets, which is called black or wastewater) for irrigation.

To what extent the initiatives mentioned in the last paragraphs can contribute to a comprehensive system for food production is still not clear. In this context, it must not be forgotten that better and stricter family planning also decreases the food problem by the corresponding reduction of food demand. China has shown that it is possible, although the forms of incentives are important. Managing population is the classic case mentioned in Garret Hardin's *Tragedy of the Commons*, in which truly the solution must be "mutual coercion, mutually agreed upon." In other words, the coercion becomes tolerable if it is agreed upon. The alternative to effective population planning is continued pressure on all natural resources, ensuring that sustainability cannot be achieved. A more comprehensive use of family planning will be discussed in the next chapter in relation to the development of the global model.

An agricultural work energy balance in developing countries – based mainly upon human labor without machines – shows that the work energy content of the products is about 10 times the labor work energy applied. In industrialized agriculture, the work energy content of the production is about 6,000 times the labor energy used. However, if we include the work energy used (gasoline, electricity included the energy used in the food industry, and energy for production of pesticides and fertilizers), the work energy applied is about 10 times the energy of the produced food (see Note 33). Therefore, the extra production in industrialized countries comes from applying much work energy in the form of fossil fuels. A significant amount of work energy is also used for transportation from farms to the food industries and further on to the consumers. The work energy consumption of agriculture in industrialized countries is a large part of the total work energy consumption − often more than 10%. A shift in the dietary habits from animal to vegetable food will reduce the work energy demand of agricultural production because animal food requires much more energy due to the respiratory and conversion losses to maintain the domestic animals. The energy saved by this shift could also be used to produce more vegetable food. The energy demand can furthermore be reduced by reducing food waste, which is estimated to be 25% of the global food production. In the industrialized countries, losses occur mainly in households, supermarkets, and restaurants and, in the developing countries, mainly by inappropriate storage facilities and transportation methods.

The objectives of agriculture have been recently expanded to include not only food and fiber but also fuel on a large scale. Agriculture has several promising possibilities for biofuel production such as bioethanol, biodiesel, and direct heat.

Sugarcane in Brazil and corn in the United States are used to produce alcohol, also called bioethanol to emphasize it is produced from plants. If the consumption of work energy for fertilizers, pesticides, and tractors are deducted from the work energy content of bioethanol, then the work energy gained is maybe only about 20% of the total work energy of bioethanol or even less; see also Table 4.1. In addition, sugarcane and corn are valuable food products.

A recently developed production method is, however, able to use waste as raw material for the production of bioethanol: straw and even different types of solid waste. Straw is a by-product produced mainly from wheat and barley harvest. To make bioethanol, the straw is treated at a high pressure and temperature to destroy the binding of carbohydrates (mainly cellulose) from lignin. Enzymes are used to decompose cellulose into lower molecular carbohydrates that by fermentation can be converted to alcohol, which is recovered by distillation from the reactor. The solid waste, after removal of the alcohol, can be used for the production of biogas. The process seems very promising because the raw material is straw and waste. Pilot plan experiments in Kalundborg, Denmark, have demonstrated that the process is realizable. Recently, an industrial scale production unit has been started in Italy using enzymes developed and improved on the basis of the experience gained by the pilot plant experiment.

Vegetable oil can be used directly as diesel oil. Cultivation of fast-growing plants and trees, such as willows or palms, is another possibility. Furthermore, plants can be used directly for production of heat energy, which can either be used for room heating or converted to electricity.

Biofuel is considered a green energy source because it is renewable and is carbon neutral, assuming it is produced without the use of fossil work energy. While burning the biomass fuel releases carbon to the atmosphere, this is equal to the amount absorbed by photosynthesis during the recent growing season. On the time scale of years or at most decades, it is carbon neutral, as opposed to fossil fuels that release ancient carbon back into the atmosphere. There are enormous possibilities for the industrialized countries in the production of biofuel. The possibilities are already there, and they will only increase in the future when fossil fuels will be more and more limited.

The logic behind the agricultural policy in the industrialized countries is not very easy to understand. Industrialized agriculture is a major polluter due to heavy use of fertilizers, causing eutrophication; medicine for domestic animals, resulting in multiple resistant bacteria; and a number of chemicals to support production, leading to chemical residues in nature. Yet, it is heavily subsidized, and the quality of some of the products is questionable. Ecological indicators clearly show that industrialized agriculture is *not* sustainable (see Note 33).

The agricultural products from the developing countries cannot compete with many of the subsidized products in the industrialized countries. It causes major problems for the economy of the developing countries that have difficulties getting started on a proper development without export possibilities for their agricultural products. The industrialized countries support the developing countries with various aid programs. However, it would be much better for the economy of the developing countries and for the agriculture of the industrialized countries, their consumers, and the entire economy of the industrialized countries if the subsidies were removed completely.

Farmers in industrialized countries make up only a small fraction of the overall population. It is therefore not understandable that this completely illogical agricultural policy continues in Europe, the United States, and Japan. A significant part of the agricultural area, probably 5–10%, should go back to nature – forests and wetlands – that would significantly increase the work energy stored in nature of the industrialized countries and thereby the maintenance of ecosystem services. A pattern of nature and agriculture in the landscape would furthermore reduce the nonpoint pollution from agriculture – mainly pesticides and nutrients. Fortunately, this possibility to reduce agricultural production has also started to be discussed in Europe. The industrialized countries should produce much fewer agricultural products but more high-quality, specialized products. That would provide healthier food production, reduce the income tax corresponding to what is applied to subsidize agriculture, and at the same time give the developing countries a chance to increase the export of agricultural products. The industrialized countries were mainly based on economically sound agricultural production 100–200 years ago, but the developing countries cannot achieve a correspondingly sound agriculture economy as long as the industrialized countries subsidize their agricultural production.

Food production provides a useful illustration of the illogic of much of the ideology of growth. The current food production is sufficient to provide the entire population of the world with an adequate diet; but while two-thirds of the world's population receive more than a subsistence diet, resulting in obesity and food waste, many millions are literally starving.

It is possible to produce agricultural goods by sustainable methods, that is, a system that does not need annual subsidies from outside, with nonrenewable work energy or money or both. It requires a new thinking based on ecological principles. This is not only theoretical because agricultural systems building on ecological principles have been tested, and the analyses of such systems show their higher sustainability compared with the widely applied agricultural systems in the industrialized countries. Integrated agriculture producing high-quality food, based on ecological principles and properties – not necessarily organic farming – can address the current industrial agriculture crisis. The main features are better resource use through tighter coupling of ecological processes such that more material and energy is reused and recirculated in a network that provides synergistic feedback. This approach will reduce pollution and produce higher quality products, which can be sold at a higher price and therefore increase the real income of the farmer.

Conclusions regarding looming concerns of agricultural management

Global agricultural development has a particular challenge: how do we continue to produce food for over 7 billion inhabitants and also find enough for an additional 1.8–2.0 billion or more people during the next 50 years? Water is the limiting factor for food production in many regions, particularly where population growth occurs. It is noticeable that the increased food demand (roughly 50%) can be produced at least partially by *not* expanding the agricultural area but simply through better water and agriculture management.

The conclusion of this section can be formulated in the following five recommendations:

1. Reduce agricultural production in the industrialized countries by gradually removing and reducing the agricultural land area. At least a 10% reduction of agricultural land is not unrealistic. The least productive agricultural land should be transformed to natural areas. The ecosystem services of this additional nature would be beneficial for the population.
2. Allow the developing countries to export their agricultural production to the industrialized countries. The industrialized countries should support the transfer of better agricultural education and management to the developing countries.
3. Agriculture in the industrialized countries should produce high-quality products based on integrated and organic farming.
4. Do not expand the agricultural area, but increase the production efficiency through better utilization of water and other natural resources. Approaches have been discussed in this section, which is completely in accordance with a recent publication in *National Geographic* in June 2014 (see Note 34). It will require massive investment in education in the developing countries but also

research to increase the efficiency of the entire global agriculture. Another possibility, which will also require research and further investigations, would be to apply the coastal areas – of course with full pollution control – to produce macroalgae.

5. Reduce food waste in all the production steps, and consider a shift at least partially from animal to vegetable dietary habits (see Note 28).

4.11 How to realize the transition to a new economy

The messages from the *Limits to Growth* books were very clear. We must ask ourselves: why has so little been changed since the first book was published in 1972? It looks like politicians and economists are living in another, very unrealistic world without consideration or awareness of the constraints inherent in the basic natural laws. This book attempts to break through the barrier between politicians and economists on the one side and reality on the other side. It emphasizes the need to change the economic system to be able to adopt the messages from *The Limits to Growth*. Neoliberal economics is not working, as the economic crisis from 2008–2013 hopefully has shown everyone. We need new economic tools to provoke a change to a green economy that is more sustainable than the present "consumption economy." We must integrate the real costs in the economy; it would provide more incentive to change from an income tax to a tax on resources and pollution. This would capture the externalities such as fossil fuel costs of climate change, acid precipitation, acid mine drainage, mercury poisoning, land disturbances, and others. When we compare the present technology with alternative green technology, we need to consider all the present and future costs and disadvantages on the one side and all the present and future advantages and gains on the other side. We need also to use realistic interest and discount rates in these calculations. Moreover, nature provides huge economic benefits to society, and we have to consider these economic benefits when we make decisions about pollution abatement or, even better, whenever we start new activities, including new productions and projects. We accept and presume that the population, at least for the coming several decades, will continue to think primarily in economic terms. Therefore, it is particularly important to include all the costs in our economic decisions. We hope that by accepting that economic cost-benefit analysis will still be dominant in our society the next decades, we will be able to persuade the politicians to use a slightly different, more realistic, and long-term economy to replace the present unrealistic and short-term economy.

We need, however, not only a new and greener economy and to leave the insatiable consumption growth, but we need a paradigm shift in our perception of the world. We need to think holistically. We need systems thinking and to understand that systems are more than the sum of their parts. We should learn from nature how to obtain the advantages of synergistic networks that have a plethora of win–win mutualistic relations. Better cooperation in all levels of society will also have a very positive economic effect. Furthermore, the best the investment society can do is to support education, research, and innovation because these will inevitably lead to better solutions that are more effective both for the economy and the environment. In addition, a high level of education is the prerequisite for a well-working democracy and for an acceptance by the population of the long-term, greener political decisions.

We admit that human nature does not readily accept steady state, but continued progress is indeed possible in a society with a green economy and holistic views. It will be in the form of qualitative development without consumption growth. A life with better quality is indeed worth fighting for. If quality and environmental factors are properly integrated into the economy, then the goals of growth and development are better aligned, which contributes to the overall well-being of the population.

The next chapter will reveal what global differences it will take to introduce the eight lessons from nature. We will use approximately the same global model as introduced by *Limits to Growth* and record the differences when using the eight lessons A–H in Section 3.17, compared with the business-as-usual approach. Introducing the eight recommendations from nature will lead to win–win situations. They are easy to apply, provided citizens and politicians expand their view from being only narrowly economic to be economic-environmental and social and to shift from a narrow short-term view to a much wider long-term view.

Chapter 9 is devoted to this theme: how can we overcome the obstacles? We have tangible suggestions to address to the problems, if we are using our knowledge prudently; but how do we change the entrenched course of business as usual in which stubborn economists and politicians view all life as only a question about economy?

5

WORKING WITH A GLOBAL MODEL

A vision without action is just a dream, an action without vision just passes time; a vision with action changes the world.

—Nelson Mandela

5.1 Introduction

Chapter 3 presented what we can learn from nature about how systems can develop sustainably. Chapter 4 depicted how it would be possible to implement nature's properties to attempt to achieve sustainable development for our society. In this chapter, we will specify the changes that are needed in society to ensure the radical shifts in development, and we apply model scenarios to compare the implementation of the changes with business as usual. We will call for concrete actions in accordance with the chapter epigraph by Nelson Mandela. The proposed actions are based on the eight changes in Section 3.17 with the goals to reach stable but dynamic equilibria regarding the input (resource use), output (waste pollution emissions), and state (population) of the global socio-ecological system. All the proposals will make radical changes in our society, and the behavior of the entire population will be altered as a consequence of these changes. They are, however, urgently needed to shift toward a sustainable society. The specific actions are formulated in detail in the next section.

The key question is: what difference will it make to carry through the changes? To answer this question, a global model, similar to the global model used in the *Limits to Growth* books, but with some slight differences, is applied in Section 5.3. It is hardly possible to assess the differences resulting from the changes without a model. A model is able to overview a complex system and relate the state of the system with the external changes imposed on the system. In model language, we say that we relate the external variables or forcing functions with the state variables or internal variables describing the state of the system. The developed model shows, not surprisingly, that if we do not change anything while both the developing and the industrialized countries continue business as usual, then human societies, as currently configured, will collapse. The collapse will be inevitably due to a lack of resources (input constraint), a too-high level of pollution (output constraint), and rapid population growth (state constraint), the last mainly in Africa and some Asian countries. These model results are completely in accordance with the results of *The Limits to Growth* model.

However, if we implement all the concrete actions presented in Section 5.2, then the model shows that we can obtain a win–win situation in the sense that it offers on average a better life than the global population enjoys today. The win–win model simulations are presented and discussed in Section 5.4, including the assumptions and equations. Section 5.5 will use the global model to demonstrate the importance of the concrete proposed actions one-by-one. The model results in this section clearly show that we need *all* the concrete proposed actions. They all contribute to solutions of the problems that we are facing, although differently. Each of the proposed changes will improve the global conditions for sustainable development – some more, some less – but if we want to ensure a sustainable win–win situation, then it is necessary to introduce all the proposed changes into our society. This is the main result of Section 5.5.

The global model does not distinguish between the various types of resources, but considers

1. investment in pollution abatement
2. adoption and wide implementation of a resource-based Pigovian tax to replace income tax
3. massive investment in education, innovation, and research
4. improved support of the developing countries by the industrialized countries.

These changes will entail:

- less use of nonrenewable resources and more use of renewable resources,
- consumption reduction – particularly of nonrenewable resources – by introducing innovative methods in industry, agriculture, and households
- more recycling and reuse and less pollution
- cooperation of more synergistic networks in industry and agriculture
- promotion of birth control and a decrease in population growth.

The action plan is presented in detail in Section 5.2, and all the details of the plan are taken implicitly into account in the global model simulations discussed in Section 5.4. The entire model can be found in the Appendix.

In addition, it is necessary to address the global warming problem as discussed in Sections 2.2, 2.3, and 4.3 by shifting from fossil fuel to renewable energy sources.

In Section 4.3, it was clearly shown that it would even be an economic advantage to make this shift because the damages that will be caused by global warming will cost significantly more on a long-term basis than the investment needed on a short-term basis to shift from fossil fuel to renewable energy. In addition, the introduction of a Pigovian tax will, as it has been shown in several countries, accelerate the shift to renewable energy sources. It is therefore presumed that the shift from fossil fuel to renewable energy sources is embodied in the elimination of resource depletion and in pollution abatement, which is quantified in the global model. In this context, it should be repeated that oil and gas resources are important raw materials for the chemical and plastic industries. The simulation results presented in Sections 5.3, 5.4, and 5.5 are very clear, but it is necessary to ask: What is the uncertainty of the simulations? How sure can we be about the results? In Section 5.5, the sensitivity of the implemented changes has been determined by model changes in the most crucial equations in context with the examinations. The intention in this context is to achieve an approximate picture of the reliability and sensitivity of the model results. The last section of the chapter, Section 5.6, summarizes the actions that are needed to achieve a win–win situation and the results that will be obtained by this shift in the structure of the society. The conclusions of this section, which are based on the model simulations, are applied in Chapters 6–8; the various scenarios presented in this chapter are elucidated using other development indicators to estimate sustainability.

5.2 An action plan is urgently needed

The message in the *Limits to Growth* books is clear: we cannot continue business as usual; we have to curb population growth, decrease pollution, and shrink our rapidly growing use of natural resources. If we do not change direction, then we will be confronted with a dramatic collapse of our living conditions, probably during the second half of the 21st century. Our impact on the Earth, which is critical in this context, is determined mainly by the three factors (see Note 35):

1. Human population: The ecological impact is roughly proportional to the population. Six billion people, as we were in year 2000, will cause roughly twice the ecological footprint as 3 billion, which was the population in 1960.
2. Consumption per capita or gross national product (GNP) per capita per year: We must strive to decouple GNP per year, as well as per capita and consumption, and turn the focus toward non-materialistic goals such as information, education, art, and science. In addition, promoting reuse, reduction, and recycling entails less resource consumption to provide materialistic needs. Pollution is roughly proportional to the consumption per capita. With an emphasis on lowering resources consumption, pollution will therefore also be reduced considerably using the three Rs.
3. Technological level: Society's impact on the Earth is regulated by the technological level. If technological development focuses on more consumption – more

electronic goods, more sophisticated chemicals (where all the eco-toxicological consequences are hardly known), and so on – then impact increases. However, when new renewable resource forms are developed, better recycling is developed, better environmental management methods are used, and wider distribution of information and knowledge occurs, then the impact can lessen. So, with enhanced investment in education, innovation, and research, the result can indeed be less pollution and reduced use of the resources due to innovative technology.

By slowing down population growth, reducing pollution, and lowering resource use, the impact on the Earth can be ameliorated. This is the core of the message from *The Limits to Growth*, but which concrete steps are needed to ensure these needed changes? The model allows us to show how specific changes will ameliorate these problems.

How can we curb population growth?

A global model by Jørgensen (1994) (see Note 36) has shown that population growth is declining significantly in the developing countries when the GNP per capita increases and birth control is supported. It is also important to raise the education level, particularly for women. Therefore, the developing countries and the industrialized countries must work together to reduce population growth. The industrialized countries must give the developing world a chance to develop and must give sufficient and proper aid. The economic support from the industrialized countries should not be projects that are beneficial for industrialized countries but should go to the root of the problem: the lack of education and insufficient family planning. Why is China today in much better economic shape that it was 20 years ago? Because China has addressed the problem of population growth. It was a top-down method, but it was needed, and many other countries could learn from China. The simulations presented in Jørgensen (1994) presume that all industrialized countries with a GNP per capita of $20,000 or more would use 0.8% (the United Nations recommended 0.7%), increasing by 0.04% per year, of their GNP to support developing countries. Today, only Norway, Sweden, Denmark, the Netherlands, and Luxembourg meet the recommended 0.7% of GNP for aid. If all the industrialized countries would follow the recommendations and in addition use 10% of this aid directly for family planning, then the global population would reach about 8.5 billion in 2040 and afterwards decline to about 6 billion toward the end of the 21st century. This corresponds to the most optimistic prediction made by the UN. This shrinkage of the global population, however, needed and evitable for the long run, will be hotly contested and challenged in the short term because so many of our institutions rely on increasing population to drive the global economic growth. The solution is not to keep raising population, which is impossible over the long run, but to use our ingenuity to discover new ways of providing well-being and social security.

The business-as-usual method is projected to reach a global population of 12–14 billion by the end of the century, if the present growth rates for the developing countries are applied for the entire 21st century. The demographics in the developing countries had still not shown a decline in 1993, but today the statistical results indicate that the number of newborn children per year in the developing countries is approximately 0.044 × the population (the birth rate is 4.4%), but decreasing by 0.005% per year. Therefore, most prognoses expect that the population will peak shortly around the middle of the 21st century at about 9.0 to 9.5 billion, although the UN cannot exclude the high-end level of 12–14 billion at the end of the century.

The following important actions to reduce population growth should be implemented.

All industrialized countries with a GNP greater than $20,000 per capita per year should pay 0.8% of the GNP, increasing by 0.04% per year. This will probably be one of most difficult changes to introduce because there is not much political will in industrialized countries to aid the developing countries. The industrialized countries are, however, today spending a lot of money on illegal refugees, and this is a major problem – particularly in Southern Europe and the southern states of the United States. In addition, the industrialized countries would profit in the long term by having developing countries demand high-tech products and know how. Unfortunately, the industrialized countries are generally far from the 0.8% recommended earlier. In addition, a significant amount of the aid is given in a form that gives no benefits to the development of the receiving countries because it is either indirect support to enterprises and industries of the donor countries or it is arms that will have no effect on the developmental potential of the developing country. Table 5.1 gives an overview of the aid in percentage of GNI (gross national income, which is GNP adjusted with the interest of debt or the interest earned by capital abroad). The table also gives the quality-adjusted aid and charitable giving expressed as GDP (%), which has deducted the aid without developmental potential but includes private charity. As seen in this table, even the Scandinavian countries use about 50% of the aid to support their own companies, enterprises, and industries. For the United States, the difference is even more remarkable in spite of the fact that the United States has private donations of more than twice as much as the foreign aid given by the federal government. It is obvious that the quality-adjusted aid and charitable giving should be increased to 0.8%. In the business-as-usual scenario presented in Section 5.3, 0.22% is presumed, as it is close to the average, with no increase by time.

1. A significant fraction of this support should be applied for family planning, with 10% proposed as a starting point. The model presented in Jørgensen (1994) has examined the effect of 0.8% foreign aid from the industrialized countries combined with the application of 10% of this aid for family planning (see Note 36).
2. An even higher fraction should be used to support education in the developing countries, namely, for instance, 40% of the total support. Supporting education

TABLE 5.1 Foreign aid for a number of countries (see Note 37).

Country	Foreign aid GNI (%)	Quality-adjusted aid + charitable giving as GDP (%)
Sweden	1.02	0.50
Norway	1.00	0.40
Luxembourg	0.99	–
Denmark	0.86	0.48
Netherlands	0.75	0.40
United Kingdom	0.56	0.19
Belgium	0.53	0.23
Finland	0.52	0.19
Ireland	0.52	0.12
France	0.46	0.26
Switzerland	0.46	0.23
Germany	0.40	0.15
Australia	0.35	0.12
Canada	0.31	0.14
Portugal	0.29	0.10
Spain	0.29	0.07
New Zealand	0.28	0.03
Austria	0.27	0.15
United States	0.20	0.07
Italy	0.19	0.07
Japan	0.18	0.09
Korea	0.12	0.02
Greece	0.11	0.07

has other positive effects, mainly on industrial and agricultural development, but for population growth it is presumed that the educational support has 10% of the effect of the direct family planning support. In particular, female education is important in this context, which has been shown to effectively lower birth rate and raise overall prosperity. Similar efforts are underway globally, such as the recent fight of the Pakistani girl Malala Yousafzai, who was awarded the European Parliament's Human Right Prize in October 2013. Recently (see Note 36), UNESCO launched a global monitoring report for 2013–2014 in which the number of children for women in the African countries south of the Sahara with different levels of education was determined. According to the report, women without any education have 6.7 children, women with seven years of education in elementary school have 5.8 children, and women with additional education have only 3.9 children. Still over the replacement rate, but moving in the right direction.

3.   GNP per year and per capita for the developing countries have a very important impact on the birth rate (number of births per 100 inhabitants per year),

as shown in Figure 5.1. Based upon the statistics from 80 developing countries, it has been found that the GNP per year and per capita is well correlated with the birth rate. The birth rate declines by 4%, starting with a birth rate of 4.4 per 100 inhabitants per year, for every $1,000 the GNP per capita per year is increased. This supports the idea that aid from industrialized countries to the developing countries will yield a decrease in the birth rate in the developing countries, particularly when it is given as support to family planning and education (see points 1 and 2), but it has under all circumstances a positive effect. In conclusion, support of education is particularly important in our effort to reduce poverty in the developing countries.

4. Evidence shows that the population of industrialized countries increases very slowly. In the so-called BRIC countries with a transition economy, there is a growing population of the middle-income families in most of the countries. In our global model, this middle-income population – estimated in year 2000 to be 300 million – is added to the 1 billion in the industrialized countries, and the growth rate of the total 1,300 million is based on an average value weighted according to the population. We decided that this gives a clearer image to presume that the 1,300 million = 1,000 million in industrialized countries plus 300 million in BRIC countries with a middle income have the same conditions with respect to birth rate, increase of income, and the general contribution to global development. As the populations of the developing countries are growing, the increase within their middle-class population is transferred to the industrialized countries. This transfer is the main reason for the increase of the "industrialized" population.

The model assumes that 0.3% of the population in the developing countries is annually transferred to the middle class and thereby to the population of the industrialized countries. This annual transfer is increasing 0.0002% per year. The value, 0.3%, corresponds to about 15–20 million per year, which matches the increase of middle class people in the developing countries from 1990–2010 – about 350 million. The final model results are, however, not very dependent on this parameter, which is easy to show using a sensitivity analysis.

The aforementioned proposals to reduce the population growth follow nature's properties, namely E, F, and G listed in Section 3.17:

E. Improve integration on and between all hierarchical levels. Emphasis in this context is on cooperation, not on control. The focus is on developing a synergistic network system in a cooperative society with a spectrum of holistic, emergent properties.

F. Appreciate diversity and understand that it gives society a wider array of resistance and buffers to destructive changes.

G. Promote and value opportunities to increase information. This requires an extensive investment in education, research, and innovation, which will have long-term benefits by making society much more effective.

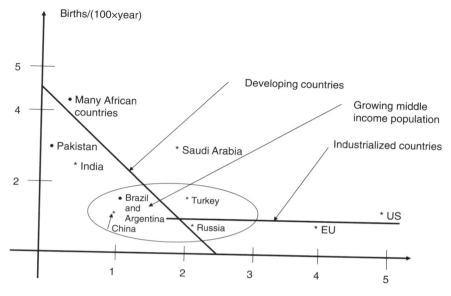

Figure 5.1 The relationship between birth rate and GNP per year and per capita. The birth rate is declining significantly for the developing countries by an increase of the GNP per year and per capita, while it is on a low level independent on the GNP/capita for the industrialized countries. The correlation coefficient is −0.69.

How can we stop pollution growth?

It is necessary to invest in pollution abatement through the introduction of a fair accounting framework, such as a Pigovian tax, based on internalizing the externalities. This means that the "invoice" to the polluter should include the costs of all the consequences of pollution, including the reduction of ecosystem services as well as the damages to nature and other humans. Pollution abatement is considered in our action plan and in the global model as follows:

1. The pollution level starts at a reference value of 100, which increases with 5% of the production in both industrialized and developing countries; 2.5% of the production value has to be allocated to pollution abatement in our action plan, and the percentage increases slightly every year. Pollution abatement is furthermore increasing the Pigovian tax annually by a factor 0.00004%. This means that a tax of 8% will increase annually the pollution abatement costs by 0.032%, or a doubling of the pollution abatement costs will take place in about 80 years. If the starting tax is 2.5%, which represents business as usual, then doubling the pollution abatement cost will take more than 300 years.

2. Pollution has several negative effects, namely increased mortality and decreased industrial and agricultural production. Therefore, not surprisingly, it is beneficial to abate the pollution. Investment in pollution abatement also has a positive effect on the nonrenewable resources, which are reduced to a lower rate. Both the agricultural and industrial production is negatively affected by the pollution and the effect is roughly proportional to the pollution level. For the effect on the industrial production is used a negative effect equal to 0.01 × the pollution. This value is not known and can indeed be discussed, but the effect is probably underestimated by this value. This entails that the model results probably do not exaggerate the negative effect of pollution.

3. Investment in pollution abatement for industrialized countries is made proportional to the pollution level divided by 100, with 100 chosen as the reference value in year 2000. Investment in pollution control will increase proportionally with the pollution level, relative to the pollution in year 2000, because it is assumed that people will demand suitable pollution controls, particularly as pollution level increases. It seems reasonable to expect that the costs of pollution control increases 30% if the pollution increases, for instance, 30%. We chose to apply this additional adjustment of the pollution abatement only for the industrialized countries due to their economic ability and higher production. It is, however, important that the industrialized countries increase the investment in pollution abatement when the pollution level is increasing. The production rate is influenced by the pollution level. In the model, the production rate decreases 0.01 × the pollution level.

4. Production is made dependent on the investment in education, innovation, and research. In accordance to the several reports from the World Bank, investment in research and education is paid back dependent on the living standards in the country with an interest of 10–20%. We assume a 15% return in the global model for the industrial countries, and for the developing countries the production is made proportional to the aid by the industrialized countries with an extra effect of the educational support by multiplying this part of the aid by a factor of four. The return of this investment in education, innovation, and research will partly be in non-materialistic productions and consumptions. In Section 5.5, we discuss how beneficial it is to invest in education, innovation, and research.

The pollution abatement is rooted in the following properties that we can adopt from nature:

A. Using the three Rs (reduce, reuse, and recycle) much more extensively.
B. Using solar radiation, directly or indirectly, as the primary energy source.
C. Transitioning from quantitative growth that requires natural resources to qualitative development. Sometimes this is expressed as a change from a growth-oriented economy to an equilibrium economy, but this is a wrong expression. The society that we hopefully can achieve will only be in equilibrium in terms of population and nonrenewable resource consumption, while it will still develop and be qualitatively dynamic.

D. Changing the scope of growth from economic profit to work energy capital of society and its natural environment. Economic profit, as it has been and still is possible for single persons and organizations, is destructive for cooperation if decoupled from society.

E. Improving society's information level, which will require an extensive investment.

F. Recognizing and accounting for the ecosystem services on which human society is dependent. Maintaining nature's work capacity means that we can continue to receive ecosystem services.

How can we slow down natural resource use?

Pollution abatement will support our effort to reduce the use of resources. Reducing global population growth will furthermore work in the same direction, as resource use is generally proportional to the population. Of course, there is here a huge difference between the use of resources in developing and industrialized countries. With a rough estimation, the use of resources is at least 10 times more per capita today in the industrialized countries than in the developing countries, which in the model is reflected by making the draw of resources proportional to the production or the consumption. Hopefully, the industrialized countries are shifting to a more qualitative growth in the future, which can be reflected in the model by accounting for the investment in education, innovation, and research; the investment in pollution abatement; and an accounting framework than internalizes the externalities.

The actions proposed to slow down the use of resources and how these actions are considered in the global model can be summarized in the following points:

1. Creating an economy that minimizes the level of unwanted wastes by coupling flows through by-product synergies is important; how to realize a proper level is already discussed earlier. In the model, resource use reduction is proportional to the investment in pollution abatement. The proportional constant is estimated to be 15, while the use of nonrenewable and renewable resources is made proportional to the production or consumption by a factor of three. It is proposed to apply 2.5% for pollution abatement in contrast to only 1% in the business as usual scenario. It can be shown that this investment in pollution abatement reduces the use of resources by 12.5% in addition to the reduction resulting from the Pigovian tax. No statistics confirm this number, but it is reasonable to expect that a proper pollution abatement slow down the use of resources at least by 12.5%. In the model calculations, similarly to the principles applied in *The Limits to Growth*, the resources are set to start at 20,000, with consumption every year due to the production in all countries starting with $108 = 3 \times$ production $= 3 \times 36$ (36 agrees with the model results of the production at year 2000). The resources will therefore last with the initial rate of 108 in $20,000/108 = 185$ years. The pollution abatement (1% of GNP is a good global average figure valid today)

and current recycling rate, which is too low, will nonetheless be able to give us 8% more time according to the model, which implies that the resources with the present consumption will last about 200 years.

If the present rate in the increase of production (at least 1.5% increase per year with the present modest increase of recycling) and thereby resource consumption will continue, then it can be foreseen that the rate of consumption of resources will be about 400 (almost four times the present level of 108). Under this scenario, resources will, at the best, last slightly more than 100 years. Let us underline that these numbers of years that the resources will last presume that the insufficient – business as usual – conditions of today are applied. Our resources consist of maybe more than 50 nonrenewable resources that have a very different importance for our production and consumption. It is therefore a simplification to lump all the resources together. Some important resources may be depleted earlier, and some not-so-important resources will last long or vice versa. With our present knowledge about resources (there are a number of statistics giving different results), it is reasonable to guess that there will be a significant shortage of at least a few important resources during the 21st century. A lumped duration of the resources without the introduction of more reuse, recycling, and reduction on 100–200 years seems therefore to be a little on the optimistic side.

2. Efficiencies in our use of the resources are, however, strongly promoted by an accounting framework that internalizes the externalities. This can take the form of a revenue-neutral Pigovian tax; see Section 4.2. In the model, a factor denoted rcy is used to divide the use of resources, assuming that the resources can be reused and recycled again and again. Therefore, implementation of tax policy that encourages resource reuse reduces the use of resources correspondingly and considerably. The value for this market-based resource reduction/reuse "incentive" is not known, as statistics for the relationship between efficiencies and an appropriate corresponding tax are not available. However, Figure 5.2 shows statistics from the United Nations about the relationship between CO_2 emission per GNP and a carbon tax rate. The effect of the incentive is evident. The linear correlation has a Pearson's correlation coefficient of -0.68. If it is assumed that the tax will have the same effect on all resources, not only the consumption of fossil fuel as in Figure 5.2, then it can roughly be presumed that a 2.2% tax will mean an rcy value of 2, corresponding to half the consumption, because 2.2% corresponds to one-half the carbon dioxide emission of no tax from about 0.75 CO_2/(GNP × 1,000) to about 0.375 CO_2/(GNP × 1,000). This is used in the model equation for the influence of the incentive on the resource efficiency.

3. Investment in education, innovation, and research will yield a further reduction in resource use because this will encourage new and more attractive methods to use renewable energy, to recycle, and to reduce the need for nonrenewable and other resources for production. Figure 5.3 shows the relationship between the investment in $1,000 per capita for a number of countries in education

(denoted TERS), innovation, and research and the CO_2/GNP. The Pearson's correlation coefficient is -0.59. The recycling coefficient rcy is made proportional to the fraction or percentage of the GNP invested in education, innovation, and research. The influence of this investment is adjusted to be roughly 1/10 of the influence on rcy by the Pigovian tax, which is therefore the dominant factor. This ratio may be questioned but seems reasonable. The accounting incentive is the dominant factor promoting the three Rs.

4. A lack of resources has a major influence on production. In both the developing countries and the industrialized countries, production decreases when resources are unavailable, which is 20,000 (the initial level) minus the present level. The adjustment in production by the declining amount of resources is five production units when the resources = 19,000 and about 11 production units when resources = 15,000; thus, overall resources are reduced by 25%. It can be claimed that this is too high an impact on production, but it should be remembered that some resources are very important for our present production and that there are no good substitutes for a major shortage of several important metals. There are no statistics that can be applied to assess the relationship between production and the available resources. Furthermore, the global model is a simplification in the sense that all the resources are lumped. Some resources may have been used up decades before

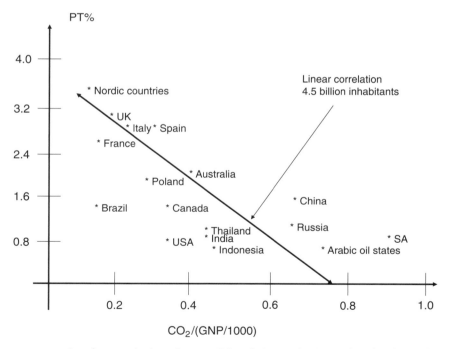

FIGURE 5.2 A carbon tax is plotted versus CO_2 relative to the GNP. The plot shows that there is a clear decline in the carbon dioxide emission relative to the GNP when the tax is increased. The correlation coefficient for the linear correlation is -0.66.

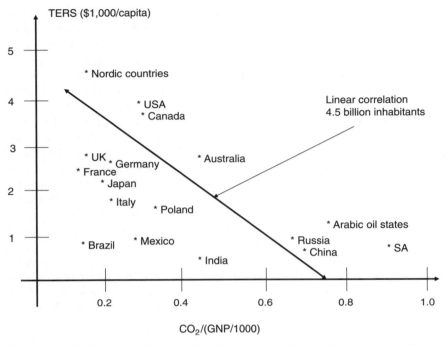

FIGURE 5.3 The investment in education, innovation, and research expressed as $1,000 per capita and per year is plotted versus CO_2/GNP. Increased investment yields a decrease in the carbon dioxide emission relative to the GNP. The correlation coefficient is -0.57.

the end of the century if we do not implement reductions and efficiencies, while some are still available. Many resources are very crucial for modern production. Just consider the use of one crucial resource such as copper in the electronic industry. Or consider the increasing use of rare elements in a number of new applications. Ninety per cent of the production of these important elements currently occurs in China, which underscores that many industrialized countries are vulnerable to the lack of rare elements in the future. It can be concluded that the global model is, on the one side, uncertain about the impact of a lack of resources on production. On the other side, however, the obtained results seem reasonable, at least from a qualitative or semi-quantitative view.

The suggested actions to be taken to avoid collapse, as the business-as-usual model inevitably will entail, are all rooted in the eight properties that we should adapt from nature. The next section presents the global model used in the business-as-usual scenario, and Section 5.4 implements the actions on the global model discussed in this section. The actions are summarized and listed in Section 5.4.

5.3 The global model

The predictions made by the Club of Rome from 1972 to the beginning of this century are largely accurate (see Note 36). We introduce a global model similar to the models used in *Beyond the Limits* (Meadows et al. 1992) and very close to the model applied in Jørgensen (1994) (see Note 36). It was used in 1993 to perform the first test of scenarios based on additional support to the developing countries, particularly for birth control and appropriate pollution control. The global model has eight state variables describing global development under different conditions. We start the model simulation in year 2000, so the initial conditions for the state variables at that time (when $t = 0$) are taken from the Club of Rome's growth model that runs up until that point. A model's complexity can always be discussed, and there are a few Club of Rome models that have slightly more state variables. A more complex model requires, however, more knowledge or more information, and, as the global models used here and by the Club of Rome inevitably have a high statistical uncertainty and only should be used to compare different scenarios, it seems important to select a model of a balanced or at least a not-too-high complexity. The eight state variables of the model are (indicated with four capital letters, also in the model details shown in the Appendix):

1. The production capacity of the industrialized countries, denoted CAPI. Meadows et al. (1992) applies a reference industrial potential in year 1962 of 100 with 75% in the industrialized countries and 25% in the developing countries. Under this scenario, the increase that has taken place since 1962 is the initial value for year 2000, such that CAPI = 340.
2. The production capacity of the developing countries, CAPD, has an initial value in year 2000 = 110, according to the reference in 1962 as indicated earlier.
3. The pollution level, POLL, has an initial value for year 2000 of 100, as already mentioned in Section 5.2. This is a relative value that increases with the production level and decreases with pollution abatement.
4. The available resources, RESS, has, as indicated in Section 5.2, an initial value of 20,000, which corresponds to about 200 years of consumption with the present initial rate of using resources and about 100 years with the expected average value of using the resources during the 21st century, based on business as usual. An annual increase of resource use of about 1.5% is presumed when the resources will be depleted in about 100 years.
5. The annual agricultural production capacity in the developing countries, AGRD, is by year 2000 defined as 100. This initial production is on the order of 20–25% lower than needed to give the entire present population in the developing countries a sufficient diet both quantitatively and qualitatively.
6. The annual agricultural production capacity in the industrialized countries, AGRI, is also a relative value 100 in year 2000.
7. The population in the developing countries, POPD, is 5,000 million in year 2000, of which 300 are included in the population of the industrialized

countries, because the United Nations statistics indicate for year 2000 that approximately 300 million, particularly in the BRIC countries, have a standard of living, birth rate, mortality rate, and consumption on the same level as the industrialized countries. Therefore, POPD in year 2000 is equal to 4,700 million.

8. The population in the industrialized countries, POPI, in year 2000 is 1,000 million (North America, Europe, Japan, Australia, and New Zealand) plus 300 million to account for the middle-class population in the BRIC countries, for a total of 1,300 million people.

The eight chosen state variables are consistent with the Meadows et al. (1992) model and the model used in Jørgensen (1994) (see Note 36). The dynamic simulation software STELLA ©ISEE Systems was used to implement the model and to generate the results. The equations and the detailed conceptual diagram of the model are presented in the Appendix. A simpler conceptual diagram (Figure 5.4) shows the state variables and the transfers but not how the rates are controlled, which are included in the STELLA conceptual diagram in the Appendix. The symbols used in the STELLA diagram are explained in the Appendix before the conceptual diagram. How to obtain the results of using the eight actions mentioned last in Section 5.2 has been discussed in detail in Section 5.2. The results will be presented in the next section. Some of the core relationships expressed in the basic model by mathematical equations, presuming a business-as-usual scenario in contrast to the use of eight actions, may be summarized in the following points:

- Pollution affects agricultural production, industrial production, and population mortality both in the industrialized and developing countries.
- Production in the industrialized countries is decreasing slightly every year, accounting for a materialistic saturation and for the difficulties to continue as an increase of the production when it already has reached a high level.
- Production in the developing countries is increasing slightly every year to express that it is easier to increase production on a low level than on a high level.
- The production capacities, CAPI and CAPD, are presumed to give an interest rate of 7.5% (see Note 38). This rate is the same as applied in *The Limits to Growth* and also about the same as in the book *2052* by J. Randers (see Chapter 2 and Note 39). This means that the production capacity is increasing in both the industrialized and developing countries by 7.5%, provided that we do not consider other factors influencing the production capacity. The rate is, however, increased by investment in education and decreased with pollution level increase and resource reduction. The increase of the annual agricultural production is considered financed by the interest rate; for details, see the equations of the model in the Appendix.
- Likewise, consumption decreases over time slightly in the industrialized countries because they are closer to the saturation and increases over time slightly for the developing countries as they have a significant need for a higher consumption. This interest rate × 0.65 is used in both the industrialized and

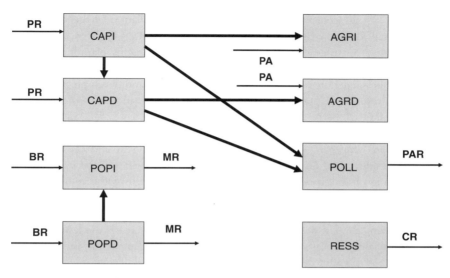

FIGURE 5.4 A simplified conceptual diagram. Only the eight state variables, the direct inputs and outputs, and the transfers are shown but not the controls. In addition, all the state variables have several important controls of rates by the other state variables; see the details about the model in the Appendix. The annual increase of the production capacities, also denoted as the interest rate, are indicated as PR. BR and MR are birth rate and mortality rate regulating the population size. PA indicates the increase in the annual agricultural production of the industrialized and developing countries. The pollution level increases proportional to the production (PR) and decreases due to pollution abatement (PAR); CR is the annual reduction in the resources.

developing countries for consumption (food, clothes, cars, housing, heating, electricity, other goods, and so on).
* The interest rate is furthermore used to determine the pollution abatement and the investment in education, innovation, and research.

The business-as-usual scenario is based on the assumption that:

* A Pigovian tax rate of 2.2% is applied. This level is used in many industrial countries today, although the average is probably slightly higher, closer to 3%.
* The investment in education, innovation, and research is 5% of the GNP, which is a reasonable estimation of the average in the industrialized countries today.
* Pollution abatement is 1% of the GNP.
* Only 0.22% of the GNP is used for support of the developing countries.
* Only 2% of the aid is used for education and innovation in the developing countries, which is very close the present situation as far as it has been possible to obtain the information. Practically no money is used for birth control in the developing countries. A small amount is used in a few countries, such as India. It is more or less the situation today.

The result of this scenario is very depressing. The population in the developing countries will be approximately 9.5 billion in 2050 and 14.8 billion at the end of the century because no investment in education and family planning has been made. Figure 5.5 shows the results of the scenario. The development during the 21st century is shown for the population in the industrialized and developing countries, for the pollution level (starting at level 100), and for the amount of the resources (starting at level 20,000).

The total GNP in the developing countries will furthermore decrease significantly toward year 2050–2060, resulting in a GNP per year and capita of only $500 (see Figure 5.6). This means that the GNP per capita will be one-sixth of the present level, and massive hunger and lack of basic needs will inevitably be the result. Massive illegal migration from the developing countries to the industrialized countries can be foreseen. The income in the developing countries will partially recover during the last decades of the century but hardly reach the level of today. The industrialized countries will also not be able to maintain the present GNP per capita. Shortly after 2045, the production capacity will decline rapidly, and the GNP per year and capita will be reduced to about $3,000 per year and capita (about 10% only of the present level), mainly due to a too-modest investment in education, innovation, and research and in the pollution abatement to reduce the impact from the increasing pollution level, which will be 42% higher in year 2050 and 80% higher in 2100 than the level in year 2000.

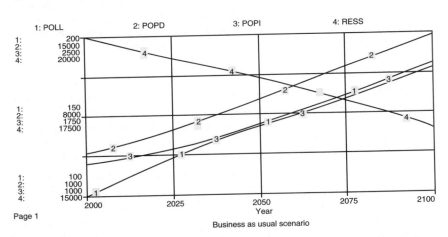

Business as usual scenario

Page 1

FIGURE 5.5 The results of the business-as-usual scenario are shown. The y-axis shows the pollution index (initial value 100), the resources (initial relative value is 20,000), and the population in the industrialized countries (POPI) and in the developing countries (POPD). The unit is millions of inhabitants. The x-axis gives the number of years starting at year 2000. The pollution level increases 89% during the century, and the resources are reduced to about 16,800 or about 16%. The population in the developing countries is increased to about 9.5 billion in year 2050 and further on to 14.8 billion because of poverty (see Figure 5.6) and no aid allocated to family planning or education. The population growth and the poverty will inevitably create an enormous stream of economic refugees.

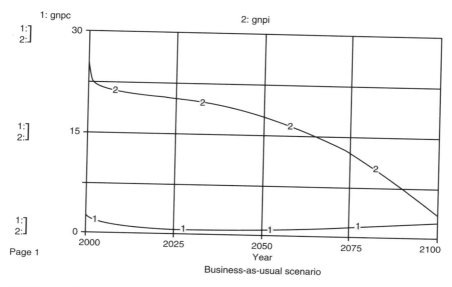

Business-as-usual scenario

FIGURE 5.6 The results of the business–as–usual scenario are shown. The y-axis shows the GNP/capita in $1,000 per year and capita. The x-axis indicates the number of year starting year 2000. The GNP/capita, gnpi, in the industrialized countries are decreasing from about 25,000 to about 17,350 about year 2050 and to as little as $3,440 per year and capita toward the end of the century. This drastic fall in life standard is due to the pollution level; lack of some resources; and too little investment in education, innovation, and research. The developing countries start at $2,850 and decrease about year 2050 to $510 but increase toward the end of the century to $2,140 per year and capita. These changes are even more catastrophic than the changes shown in Figure 5.5 because the low GNP per year and capita in the developing countries will probably inevitably leads to wars, starvation, and economic refugees. However, the industrialized countries are not doing much better, and the results will probably be a complete collapse of the societies.

The disastrous consequences of continuing business as usual have again and again been shouted to the entire global population by *The Limits to Growth* and other books in the last 40 years, but they have been shouted in vain. Why do people not listen? Is it because they do not understand that nature has limits? Or is it because they are rigid and only want to listen to one voice, that of the immediate, short-term economy? Are people so fixated on economic growth (understood as consumption per capita) that they lose sight of other important aspects of human and natural well-being? Our hope is that the proposals in this book can encourage concrete changes that can be implemented so easily that politicians will take the needed steps before we are forced by the circumstances when there will be fewer options, less control, and many more difficulties to overcome. If we blindly follow business as usual, then such unfortunate circumstances will probably emerge more or less unexpectedly in 20, 30, or – at the most – 40 years.

We urgently need to take action and follow an action plan similar to the one that we are presenting in this book. The next section will show how the proposed action plan (following the recommendations that nature has shown us) will lead to a win–win situation. It may, however, be necessary that the changes are coming through the bottom–up scenario and not by top-down methods. Therefore, this is an appeal to everybody to contribute to the shifts and changes in our everyday life and to use all possible effort to elect new politicians who understand how serious the situation is, are willing to make the urgently needed changes, and will implement the proposed actions. In a "new" society, the citizens will understand that it is an advantage to follow the changes, support the necessary actions, and institute long-term planning. They will force the politicians to consider all aspects of a healthy society – not only economy. The future will probably look backward on the period 1990–2030 as the period that was completely dominated by economics, and they will not understand why we could be so narrow-minded.

5.4 Global implementation of a needed action plan

Section 3.17 lists eight lessons, A–H, that nature has taught us. A six-step action plan based on these eight lessons is presumed implemented. The actions, that will be taken and introduced to see the effects in the global model, are:

1. All industrialized countries with a GNP/capita of more than $20,000 per year pay 0.8% of GNP, increasing by 0.04% per year.
2. Ten per cent of this support is used for family planning.
3. Forty per cent of the support is used to improve education in the developing countries, while the remaining 50% is negotiated between the donor and the receptor country. Particularly, education in better agricultural management is urgently needed. The agricultural yield per ha in many developing countries could easily be increased a factor of two to three, or even four, which would reduce the poverty in many developing countries significantly without increasing the agricultural area.

By the actions 1–3, the GNP per year and per capita in the developing countries will increase, which will have a significant positive affect on reducing the birth rate in the developing countries. The birth rate declines by 4%, starting with a birth rate of 4.4 per 100 inhabitants per year, for every $1,000 the GNP per capita and year is increased.

4. Pollution control accounts for 2.5% of the production value. This investment is assumed to be sufficient to control the pollution and has a positive effect on resource maintenance. It is assumed that pollution is proportional to the production value by a factor (parameter) 0.05. Or expressed differently, if the production value increases 100 units, then the pollution increases five units.
5. The Pigovian tax is increased to 8% on average. This tax promotes efficiency and increased recycling and reuse. The effect snowballs because recycling technology is presumed to increase. The pollution abatement has an annual increase, which is slightly dependent on the tax rate.

6. A massive investment, at least 10% of GNP, is made in education, innovation, and research in the industrialized countries, which has a positive impact on production as well as application of the three Rs, and thereby on the mainte-nance of resources.

Each of six steps has a quantitative indication of how resources should be allo-cated to realize the action plan. The quantitative indications are reasonable with the discussion in Section 5.2, and they will furthermore be examined in Section 5.5, when we discuss how much it will change the scenarios to use slightly more or less resources.

The results of using these six changes are presented in Table 5.2 and Fig-ures 5.7–5.8. The last result is the percentage of agricultural growth of the total growth in the developing countries. Not surprisingly, agricultural growth is signifi-cant in the first part of the century (75% in year 2000 and 74% in year 2054 of the total growth, industrial + agricultural), and the massive growth of the developing countries in the last part of the century is mainly non-agricultural (84%). What is directly denoted qualitative growth in the table is calculated based on what is invested in pollution abatement, recycling, and education. In addition, it is expected that there will be a significant growth in biotechnology, information technology, and energy technology that is qualitative. The model cannot quantify this qualita-tive development.

TABLE 5.2 The results of using the action plan with the six changes.

State variable	Unit	Initial value (year 2000)	2054	2100
CAPI	rel.	340	539	814
CAPD	rel.	110	158	659
POPI	10^6	1,300	1,590	1,900
POPD	10^6	4,700	6,768	3,860
TOTAL POPUL.	10^6	6,000	8,358	5,760
AGRI	rel.	100	121	186
ADRD	rel.	100	172	252
POLL	rel.	100	122	104
RES	rel. (1,000)	20	19.4	18.8
GNP/cap. ind.c.	$1,000/cap	29.5	32.4	44.4
GNP/cap. dev.c	$1,000/cap	2.7	3.2	19.5
% qualitative	GNP/cap ind.c.	6.3	22	25
% qualitative	GNP/cap dev.c.	4.4	20	18
Agricultural growth, dev. countries	as % of total growth	75	74	16

As illustrated in Figure 5.7, the population will reach a maximum of 8,358 million global inhabitants toward the decade 2050–2060 but by 2100 decline to about 5,800 million, which is about 15% lower than the current population in 2014. The GDP per year and per capita in the industrialized countries, including a few hundred million middle-class inhabitants in the intermediate countries, will reach a maximum about year 2100 at $44,400 per year and per capita (see Figure 5.7). The developing countries will, however, due to increased quantitative and qualitative growth and to a declining population, have a significant increase in GNP per year and per capita the last decades of the century, but the value will be stagnant or only increase slightly (about 10% only) toward the decade 2050–2060 due to the increased population. However, if we include in the GNP per year and per capita the 600 million middle-class people in the developing countries, then the GNP per year and per capita will have increased about 50% at year 2054 compared with today. This is consistent with the observations today: the increase of GNP in the BRIC countries is mainly going to the middle class. When a developing country achieves higher qualitative and quantitative production, there is, as we have seen in Russia, South Africa, India, and China, a tendency toward increased inequality, which is expressed by the increasing middle-class income population and often a decreased GNP per year and per capita for the population with a lower income.

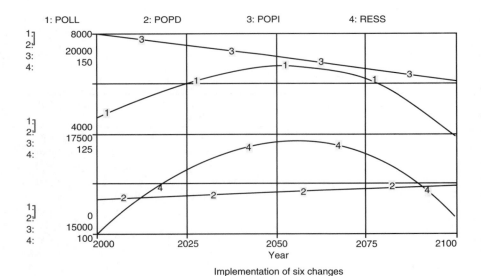

Implementation of six changes

FIGURE 5.7 Implementation of the six changes is foreseen. The relative level of pollution, POLL; the population in developing countries in million inhabitants, POPD; the population in millions of inhabitants in the industrialized countries + the middle class in the BRIC countries; and the relative amount of resources (initial value 20,000) are shown from time = 0 corresponding to year 2000 and to time = 100 corresponding to year 2100. The increasing population in the industrialized countries is mainly due to the increasing middle class in the developing countries.

The rapid growth of GNP per year and per capita in the developing countries toward the end of the century is due to full control of the population growth. Implementation and effects will inevitably take at least a generation before the family planning program will be fully implemented. Once in place, the results are significantly shown in the population statistic. Efforts toward this demographic shift are considered in the model by having an increasing effect on the investment in family planning and education in the developing countries.

Pollution will increase about 20% during the first 50 years of the 21st century, but this is much less than the business-as-usual scenario. Toward the end of the 21st century, pollution levels will return to the same as in 2000, despite increased production. Resources decline but at a smaller rate than under the business-as-usual scenario in spite of continuous growth. Only about 6% of the resources are used by the end of the century. With an increasing production capacity and without pollution control and application of the three Rs, the resources would decline between 108 and 300 units per year, implying a decrease to less than 10,000 at the end of the century. Under the business-as-usual scenario, resources will decline three times as much in spite of a lower production level. The difference is crucial for maintenance of a high qualitative and quantitative production and to avoid collapse due to a lack of resources, high pollution level, and high population growth.

All in all, it is possible to conclude that the six changes introduced are able to provide acceptable results for the global population, both in the industrialized and developing countries. The obvious question is: are the model results at least approximately reliable? The sensitivity of the effects of each of the six changes is examined in the next section and can be used to estimate the uncertainty of the model results.

While all the equations applied are reasonable, have causality, and are based on the statistical information that is available, they still have an uncertainty that may affect the results of the model scenarios because the statistical data are unfortunately limited, as pointed out a few times. In this context, it is important to underline that the presented results are only scenarios – not predictions. The scenarios require that all the six changes are realized; in a dynamic world, other unexpected changes may take place. The results of the scenarios tell us the approximate relative effect of the implemented changes compared with the business-as-usual scenario. Of course, the model cannot account for unexpected natural or human-controlled changes that we have not the slightest idea about today; on the other hand, new experience will be gained and can be applied to adjust the model currently and thereby increase the reliability of the model results.

5.5 Examination of the effects of the six proposed changes, one-by-one

We have the results of two comparable scenarios: 1) business as usual and 2) implementation of changes based on nature's properties. Clearly, the changes of the proposed action plan have a significant effect as they prevent a collapse, ensure

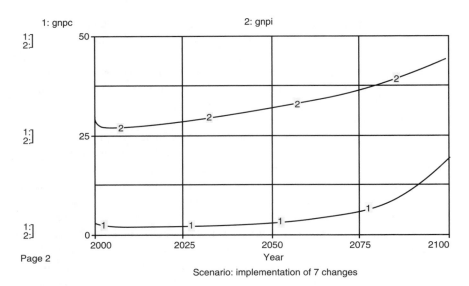

Scenario: implementation of 7 changes

FIGURE 5.8 The GNP per capita is $1,000 per year for the developing countries, gnpc, and the industrialized countries inclusive of the middle class in the BRICS countries, gnpi, are shown from time = 0 corresponding to year 2000 to time = 100 corresponding to year 2100. The GNP per capita and year in the industrialized countries is slightly decreasing during the first decade of the century, which is due to the increasing population of the middle class in the developing countries, as they are included in the population of the industrialized countries. The income per capita will increase in the industrialized countries about 50% during the century, which will be rooted in an increased life quality rather than in increased consumption. The developing countries minus the middle class in these countries will increase their income by a factor of more than six, mainly due to decreased population.

sufficient agricultural production to prevent hunger, yield reasonable pollution control, considerably reduce resource decline, improve the living standards particularly for developing countries, stop population growth, and give a significant boost to the educational levels in all countries. We address the importance of each of the six changes by making univariate changes. The results are shown in Tables 5.3–5.7.

The results if we would only support the developing countries by 0.22%, which is the present level, instead of the recommended 0.8% are shown in Table 5.3. These results are unacceptable because the developing countries will not increase their GNP per capita at all, but a small decrease will even take place – while the industrialized countries will only obtain a slightly higher GNP per capita. The low GNP per capita in the developing countries is due to a population explosion – the result of the scenario says almost 13 billion people in year 2100. The industrialized countries will, under these circumstances, receive a massive stream of poverty refugees, which will be difficult to manage. Most probably, this scenario will never

TABLE 5.3 The results of using the six changes, except the aid to developing countries, in which only 0.22% of the GNP is used in year 2000 and no annual increase is presumed.

State variable	Unit	Initial value (year 2000)	2054	2100
CAPI	rel.	340	570	954
CAPD	rel.	110	70	115
POPI	10^6	1,300	1,656	2,169
POPD	10^6	4,700	9,064	12,731
TOTAL POPUL.	10^6	6,000	10,720	14,900
AGRI	rel.	100	123	201
ADRD	rel.	100	172	243
POLL	rel.	100	121	103
RES	rel. (1,000)	20	19.4	18.9
GNP/cap. ind.c.	$1,000/cap	29.5	34.1	47.1
GNP/cap. dev.c	$1,000/cap	2.7	1.4	1.9

be realized because the poverty may lead to higher mortalities. Wars may also be a possible consequence or other negative political initiatives. The scenario is clearly a lose–lose scenario.

Support levels of 0.8% have been applied in Section 5.4 as the percentage of the GNP in the industrialized countries that should be the aid to the developing countries. The 0.8% is a recommendation by the United Nations, and we have seen that business as usual, which is about 0.22%, is too low. Examining the sensitivity of 0.8% value, we see that if it is increased or decreased 0.1%, then industrialized countries will lose or gain 2–3% in GNP per year and per capita at the end of the century, while the developing countries will get 25% more or less in GNP per year and capita. The population will, however, be much higher in the developing countries – about 300 million more at about 2054 and 800 million more at the end of the century – if the 0.8% is reduced to 0.7%. It is therefore strongly recommended to maintain the 0.8%, according to the United Nations, or even consider a higher level. The result of the scenario in Section 5.4 is based on the relationship between the birth rate and the GNP per capita shown in Figure 5.1. The relationship is causal and has a reasonable correlation coefficient (-0.69). Of course, there are additional factors influencing the birth rate, but it is very difficult to play on these factors as they are strongly dependent on the cultural traditions and a number of political issues in the various countries. It should again be remembered that the results are based on scenarios and cannot be considered as predictions. The scenarios apply the same relationships for the entire 21st century, while in practice it will be politically possible to adjust the percentage of aid. Moreover, it will be possible to apply other relationships if new experience in the future will change the relationship between the birthrate and the GNP per capita in developing countries. Overall, it should be possible to conclude that there is a good basis for an aid percentage of 0.8%, which is increasing slightly year-by-year, and that the aid seems beneficial for both the

TABLE 5.4 The results of using the six changes, except the aid to developing countries does not consider the support of birth control and education, although the aid is still the recommended 0.8%. The results in parentheses correspond to one-fourth of the support applied in Table 5.2 for birth control, and education is maintained.

State variable	Unit	Initial value (year 2000)	2054	2100
CAPI	rel.	340	543 (542)	834 (828)
CAPD	rel.	110	109 (120)	308 (370)
POPI	10^6	1,300	1,632 (1,629)	1,998 (1,973)
POPD	10^6	4,700	7,650 (7,424)	6,768 (5,961)
TOTAL POPUL.	10^6	6,000	9,282 (9,294)	8,766 (8,543)
AGRI	rel.	100	123 (122)	190 (188)
ADRD	rel.	100	175	250
POLL	rel.	100	122	104
RES	rel. (1,000)	20	19.4 (19.5)	18.9 (19.2)
GNP/cap. ind.c.	$1,000/cap	29.5	32.6 (32.6)	43.7 (43.9)
GNP/cap. dev.c	$1,000/cap	2.7	2.2 (2.4)	6.3 (8.1)

industrialized countries and the developing countries, particularly when the impact on the industrialized countries by poverty refugees are considered.

Changes 2 and 3 are the allocation of aid to developing countries toward birth control (10%) and education (40%). If the aid is given to the developing countries as today by supporting developing projects that are also beneficial for the industrialized countries, mainly development of infrastructure, industries, and agriculture, then the scenario gives the results shown in Table 5.4. The main difference from Table 5.2 is a higher population in the developing countries, which again means a lower GNP per year and capita in these countries. Agricultural production, resources, and pollution are only affected slightly.

The equations used for accounting for the effect of 10% support for birth control and 40% used for education are not very certain. There seems to be no doubt about the causality of the applied equations in the sense that the birth control and the rise of the educational level in the developing countries inevitably must decrease population growth and therefore increase GNP per capita in the developing countries because a lower population shares the GNP. This has been tested to maintain the support for birth control and education but by 2.5% and 10%, respectively (one-fourth of the level applied in Table 5.2). The results of the reduction of the support to 25% of the level in Table 5.1 are shown in parentheses in Table 5.4.

Supporting birth control and education in the full amount proposed results in reducing population by about 900 million people in 2054. Without the two supports, the population in the developing countries will be 7,650 million and with the support 6,768 million. The difference is even more significant in year 2100. The results of 25% of the support for birth control and education shows by comparison with

Table 5.2 that the effect on the population in year 2054 means that the reduction of the population in the developing countries is decreased from about 900 million to about 660 million. Consequently, the 10% and 40% application of the aid applied for birth control and education, respectively, should indeed be implemented. The effect on the population in year 2100 in the developing countries is more complex because as the developing countries achieve a higher GNP per capita, the effect of this factor becomes more dominant and the effect of the supports becomes less clear.

The results of these model tests are, however, quite clear. The effect of the support in 40 years on the population in developing countries – the population reduction of 900 million – seems reasonable, although the equation applied for the effect still can be questioned. It is certain that the support for birth control and education has a clear and understandable effect, but it is hardly possible to assess whether it is 900 million or 600 million or maybe even 1,200 million. As the effect is clear, the results should be accepted qualitatively or even semi-quantitatively. Therefore, it is strongly recommended to apply the support and follow the results of the effects and to adjust the support accordingly, using an adaptive management approach. It is crucial for the developing countries to reduce their population growth considerably because it is the key to a higher living standard both qualitatively and quantitatively, which will be very beneficial for the industrialized countries, too. In this context, it should not be forgotten that an adjustment of the aid to the developing countries in both the amount and the allocation of the aid to cover different purposes can be re-assessed as better statistical material about the effects of the aid will be accessible. The results are, however, very clear: let us get started – sooner better than later – with higher support to the developing countries.

The fourth factor to change, use of 2.5% of the GNP for pollution abatement, makes it possible to maintain the pollution level at 121 (21% higher than in year 2000) or lower until year 2054. Thereafter, the pollution level will be reduced toward the end of the century to about the same level as year 2000. The 2.5% increases slightly year by year and also if the pollution level increases. If only 1.5% is used, corresponding to a level closer to the business-as-usual approach, then the pollution level will reach 40% above the present level in year 2000. It is important to underline that the pollution level has an impact on all the other state variables. Industrial and agricultural production, population growth, and resources are all decreasing under a higher pollution level. The model has been used to assess the consequences of using 3.5% instead of the strongly recommended 2.5%. The results of these scenarios are summarized in Table 5.5.

The results in Table 5.5 show that the pollution level, and therefore also the pollution abatement, have a significant impact on the population growth due to higher mortality at a higher pollution level. A reduced population growth is beneficial, but to control the population growth by increasing the pollution level is unacceptable due to a higher mortality; the most effective and still acceptable method is family planning. This result is akin to the statement by Paul Ehrlich – author of the *Population Bomb* – that eventually we have either death control or birth control. It is possible on the basis of the results to conclude that pollution control has a strong

TABLE 5.5 The results of using the six changes. The pollution abatement is, however, starting with 1.5% and 3.5% instead of 2.5% as used in Table 5.2. The increases with time and the determination of the pollution level are unchanged.

State variable	Unit	Initial value (year 2000)	2054		2100	
			1.5%	3.5%	1.5%	3.5%
CAPI	rel.	340	553	529	831	809
CAPD	rel.	110	162	151	807	549
POPI	10^6	1,300	1,610	1,623	1,862	1,936
POPD	10^6	4,700	6,562	6,966	3,258	4,510
TOTAL POPUL.	10^6	6,000	8,172	8,589	5,120	6,546
AGRI	rel.	100	121	122	179	186
ADRD	rel.	100	187	181	227	269
POLL	rel.	100	142	106	138	74
RES	rel. (1,000)	20	19.3	19.2	18.7	18.5
GNP/cap. ind.c	$1,000/cap	29.5	38.6	31.9	45.9	43.3
CNP/cap. dev.c	$1,000/cap	2.7	3.4	3.1	27.0	14.6

positive health effect. Pollution abatement increases, particularly in the developing countries, when those countries can afford it during the second half of this century. Therefore, the overall effect of pollution abatement is most pronounced after year 2054. GNP per year and per capita increases less in the developing countries due to the pollution abatement cost, as a comparison between 1.5% and 3.5% and Table 5.2 clearly shows. The influence of pollution control on the GNP per year and per capita in the industrialized countries and on the resources is minor. The effect on resources comes more from using the three Rs – mainly recycling – which is examined later. The positive effect of the pollution level on recycling is covered by the equations, and it is therefore reflected in the results.

The model results that include a Pigovian tax of 7% and 9% are tested to see the effect of changing this tax rate. The results are summarized in Table 5.6. The main effect of the tax is on the production and the pollution level, as the tax levels the playing field, making greater use of the three Rs, which is able to more than neutralize the effect of declining resources on production and simultaneously reduce the pollution level. Provided the expressions used in the model account for the influence of the declining resources and the increased pollution level, application of the three Rs is very important for maintenance of the production level, although implementation of the three Rs may shift production to less quantitative and more qualitative endeavors. Resources are only slightly influenced by the tax rate, at least as long as the changes are relatively modest, because the increased production implies increased use of resources. This, however, is neutralized by an increased use of the three Rs. The most significant difference between the consumption of resources at a high and a low tax is seen in the first 40–50 years of the century.

TABLE 5.6 The results of using the six changes. The Pigovian tax is, however, 7% and 9% instead of the 8% used in Table 5.2.

State variable	Unit	Initial value (year 2000)	2054		2100	
			7%	9%	7%	9%
CAPI	rel.	340	534	543	793	833
CAPD	rel.	110	152	161	637	678
POPI	10^6	1,300	1,617	1,614	1,945	1,901
POPD	10^6	4,700	6,795	6,345	3,944	3,844
TOTAL POPUL.	10^6	6,000	8,412	7,959	5,889	5,745
AGRI	rel.	100	122	122	186	183
ADRD	rel.	100	174	175	242	254
POLL	rel.	100	125	121	112	95
RES	rel. (1,000)	20	19.4	19.8	18.7	18.9
GNP/cap. ind.c	$1,000/cap	29.5	32.1	32.9	42.9	45.9
CNP/cap. dev.c	$1,000/cap	2.7	3.1	3.3	18.6	20.2

The decrease of resources has a strong impact on production, according to the first part of the century in the model. Policy makers can discuss whether this impact is too strong; on the other hand, our societies are very dependent on a number of resources that will be depleted if we do not start to reduce, reuse, and recycle much more aggressively. For instance, the electronics industry is very dependent on a number of metals that are reused or recycled today only on a very small scale, although we know that the presently *known* resources are depleted within a few decades.

Implementation of the recycling and reuse technology will also add to the production. The Pigovian tax has a clearly positive effect on the general development. It could therefore be considered to increase the rate, as the results demonstrate. In this context, it should be emphasized that income tax is assumed to be reduced correspondingly to maintain approximately the same tax level. A declining income tax, balanced with an increased Pigovian tax, will have a significantly positive effect on production and the maintenance of resources.

Finally, the sensitivity to investment in education, research, and innovation has been investigated by changing the investment to 8% and 12% instead of 10% of the total production value used in Section 5.4. The results are presented in Table 5.7. The main influence of the investment in education, research, and innovation is on the production capacity and the population in both the industrialized countries as in the developing countries. This indicates that GNP/capita is affected even more significantly. It is generally acknowledged that investment in education, research, and innovation is very beneficial for a country. However, this investment yields long-term dividends, beyond the term of office for elected officials who are more concerned with reelection. Consequently, the democratically

TABLE 5.7 Results of using the six changes. The investment in education, research, and innovation is, however, 8% and 12% instead of the 10% used in Table 5.1.

State variable	Unit	Initial value (year 2000)	2054 8%	2054 12%	2100 8%	2100 12%
CAPI	rel.	340	518	558	740	882
CAPD	rel.	110	143	168	560	758
POPI	10^6	1,300	1,619	1,615	1,918	1,857
POPD	10^6	4,700	7,031	6,916	4,627	4,095
TOTAL POPUL.	10^6	6,000	8,650	8,531	6,545	5,952
AGRI	rel.	100	122	122	184	182
ADRD	rel.	100	175	174	251	250
POLL	rel.	100	122	124	105	103
RES	rel. (1,000)	20	19.3	19.4	18.7	18.8
GNP/cap. ind.c	$1,000/cap	29.5	30.0	34.9	38.6	50.0
CNP/cap. dev.c	$1,000/cap	2.7	2.9	3.5	15.2	24.0

elected officials' policies run counter to goals of long-term betterment of the society. Ironically, the higher the educational level in a country, the better the population understands the importance of education and the more it will be inclined not to vote for shortsighted politicians who do not prioritize education, research, and innovation.

5.6 Conclusions based on the model results

Generally, it can be concluded by comparing the business-as-usual scenario with the scenario based on the six changes that it is important to implement *all* the changes of the proposed action plan:

- use 0.8% of GNP for aid to the developing countries
- massive use of the aid for birth control and education, 10% and 40%, respectively
- use 2.5% of GNP for pollution control
- internalize the externalities by introducing a Pigovian tax of about 8%, and simultaneously decrease income tax to remain revenue neutral
- use about 10% of GNP for education, research, and innovation.

Section 5.5 has examined the effect of the six proposed changes one by one. Our results demonstrate the importance of aid to developing countries to stabilize population growth. Likewise, it is clear that the effect on population growth is significantly better when the aid is applied for birth control and education. Pollution control using 2.5% of aid seems to be close to optimal, provided that the model draws the right picture, which is probably at least qualitatively correct. A modest

Pigovian tax has a major impact on the pollution level and resources and thereby on the production capacity. Particularly, there is a sharp decline in resource use due to a high production capacity. The resources can be maintained at a level that still makes a high qualitative and quantitative production capacity possible. Under the business-as-usual scenario, the resources are also maintained but only due to the collapse of the production capacity. It would furthermore be beneficial to raise the tax rate from 8% to 9% or maybe even higher. The use of the three Rs, which is enhanced considerably by introducing the tax, contributes to the GNP per year and per capita by the work needed to apply the three Rs. Our knowledge about the effects of a wide use of a high Pigovian tax is unfortunately very limited. Therefore, while we conclude that this tax has a positive and clearly causal and understandable effect on the resources and production capacity, it is hard to indicate the right level of the tax rate. However, once such a policy is introduced more widely, it will be possible to gain experience and adjust the rate accordingly. The conclusion is, however, clear: do not delay internalizing the externalities with a rate of at least 8%.

The main influence of a massive investment in education, research, and innovation is not surprisingly on the production capacity and population growth, although there is also a minor effect on the pollution level and the consumption of resources. However, maybe the indirect effect of the educational level is the most pronounced. A higher educated population will generally require and select better politicians and can better accept that many investments will have a long-term positive effect, such as the effect of renewable energy to mitigate climate changes. The model has, of course, not been able to include this indirect effect.

Nature has shown us (Chapter 3) that all the proposed changes are beneficial to sustain the focal systems. In nature, this encompasses ecosystems and the environmental conditions of their organisms, and for us it is society and the living standards that are offered to us. The proposed changes offer a win–win situation in which both the environment and society realize improved conditions. This goes for societies in both the industrialized and developing countries. It is a puzzle why the politicians do not rush to introduce the changes. *Homo sapiens* are easily conditioned to focus only on the shortsighted and narrow-minded question of "what can *I* gain – preferably here and now?" Furthermore, the democratic countries that should lead the changes have maybe the most shortsighted political systems: the politicians are encouraged to provide immediate gratification to the voters to ensure reelection, as quoted by the economist Dambisa Moyo (see Note 40). She also emphasizes the importance of education, as it will lead to a strong and well-educated middle class that will require and understand the needed long-term investments in infrastructure, education, research, pollution abatement, the right aid to developing countries, and renewable energy sources. She is very critical of the present aid to African countries because it is given more as support to activities in Africa for companies in the industrialized countries, and this includes the African involvement by China.

The needed changes are difficult to introduce because we are generally skeptical of politicians, which is often unfortunately legitimate, and we are hardheaded when defending our rights. We do not at all consider the global population but are preoccupied with our local cares and concerns of maybe a few hundred individuals. Our holistic mind is very underdeveloped.

We are aware of the skepticism in the United States of introducing a resource-based consumption tax to replace income tax. But the experience in Europe is that it significantly reduces fossil fuel consumption. The reaction in the United States expresses both the skepticism to the politicians and also our shortsightedness.

Our global model does not consider changes to the financial structure that are needed to reign in the Wall Street wolves and create a fairer playing field. Policies in this direction would make society more equal, which is a prerequisite for a broad acceptance of long-term decision making. Moreover, the damage caused by inequality in society has been clearly demonstrated (see Note 41). Health and social problems increase with income inequality; life expectancy, child well-being, literacy, social mobility, and trust are all better in more equal societies; infant mortality, obesity, teenage pregnancy, homicide rates, criminality, and incidence of mental illness are all worse in less equal societies. The current realization of neo-liberal capitalism has made societies more unequal. In the United States, where this doctrine has been most dominant, the 400 richest people have more capital than the other 320 million U.S. citizens (see Note 42). Therefore, it is absolutely necessary to make structural changes in addition to the recommendations from the global model exercise shown earlier. The states have to limit financial speculation and support policies that result in more equity in society. Such approaches have started in Europe, particularly Northern Europe, very slowly. Such changes toward a more real democracy in the original meaning with democracy have to take place if we want to solve the problems of the business-as-usual scenario. The present neoliberalism encourages shortsightedness and narrow-mindedness. Currently, many decisions are distilled to a matter of simple, short-term, cost-benefit economics. Therefore, the current system presents hurdles to implement the needed changes to society. Economic analyses, however, very often give wrong and biased results:

1. They do not consider that nonrenewable resources are limited and have to account for their loss in capital values when they are decreasing due to consumption.
2. They hardly consider the benefits by implementing green technology in the future due to decreased likelihood of natural catastrophes such as hurricanes, fires, flooding, and so on.
3. They fail to adequately account for the loss of ecosystem services, although the loss of nature's free services can be very costly for society.
4. If future benefits are considered in the economic analysis, then the values are adjusted to the present value by deducting an annual discount rate, which the economists do not know but have to guess.

Points 2 and 3 refer to what economists call externalities, and particularly the environmental economists admit that these costs should be included in the economic analysis. The false picture that economic analyses give can best be exemplified by the total lack of warning from the economists leading up to the 2008 crisis. Most economists gave very optimistic messages just a few months before the crisis started. Therefore, we need tools to make better decisions than the present narrow-minded and shortsighted economic analyses. We need to have tools that overcome the four flaws listed earlier. Unfortunately, rather than develop better tools, a more likely response is for the status-quo proponents (economists and some policy makers) to criticize and challenge the model results with arguments such as:

1. It does not pay to abate the greenhouse effect because the economic calculations cannot account for benefits that are more than 10, maybe even 20 years ahead.

2. We cannot calculate the benefits of fewer hurricanes or a better environment when we are accounting for more than 20 years ahead because the predictions about economic conditions will be so vague that it will be impossible to conclude anything. The benefits are adjusted to the value today according to the discount rate over the considered period.

3. If the investment in greenhouse gas abatement has to be justified, all countries must do their share. If, for instance, 1% of the global population makes the necessary investment and the other countries do nothing, then the benefit for the 1% will only be 1% of what they actually should gain. This explains why the many global meetings about climate change have resulted in very vague statements without hardly any effect. None of the countries want to be the first to make the investment needed and then after some time admit that it has been in vain. Therefore, all countries are sitting on the fence at the global climate meetings.

4. Similarly, for recycling of a number of nonrenewable metals, we know that there will be a shortage later in this century. Although recycling will be beneficial for the market price of the metals for all countries and delay the economic disaster of shortage considerably, it does not pay here and now to invest in recycling, unless almost all countries do it and thereby keep the consumption sufficiently low to stabilize the prices.

5. We admit the costs of externalities are very rarely included in economic analyses, but the methods to include them are not yet very developed, and it is not the tradition to include them, although there are exceptions.

6. Generally, it is hard for us economists to make calculations for a period even as short as five years because our calculations are dependent on the interest rate, and it is impossible to predict the rate more than one or maybe at the most two years ahead. In addition, as soon as our forecasts are more than five years, the interest rate has a major influence (which is easy to demonstrate) on the value of benefits which are four, five, six, or even more years ahead.

These criticisms are addressed in Chapter 9.

Economists mostly admit when they are confronted with the obvious shortcomings that limit reliability of economic development, but unfortunately politicians still believe blindly in economic analyses that are most often based on neoliberal concepts. Therefore, we need these economists to speak more openly about the limitations in their analyses and make it clear to all the managers of our society that these shortcomings have to be considered. It is absolutely necessary to supplement an economic analysis with environmental and social analyses, and together these analyses are equally important for the final decisions. This is a prerequisite for the realization of our action plan, in coordination with the results from our global model. In this manner, we may influence traditional neoliberal economists to consider the aforementioned shortcomings in their analytical methods and possibilities.

It will be particularly difficult to persuade the American people, who are generally anti-state control, about the benefits of a consumption-based tax, stronger environmental legislation, aid to developing countries, and state-supported education of high quality. The present economic difficulties demonstrate that the current system is not working; we need to revise our economic system. Meanwhile and hopefully, there will be some changes in Europe and the rest of the world that demonstrate clearly the need for changes, or the real democratic forces will be sufficiently strong to take more responsibility and power.

The model exercises have shown that there is an uncertainty – of course – in the model results, but it can be concluded qualitatively and even semi-quantitatively that it is absolutely necessary that we get started to implement the six changes. With these, there is a high probability for a much brighter and more sustainable future for our global standard of living than under the business-as-usual scenario. The model results show not only that the wolf is coming but also how we can meet the wolf. But do not listen to the economists that claim that the wolf is not coming because then we cannot prevent the attack, which may come as a surprise. Let us get started to meet the global challenges with actions that will make a difference.

Even with the model results in hand, we cannot conclude that the six changes will ensure sustainable development. The model focuses on how we can solve the problems of population growth, resource depletion, and pollution abatement and how we can maintain a reasonably high, although more and more qualitative production, to ensure a good economic basis. Solutions to these core problems are prerequisites for sustainable development. Their solutions are necessary but not sufficient. Therefore, it is necessary to supplement the model results with the use of indicators to analyze the sustainability. Chapters 7 and 8 will introduce and use two important sustainability indicators: ecological footprint and work energy capacity.

6

TO THINK LIKE AN ECOSYSTEM IS KEY TO WIN–WIN OUTCOMES FOR HUMANS AND ENVIRONMENT

An Invitation – Thinking Like an Ecosystem. Now we are realizing that ecology is not merely a particular field of science; it is a new way of understanding life that frees us from the failing mechanical worldview's assumptions of separateness and scarcity.

—Frances Moore Lappé, *EcoMind*, 2011

Think Win–Win

—Stephen Covey, *The 7 Habits of Highly Effective People*, 1997

6.1 Introduction

In previous chapters, we raised the question of why world leaders and citizens have not heeded the warnings and predictions of the *Limits to Growth* books and related work. We also suggested that change may be impossible in the context of the current mainstream neoliberal economic system. We presented eight lessons to learn from nature and how coordination of eight changes related to these lessons – if all done in concert – could lead to real progress. We have proposed the need for a paradigm shift in our perception of the world, for thinking holistically, and for systems thinking. We have also identified the need for a high level of education and believe this is essential for a working democracy and for success in meeting the challenges of sustainability.

In Chapter 3, we described 14 propositions of an ecosystem theory and explained how these produce the four-billion-year success story of self-sustaining living systems. We also showed how human systems do not follow these basic tenets of ecosystem organization and how this leads to our unsustainable impacts on Earth. In Chapter 4, we described governance, policy, and development changes that

would steer us toward a more sustainable path by implementing the 14 propositions. These efforts, which we may view as largely *top-down* solutions implemented
through active leadership at higher levels of government and society, include Pigovian taxes and related laws and policies intended to penalize unsustainable practices
and reward sustainable ones on the part of corporations, communities, and citizens.

In this chapter, we develop a set of complementary ideas and supporting case
studies to bolster the necessity of a whole-scale transition from a focus on growth
to a focus on development as the primary goal of human endeavor. The transition
can lead to life-enhancing, win–win outcomes. This chapter again explores the
view that our problem is in understanding fully the current human–environment
crisis and also in seeing clearly that nature and living ecosystems provide pragmatic
examples of how to solve the crisis. But here we present a unique attempt to for-
malize a holistic understanding of life and the life–environment relation that can
provide the basis for a specific and new kind of education and literacy related to
the environment. Most importantly, we propose here several key aspects to aid a
bottom-up groundswell of new thinking.

Clearly, the action plan needed as a result of the global model and the evidence
in Chapters 1–5 calls for a top-down solution, but if we want to be successful with
the proposed changes, we need a simultaneous bottom-up movement. We need all
people to work together on the solution and the corresponding action plan, otherwise it will fail. Both top-down and bottom-up solutions are needed and should
work hand in hand. To realize the bottom-up solutions, in this chapter we present:

1. The critical need for a paradigm shift in our scientific as well as everyday
   thinking, which would also require revised textbooks and definitions of life;
   new ways to teach biology, ecology, and life science; and a new cultural mindset
   and mental model of "what is life?"
2. A depiction of this paradigm shift as linked to the central systemic cause of
   why we continue to degrade the environment despite knowing better.
3. Strategies from systems modeling, including the intentional choice of system
   boundaries, which can aid the cognitive shift to new and more holistic everyday thinking and foster a culture in which most people naturally "think like an
   ecosystem."
4. Three inspiring case studies demonstrating how such holistic thinking leads to
   real world success and win–win outcomes between humans and environment.

We see the ideas and bottom-up strategy in this chapter as a powerful com-
plement to the governmental and top-down approaches presented earlier. This
bottom-up approach works at the "grassroots" level of challenging, correcting,
aligning, and renormalizing the everyday thoughts, assumptions, and worldview of
citizens away from a mechanical separation of life–environment and toward holistic
reintegration of life–environment. Unless a majority or critical mass of citizens
think this way, then people may resist, reject, and push back against the top-down
taxes and policy reforms imposed by leaders and experts. If we work from both top

down and bottom up in coordinated fashion, then we have the best chance to succeed in creating ecologically oriented, sustainable communities.

To recap our global circumstances briefly, as we have said, many now characterize the current situation as a human–environment crisis or global ecological crisis, and the evidence clearly supports this mental framing of our predicament and the many simultaneous challenges we face (climate disruption, excess CO_2 emissions, peak oil, species extinctions, water quality and quantity problems, etc.). But does it have to be this way? Must it be true that the actions of more than 7 billion (and every day more) humans necessarily lead to degradation of the natural environment and jeopardize the life support and ecosystem services on which we fully depend for every breath we take, every drop of water we drink, all the food we eat, and all the beauty and diversity we think of as "life on Earth"?

We submit that this outcome – what Garrett Hardin described as the inevitable "tragedy of the commons" – does not need to occur, that we have alternatives, and that we can be successful. Living systems integrate and utilize resources in ways that are not always tragic but also mutualistic, synergistic, and life enhancing, resulting in a "beneficence of the commons" not typically recognized nor given credit for the sustainable complexity of these systems. And as we have shown, natural ecosystems organize themselves in ways that are successful and by which a win–win life–environment relation is a real possibility and practically achievable.

Next, we propose that a truly sustainable human–environment relationship, including outcomes that solve our current suite of dire systemic problems, cannot and will not be achieved unless we change dramatically our thinking, perspective, and conceptual framing of the problem and solution cases. If we are able to update our most basic understanding of how the world works and what the current symptoms signify, then we see great hope for making better decisions, choosing and implementing better actions, and realizing better outcomes. In analogy with health care, a cure depends fully on a proper diagnosis. And, in analogy with the growth and development of an individual person, when one reaches adulthood, one must adopt a new understanding of the self, the world, and the self–world relation in order to change behavior in an appropriate way, to stop acting like a teenager and start acting like an adult. When a human individual reaches a fully grown adult condition, the body stops growing in size and mass, and the person shifts emphasis – consciously and naturally – toward development of mind, skills, and capacities. In similar fashion, we believe the "body" of humanity has grown to a full size that has matched the scale of life support capacity of the planet, and we as a species should now shift toward development of personal, social, national and global skills; capacities and non-consumptive activities such as arts, recreation, and spirituality; and similar social, cultural, and personal development endeavors.

To accompany and catalyze this transition to a form of planetary human maturity, we propose the need to revise our most basic ideas and mental models of life, environment, and the relationship between life and environment. Our current scientific paradigm of life science, and our current mainstream image of life in modern industrial culture, focuses on organisms and individuals as fundamental, independent, objectified, and isolated units of life (and fundamental units of economies, i.e., the rational individual). As long as this remains our sole scientific model and single cultural image, we mainly study isolated population dynamics, and we get stuck grappling with seemingly irreconcilable choices between either using the environment for human needs or in saving the environment for itself. If we adopted a new paradigm of life and environment in which the two are integrated into a single holistic, co-supporting life–environment system, then this apparent paradox goes away. We then can see the system as a whole and can actualize the "humans-and-environment system" developing with complementary, synergistic, and mutually beneficial structural, functional, and dynamic relations between humans and environment.

We present and continue to develop a holistic science paradigm that integrates major subdisciplines of biology and ecology to provide an innovative view of life and nature and that we believe then provides better means to apply nature's lessons, successes, and role models to solve human–environment problems. The proposed paradigm involves dual and complementary models of life, analogous to dual and complementary models of light in physics. We propose that organisms and individuals represent "discrete life" (similar to particles or photons of light), while communities, ecosystems, and the biosphere represent "sustained life" (similar to nonlocal and wave aspects of light). We also propose a means to integrate core models focused on 1) organism/individual, 2) community/ecosystem, and 3) biosphere/planet into a single holistic multimodel.

Some key examples of win–win human–environment relations are presented, and we examine specific details that make these cases successful in achieving local/regional environmental sustainability. Finally, we explore how such a revised foundation for life–environment science can be applied to serve human needs and consider links to ethics and social movements for change.

6.2 The proposed paradigm shift – to think like an ecosystem

In this section, we recap and update an existing portrayal of the proposed paradigm previously presented (see Note 43).

We suggest that we (those in industrial and Western scientific cultures) now think with, and live by, a central error in our understanding that is codified into all biology textbooks and dictionary definitions of life. The essential error we see is that *our current paradigm fragments life from environment* and treats life and environment as separate and separable categories. From this foundational idea, we see that formal education is misguided and leads to errors in understanding, which further cause 1) the inappropriate emphasis on growth and overemphasis on competition, 2) a kind of social Darwinism that is used to justify hyper-competitive economics and business practices, 3) a belief in trickle-down economic benefits, and 4) antagonism between rich and poor, as well as many other notions and practices that continue to drive environmental and social degradation. This starting wrong idea and worldview predictably does generate the tragedy of the commons – it is like a self-fulfilling prophecy. This negative influence travels upward from the thoughts and actions of many individuals and results in global impacts, and this is why we suggest the need for a bottom-up approach toward solutions.

Contrary to the dominant mainstream view, the basis of all current biology and life science education, it now is becoming clear that *life is not only (or even primarily) an organismal property*. In the view actively emerging, life is not centered, situated, located, or emanating from organisms, nor is it primarily a localized, objectified, or material phenomenon. Instead, *life has inherently relational, distributed, and non-localized* qualities that are essential for understanding life itself, for framing the current problem correctly, and for success in envisioning and actualizing the solution. Since this is increasingly seen as true, we need to rewrite all biology textbooks and change our dictionary definitions – we need to change our minds, mindsets, and collective intelligence at the individual and grassroots level – about the basic nature of life and environment.

The view of life as organism may have made sense during previous eras of human history. It was a useful, simplifying assumption that helped to focus attention on organisms and their growth, development, anatomy, physiology, evolution, and more. But this mental model equating life with the unit of organism was a limited construction – shorthand that left out crucial details about the intimate, continual, and necessary relation between life and environment. This limited construction and narrow abstraction must now be updated to fit our new global environmental context and reality.

More comprehensive mental models and holistic views similar to what we propose already exist, but these must be amplified and elevated in importance and recognition. These must renovate our first principles of life. A few textbook authors recognize this, paving the way for this new understanding. Keller and Botkin (see Note 44), for example, stated:

> To understand how life persists on Earth, we have to understand ecosystems. We tend to think about life in terms of individuals, because it is individuals that are alive. But sustaining life on Earth requires more than individuals or even single populations or species. . . . Living things require 24 chemical elements, and these must cycle from the environment into organisms and back to the environment. Life also requires a flow of energy. . . . Although alive, an individual cannot by itself maintain all the necessary chemical cycling or energy flow. Those processes are maintained by a group of individuals of various species and their non-living environment. . . . Sustained life on Earth, then, is a characteristic of ecosystems, not of individual organisms or populations.

Harold Morowitz and others have similarly hinted at an essential distinction between the "discrete life" of organisms, individuals, and even populations compared to the "sustained life" of ecosystems and the biosphere.

We develop and add corroborating evidence and concepts to this new perspective, emphasizing "sustained life" that is actively emerging now in work in ecological network analysis, systems sciences and systems ecology, energy network science, and relational systems theory (see Note 45). This alternative perspective integrates relational, network, systems, holistic, pragmatic, evidence-based, and win–win approaches. We propose this holistic life–environment system approach can actually work to solve our current suite of chronic and systemic environmental disease symptoms, and we assert that it fits better with real data and evidence of how the world works. This perspective also builds on key principles described in Chapter 3, including the high degree of recirculation of matter and energy in ecosystems; the increased efficiency of ecosystem organization; the example in nature of the 3 Rs; and the cooperative mutualistic relations that arise from higher order, indirect interactions (see Sections 3.3, 3.4, and 3.13).

The perspective we propose has four core tenets:

1. Life and environment are best understood and modeled as unified as a single life–environment system.
2. The "discrete life" of organisms and individuals is distinct in category or type from the "sustained life" of ecosystems and biosphere, and these dual models must always be used in concert in both thought and action (neither model nor concept of life is sufficient on its own) analogous to complementary models of light as both particle and wave.
3. Three holons (or submodels) of life – organism, ecosystem, and biosphere – are conceptually integrated into one hyper-holon (or multimodel) that is the life–environment system.
4. A hyperset equation (with inherent self-reference) serves to unify formally life and environment, discrete and sustained life, and three submodels of life and thus serves to explicitly and formally *prohibit fragmentation of life from environment* (an essential unity), of discrete from sustained life, and of any of the submodels of life. This equation is: life–environment = {environment{ecosystems {organisms{environment}}}}.

This formalism *prohibits fragmentation of life from environment* (repeated emphasis to note how essential and how different from the mainstream paradigm) by defining the whole right side of the equation as a single entity. The way that environment appears twice in this equation – at the outer level to signify the planetary environment and biosphere and at the inner level representing the similarly "abiotic" chemical components, such as those inside cells and organisms – also serves to unify this model of life as a seamless yet hierarchical unity.

In Figure 6.1, we depict a holistic representation of our current problem context. Rather than emphasize one of the current problem trends – many of which are full-scale global disasters and crises in their own rights – we seek to understand how all of these negative symptoms are related and similar. As earlier, we propose that an important way to imagine the central factor that serves to unify the causal understanding of these harmful environmental side effects is our paradigm of life and life science. This is the shared mental model of life at the center, and this

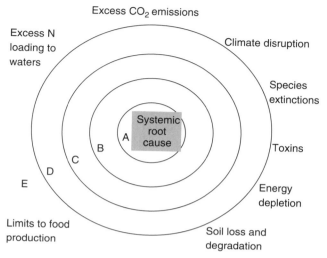

FIGURE 6.1 Superficial symptoms of global ecological crisis emanating from central systemic cause – shared mental model "life = organism only." Modified from Fiscus et al. (2012). See text for explanation of links A to E.

is linked to tragedy of the commons outcomes by a simple set of relationships that radiate outward (and influence travels from bottom upward, from individual thoughts-actions to global impacts) in stepwise fashion:

A. A mental model, "life = organism only," is shared by science and promulgated via education to most people in industrial culture. It is the assumed and shared normative idea for life.
B. Inherent in this mindset, *life is separated from environment* in mind and action. This is the key error (or outdated paradigm) that severs the unity of life and life support systems (carrying capacity).
C. Once fragmented, it is possible and likely that *the value of environment is seen and treated as less than the value of life.* Note that it is not possible for this relative devaluation of environment to occur if life–environment remains unified as a single focal entity and system of study.
D. Individuals act for self-interest primarily and compete for what they perceive as limited, scarce, and zero-sum resources.
E. Environment is consumed and degraded as manifest in many symptoms of ecological crisis, and the influence of the citizens' mental fragmentation and devaluation of environment travels upward to larger scales and produces the global crisis.

The essential goal and outcome of the new framing of the problem and solution we propose is that it opens the way to more tractable and *systemically effectively* actions for change. Using this comparison of life–environment models as our lens, we see that our current human–environment relation is win–lose – as we live and operate (grow, gain, and win), the environment degrades (and loses or is diminished) and that this antagonism and conflict begins with our fragmented model of life and environment held and operating at the individual, citizen, grassroots cultural level. The proposed unified life–environment paradigm – as a key component of a bottom-up solution strategy and effort via education and communication – prevents this antagonism and win–lose outcomes, thus making possible a win–win relation in which both humans and environment are enhanced in concert. This ensures sustainability for life and environment over the long term. This is another way to argue for the necessity of the eight coordinated changes described and modeled in Chapters 4 and 5.

Using network analysis, it has been shown that mutualism is the norm in ecological networks; when all direct effects (from first-order, proximate interactions) and indirect effects (from higher-order interactions) are integrated, most pair-wise relations between species or components in ecosystem networks are win–win (see also Section 3.13). Despite this widespread pattern of mutually beneficial relations between living entities, humans (mainly in modern industrial cultures) defy this pattern and clearly show negative impacts on other species, the atmosphere, soils, and other integral components of the biosphere. Understanding why humans are aberrant in this respect, why we continue to resist change, and conceptualizing and developing the real capacity to alter this detrimental relationship are top priorities.

Admittedly, the site-specific implementation of sustainable win–win human–environment systems, and scaling these up to the global scale, are difficult, but the first key mental shift is immediately doable – it just depends on where we draw the system boundary and whether we conceive of life and environment as separate, isolated, and different in type or category versus a concept of life–environment as a single, integrated, complex, and dynamic system. In the unity of life–environment, we see the fates of ourselves (our individual lives) and our life support systems (environmental carrying capacity) as forever tied. Once tied in this way, we are able to think, plan, and act for the continued health and well-being of both. This is to "think like an ecosystem," and it is ostensibly the best mindset to generate the sustainability, diversity, and resilience successes that ecosystems have achieved over millennia.

6.3 Boundaries and modeling strategies

Systems theory is about a distinction of boundaries, and the first step to systems analysis usually entails the drawing of a system boundary to identify the focal system of study and to specify clearly which aspects of the world are excluded from analysis or modeling. But if one adopts the view that our current ecological crisis stems from a mental and subsequent actual fragmentation of life from environment, then the potential arises that the real solution lies in a non–objectification paradigm in the first place. Another way to say this and to operationalize and utilize this idea is to integrate the works of Patten on environ theory and Elbow on dialectical thinking (see Note 46).

Elbow proposed a dual and complementary modeling approach as a kind of fundamental method for thinking and cognition. Writing about such dilemmas as the Heisenberg uncertainty principle, he said:

> The dialectical pattern of thinking provides some relief from this structural difficulty inherent in knowing. Since perception and cognition are processes in which the organism "constructs" what it sees or thinks according to models already there, the organism tends to throw away or distort material that does not fit this model. The surest way to get hold of what your present frame blinds you to is to try to adopt the opposite frame, that is, to reverse your model. A person who can live with contradiction and exploit it – who can use conflicting models – can simply see and think more.
>
> *(p. 241)*

Illustrating a similar idea in the realm of life–environment relations, Patten (2001) wrote:

> In the history of human interactions with the external world, entities and environments became separated into two distinct categories, the first concrete and the second vague. This was due to a cognitive machinery that discerns objects but not, at least not directly, their covert linkages. Objects are local, whereas environments based on the transactions and relations between these are more extended, and boundaries which may be real or perceived separate the two.
>
> *(pp. 425–426)*

> So it is natural for man that things and their environments are viewed as separate, and separated, and this *entity–environment duality* is registered strongly in physics' basic categories of open and nonisolated systems. The opposite, where environment and its defining entities are continuous and inseparable, is *entity–environment synergy*.
>
> *(p. 426)*

Figure 6.2 depicts, in very simple form, both the entity–environment duality (A) and the entity–environment synergy (B) of Patten. To carry along and forever utilize both models would be to practice dialectical thinking as advocated by Elbow. We propose the same basic dialectical approach is needed for models of discrete and sustained life and that – as Elbow says – using both allows one to "see and think more." By extension, we propose this expanded seeing and knowing opens up new vistas in which we can find the systemic solution (or system of solutions – the eight coordinated changes) and actualize human–environment sustainability.

In a more general sense, where we draw system boundaries relates to what we choose to be "in" and "self" versus "out" and "other." These aspects of modeling

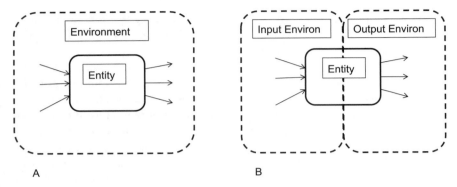

A   B

FIGURE 6.2 Alternative depictions of a living entity and its environment. A) entity–environment dualism. B) entity–environment synergy. Modified from Patten, 1981; see Note 46.

are also similar to efforts to internalize what had previously been externalities in economics. And we could say that the emerging view of a unified life–environment system and the ecosystem and biosphere as fundamental units of sustained life are compatible with the transition from an "empty world" to a "full world" (see Note 47).

The skill to use dialectical mental models, and the habit to conceive of an individual human self as both discrete and localized as well as extensive and integrated with environmental context and life support capacity, may be seen as a higher-order skill developed and utilized by more mature and wise individuals. (Note: this view may apply more to industrial cultures, whereas this "higher-order skill" may be natural and inherent for many indigenous cultures.) This more complex modern intelligence must be supported and promoted by education in life science at all levels as part of the bottom-up solution strategy, which then can transform our culturally shared mental model. This higher-level consciousness evolves our thinking beyond the simplistic black/white, either/or, true/false pattern that is associated with our current problems as well as social and political polarization and conflict. F. Scott Fitzgerald said, "The test of a first-rate intelligence is the ability to hold two opposing ideas in mind at the same time and still retain the ability to function." We need to help stimulate "first-rate intelligence" throughout all culture and support mature, wise, systems thinkers able to understand and act on the new, emerging ecological view that we are all at once individuals and interdependent parts of ecosystems and biospheres.

6.4 Real examples where win–win works

Before reporting on real world cases in which win–win synergism has been achieved in human–environment relations, we discuss why it is difficult to analyze and study this general idea.

This topic is difficult in part because it is not obvious how to define or assign a winning or positive impact in reference to the environment. In mainstream conventional wisdom, "environment" has no basis for value, good/bad, or right/wrong on its own. In addition to the value-neutral image of the environment in science, it also appears in philosophical traditions, such as Buddhism and Taoism, as in this quote from Alan Watts (see Note 48):

> Looking out into [the universe] at night, we make no comparisons between right and wrong stars, nor between well and badly arranged constellations.
>
> *(p. 5)*

While this quote mentions extraterrestrial aspects of environment, many use similar logic to characterize species extinctions, a lack of any direction or progress in evolution, climate change, soil degradation and similar natural principles, and side effects of human actions as essentially the same as storms, floods, and natural disasters – they are treated like either "random events" or "acts of God" that cannot be labeled with any absolute or solid determination as "good" or "bad."

Thus, it appears the only strongly justifiable way to conceive of win, good, benefit, gain, and what is right for environment is *self-referential* with respect to life and human life. What is good for the environment is something that allows the environment to aid life and by extension humans.

While self-referential definitions have historically been taboo in mathematics (e.g., Whitehead, Russell) and at times can be pathological in math, computing, and some science realms, here we see that a self-referential definition for value is fully necessary. Similar developments are occurring in allied studies where complex systems are treated in non-fractionable ways.

Given this starting place for value – what is good for the environment is something that allows environment to aid life – we assert that life is the central basis for all value. This is compatible with Aldo Leopold's *Land Ethic* in which he wrote "A thing is right when it tends to preserve the integrity, stability and beauty of the biotic community. It is wrong when it tends otherwise" (see Note 49). And it fits with views of many others in biocentrism, deep ecology, and other schools of thought. But this basis for value is also logical and valid: life is certainly important and special, it can be destroyed and thus requires care and stewardship, it is shared by all humans, and it is thus an excellent and fitting basis for unity among people and nations. Therefore, we choose this value basis as the foundation for understanding the win–win human–environment relation.

Given this philosophical context, we next examine cases that we see to exhibit win–win outcomes and explore how and why they work.

Three nonhuman examples of win–win life–environment relations on Earth are 1) the oxygen atmosphere, 2) the ozone layer, and 3) soils. In each of these cases, environment has improved (in terms of moving further from thermodynamic equilibrium) over time in that the environment has become increasingly complex and beneficial for life.

The oxygenated atmosphere of Earth is unique compared to other planets, and the associated higher-oxidation potential serves to make higher rates of energy and metabolism – and thus life forms like mammals – possible. While the excess oxygen is produced by green plants, this is done in an ecosystemic and biospheric context in which animals and microbes are intimately linked to and interdependent with plants, and many chemical and physical processes alter the composition of the atmosphere, all in the "sustained life" sense of the unified life–environment system.

The presence of an oxygenated atmosphere had further secondary benefits for the development of complex life forms on Earth. Early life forms originated in water bodies, not only due to the need for water but also due to the protective layer that the water provided from solar ultraviolet (UV) radiation. On land, exposure to the UV radiation would cause increased mutation and cell damage. Oxygen, once abundant in the atmosphere from photosynthesis, could migrate to the stratosphere, dissociate under the UV energy, and reform as ozone, which effectively absorbs energy in the 0.1 to 0.3 micron wavelength, the range at which most UVB is transmitted. The naturally occurring ozone layer, formed around 600 million years ago, provided a protective shield, allowing aquatic organisms to colonize and biogenesize land surfaces on Earth.

Soils are a third item of evidence that a win–win life–environment relation is possible (see Note 50). In forests and grasslands, for example, soils naturally and spontaneously develop and increase in depth, fertility, and functionality in ways that support greater diversity and resilience of living communities existing on those soils. As systems thinker Jane Jacobs said, we have a situation in which "The ensemble itself made the environment rich by expanding." Positive feedbacks enhance the system complexity in a way that creates new niches and opportunities for development of the entire ecosystem (see Note 51).

We could also consider the generation and maintenance of species diversity, creation of those deposits that became fossil fuels, and other aspects of biogeochemical cycles as evidence that a mutualistic life–environment relation is not only possible but is perhaps the norm when considering nonhuman or preindustrial human life. Emphasizing the networks of self-reinforcing relationships in ecosystems, Ulanowicz proposed that mutualism is ontological prior to competition, which supports this view of an inherently mutualistic aspect to the fundamental nature of life (see Note 52).

Thus, we have solid evidence of nonhuman life–environment synergy and win–win relations. We next explore three human examples: a modern case of forests in Nepal (see Note 53), a rural development project now underway in Appalachia in the United States (Frostburg Grows), and *terra preta* (dark earth) soils of indigenous people in the Amazon (see Note 54).

Forests in Nepal

The first case study we present is based on work of Nagendra and others (see Note 53). Forests in Nepal provide a cautiously optimistic example of win–win relationships that are possible between people and their local environment. In the context of overall massive tropical and subtropical deforestation globally, the degree of successful reforestation in Nepal provides hope. Nagendra presents important details on which specific actions and structures have been most successful, and the specific socioecological system variables Nagendra analyzes are the same ones proposed by Ostrom (see Section 6.5) as key to avoiding the tragedy of the commons.

Studying 55 forests spanning a variety of topographic, ecological, social, and government policy circumstances, Nagendra found that forest density increased the most in cases where 1) the land tenure regime was of the leasehold forest type; 2) monitoring of forest condition and use and sanctioning of violators occurred seasonally; and 3) the group size per unit area of forest was intermediate, in the range of 5–15 individuals per hectare of forest. All of these variables were statistically significant as drivers of positive impact on reforestation. Two other land tenure regimes – national forests and community forests – each with different patterns of forest size and management practices – were not as successful for increasing reforestation. Nagendra stated that all forests in Nepal are owned by the government, but these three major tenure regimes vary significantly in details of the relationships between the people and the forest. For the monitoring and sanctioning variable, seasonal monitoring was more effective than occasional and year-round monitoring and much more effective than a total lack of monitoring. Moderate group size to forest size ratio was more successful than smaller or larger groups. Nagendra interpreted this result this way:

> When the number of users is too few relative to the total forest area, forest planting, maintenance, monitoring, and other critical tasks cannot be carried out effectively. When the number of users increases beyond a point, however, coordination becomes difficult and cooperation tends to break down, making the task of forest protection even more difficult.

Other variables tested, such as the presence of skilled leadership in the local forest community, were not significantly correlated with increased forest density. However, Nagendra acknowledged that this variable is very hard to measure. Several more variables had enough data to be tested, including steepness of the terrain, forest size, forest condition, likelihood of adoption of new technologies, and degree of forest dependence, but these were found to be correlated with the four main variables and were not analyzed separately.

Stewardship of forest ecosystems in Nepal has defied the negative global trend of massive deforestation by way of both natural regeneration and active tree planting. This country and other countries with "poor, forest-dependent, rural inhabitants" have developed diverse policies and practices, and some of them are clearly effective in aiding increased forest density. Increased forests will enhance carbon sequestration, reduce soil erosion, improve water quality, aid species conservation, and provide additional key ecosystem services. Nagendra makes the point that "there are no panaceas," and no single policy, structure, or plan can work in all local communities for all natural resources. But this author, as well as Ostrom (discussed in Section 6.5), provides a valuable strategic framework and diagnostic approach to help tailor studies and designs to best fit the real condition in each special context of socioecological system. Working under this framework, human–environment win–win situations are being realized.

Frostburg Grows

Frostburg Grows (Frostburg, Maryland) is a university and community project that seeks to implement the theories, principles, and values presented in this book. Frostburg Grows is an innovative and ambitious two-hectare (five-acre) project that combines multiple interconnected and scaled interventions:

1. local food production in high tunnel greenhouses
2. a native tree nursery growing trees for restoration, reforestation, and carbon sequestration
3. composting of municipal organic yard materials (leaves, grass, and brush)
4. renewable solar energy
5. rainwater collection and storage for irrigation
6. training and workshops to teach local citizens these sustainability methods
7. experiential education, service learning, undergraduate research, and leadership opportunities for university students
8. economic development through job creation and an incubator function to support food entrepreneurs.

The lead project organization, Western Maryland Resource Conservation and Development Council, received grant funding in 2012 from the U.S. Environmental Protection Agency and the nonprofit organization American Rivers due to its location on a former strip mine (from coal mining) and the goals to improve water quality for the Potomac River.

Frostburg Grows seeks simultaneously to create jobs and improve the environment, which are two great needs in the impoverished Appalachian region in Western Maryland, where environmental degradation from coal mining often persists for decades and longer. The eight activities and subprojects listed earlier are being developed in coordinated fashion, so they are mutually beneficial. For example, the compost produced will provide a soil amendment input for both the tree nursery and local food production and in turn also serves as a place to dispose of dead plants and unusable fruits and vegetables. The composting operation is also saving money for Frostburg State University and the city of Frostburg. By diverting organic yard waste, and eventually cafeteria and food services scraps, the local government and university save much of the $45 per ton cost of dumping waste into the landfill. Instead, the organic material is channeled into a composting enterprise that turns it into soil and soil amendments (organic fertilizer, soil-improving additives, etc.). When fully operational, the compost, mulch, and related products from this new enterprise also can be sold, thus contributing to the local economy (while preventing outflow of money from the region via larger corporate sales of compost and mulch). In this way, interlinked, mutually enhancing, environmentally sound enterprises increase local jobs, businesses, money circulation, resilience, and vitality at the same time as helping restore the environment. By enlarging the boundary to include multiple socioecological processes, it became possible to realize win–win synergies. This project demonstrates an intentional strategy to redirect exports and recycle wastes to increase the number of local and internal system cycles – a direct mimicry of the ways ecosystems are organized. In this realization of a human–environment system modeled after ecosystems, Frostburg Grows holds promise for a win–win relationship that covers flows of carbon, nitrogen, energy, and water. While the region is not currently increasing in population, such restoration projects serve to increase the carrying capacity of the land.

Terra preta in Amazonian soils

In Brazil and other countries of the Amazon region, archaeologists and other researchers have studied rich, fertile, black soils that were altered by indigenous people thousands of years ago. Called *terra preta do indio* (Indian dark earth) or just *terra preta*, these soils were amended with charcoal plus high-nutrient excrement, animal wastes, and bones. These organic materials then coincided with (and likely stimulated) high biomass of special soil microorganisms, and all interact to generate high soil fertility that has lasted for millennia and still enables lush vegetation and agricultural production. One researcher stated that the pre-European contact Amerindians "practiced agriculture here for centuries . . . but instead of destroying the soil they improved it." Another stated "sustainable, intensive agriculture is possible in the Amazon, after all. If we can learn the principles behind it, we may be able to make a substantial contribution to human welfare and the environment" (see Note 55).

Other workers have studied the chemical, physical, organic, and nutrient properties of *terra preta* and have documented some of its special qualities, such as comparing the fertility properties of *terra preta* with ferralsols with no anthropogenic A horizon (see Note 55). *Terra preta* had higher soil fertility based on higher pH, higher cation exchange capacity, higher sum of bases, higher base saturation, and higher total soil carbon. They also reported that these fertility properties were associated with the "highly stable soil organic matter fraction" of humin, thus holding promise for "sustainable soil fertility management models in tropical ecosystems." Thus, the indigenous peoples who lived in these regions understood how to live in ways such that their actions led to increase in the quantity and quality of soils, much like the effects that forests and grasslands have on soils.

In addition to these three specific cases, we are aware of many others in which people have managed to unify the value, and integrate the improvement of, human and environmental quality of life. For example, the work of Bakshi and Fiksel (see

Note 56) intentionally seeks synergy between 1) human technology; 2) building, site, and system designs; and 3) the local natural environmental context. We suggest that a common denominator that links all these cases and success stories is a shared paradigm, a worldview and value system in which the value of environment is seen as equal to the value of human quality of life. A culture where this equality of value is asserted (or unquestioned and assumed) is compatible with a paradigm or shared cultural mindset in which life and environment are conceived as a single unified system.

6.5 Toward practical implementation of the presented theory

This section addresses ways this holistic perspective could be employed realistically at more sites and at larger scales, what its use would look like, how the actions would be different than current approaches, and how the outcome would be different. Here we summarize Ostrom's findings of characteristics shared by communities where self-organization of local rules to prevent the tragedy of commons has been successfully implemented.

In multiple works, for which Elinor Ostrom won the Nobel Prize in Economics, she studied ways locally self-organized rules and norms resulting in sustainability of an environmental commons can work (see Note 57). She identified a set of 10 socio-ecological system (SES) variables regularly linked to the success of local communities self-organizing to achieve sustainability. She applied these 10 variables to answer the question: "When will the users of a resource invest time and energy to avert a tragedy of the commons?" citing Hardin's concept. She subdivided these SES's into 1) natural resource systems, 2) governance systems, 3) natural resource units, 4) users (the people involved), 5) interactions and linked outcomes, and 6) related ecosystems. Her top 10 system variables from across these six subsystem categories that make self-organization (S.O.) more likely to succeed are:

1. Size of the resource system – moderate size is most conducive. For example, the moderate sizes of coastal zone, lake, and river fisheries are more conducive to S.O. than open ocean.
2. Productivity of system – users need to experience productivity with some scarcity to invest in S.O., whereas resources that are either exhausted or very abundant are less conducive.
3. Predictability of system dynamics – sufficient predictability allows people to forecast impacts and outcomes of no-harvest zones and other rules reliably.
4. Resource unit mobility – stationary resources are more conducive for S.O. than mobile resource units. Costs of observing and managing mobile units like game animals or even flowing water are higher than for trees or water in a lake.
5. Number of users – community size matters but is context dependent – sometimes smaller is better for communication and trust, while in other cases more people helps to mobilize resources.
6. Leadership – entrepreneurial skills and respected local leaders help S.O. succeed.

7. Norms and social capital – shared morals and ethics, norms of reciprocity, and sufficient trust help agreements to last and reduce costs of monitoring.
8. Knowledge of the SES – knowledge of the system, its carrying capacity, each other, and rules used in other systems lowers perceived costs of S.O.
9. Importance of resource to users – true dependence of people on the resource for livelihoods, and/or high perceived value of sustainability of the resource, aid S.O.
10. Collective-choice rules – autonomy to create and enforce their own local rules aids S.O.

Overall, Ostrom wrote that "long-term sustainability depends on rules matching the attributes of the resource system, resource units and users" (see Note 57, p. 421). These 10 attributes, in addition to others she identified, could be combined with information about population centers, watersheds, physiographic provinces, eco-regions, and similar factors to make *specific and meaningful boundaries around a local system* to aid conscious community efforts for sustainability of the unified life–environment system. These principles also are compatible with proposals in previous chapters for changes to tax policy and educational efforts to shift the relation between humans and the natural environment on which we depend. Ostrom and fellow workers employ the term "users" for humans in relation to local ecosystems, and this seems as bad as the term "consumers," which is used in everyday discourse. Perhaps a new term like "stewards," "citizens," or some more positive term would be better and more compatible with the ideas of win–win relations and interdependence of unified human–environment systems.

6.6 Summary and conclusion

These ideas grow out from "hard science" of ecosystems and networks, but they are also compatible with many spiritual, philosophical, psychological, moral, ethical, social, and emerging ideas in these fields. Thus, we suggest that efforts for theory and action for sustainability can also benefit from increased dialogue and synergy between science and ethics, philosophy, arts, and humanities. As we search for answers to why people and governments do not change despite clear information and evidence of the necessity of change, we inevitably extend beyond science into all realms of culture.

It will be necessary to reach a majority of people in order to achieve lasting change; our science must fit in with a larger program able to inspire, to win hearts as well as minds, and to instigate a widespread movement for sustainability and win–win human–environment relations. Thus, we could seek to express not only cold hard facts and better ideas, measures, analysis, and rationale but also provide a worldview and action program that is motivating and deeply meaningful. By developing both a science and ethics that value service to humans, service to life, service to our children and grandchildren, and service to the environment, we can realize a vision of humanity as leaders and heroes aiding all of life, all species and ecosystems, in life's epic and billion-year journey, from origin to destiny.

A human developmental or evolutionary project able to integrate science, ethics, and culture could include a process of nurturing and increasing wisdom. Similar to other scientific revolutions and paradigms shifts – Darwin's and Wallace's evolutionary worldview or Einstein's relativistic one – the currently emerging ecological worldview is not only a great leap in science. Prior paradigm shifts and the current one also have served to transform totally our sense of ourselves in relation to our world and universe. Darwin's and Wallace's insights resulted in a shift from a sense of human self as created by God to a view of humans as descended from previous life forms. The current ecological and sustainability revolutions require a new image of the human self as fully interdependent and coevolving with the complex web of environmental life support systems, including other species with their own inherent life and value. Awareness of this interdependence can help motivate actionable change toward socio-ecological sustainability.

As part of this evolution and maturity in the human sense of self – toward the "ecological self" of Arne Naess – we can work to be more anticipatory and less reactionary (see Note 58). We do not need to wait for a global ecological crisis of mass apocalyptic proportion to mobilize the political will and social mandate for systemic change. Our cognitive, technological, ethical, and other capacities are powerful enough to allow us to look into the future, to develop and evaluate alternative scenarios, to understand the comparative outcomes, and to choose the better path. Prevention of disaster is always better and cheaper (although not as dramatic, exciting, or urgent) than attempts at cure, remedy, and recovery after disaster has struck.

Another part of maturity is in forms of mental discipline. Rather than seeking understanding via simple, mechanical, linear causality (as in one or a few independent variables influencing one or a few directly connected dependent variables), we need to be able to analyze and synthesize vast webs of relations and distill the influence of both direct and indirect causal links. As in works of Patten and colleagues (see Note 59 and Section 3.13), ecological network analysis has shown that *indirect effects dominate* in complex systems like food webs and ecosystems.

Our work then may need to be predominantly indirect. Rather than tackle the environmental problems represented in Figure 6.1 head on, we may need to nurture an overall context in which problems like this never arise in the first place or in which all such problems can be solved in concert. This shift in strategic approach is akin to the adage about gardening: for best results, don't feed the plants; feed the soil, and let the soil feed the plants.

Mental discipline and higher consciousness also require the ability to hold two contradictory thoughts in mind at the same time. This skill is associated with the dialectical modeling of Elbow cited earlier, and we see it as needed when we employ complementary models of life as both discrete and sustained. The discrete life of organisms is localized in space and logically simpler; an organism is either alive or dead. The sustained life of community, ecosystems, and biosphere, however, is not easy to identify in terms of spatial boundaries and logically complex as ecosystems integrate both living and dead components. The recursive and self-organized life–environment complex sustains life. As in the hyperset formalism earlier, the complexity of life requires many new ideas and forms of thought, including those being developed in impredicative logic. One challenge of this worldview is the interpretation of self-reflexive and inward-outward orientation of environment; it resides in us and surrounds us. A sustained life paradigm finds harmony, peace, and productivity with this duality.

Having the wisdom, intelligence, maturity, discipline, and skill for sustainability efforts can also benefit following the Golden Rule in our actions toward other humans. Having the courage to move beyond "fight or flight" reactions to other people, we can shift toward a predominance of relations more aligned with "tend or befriend" relations. Increasing our love and trust for others can be a natural counterpart to the environmental message the planet is now sending us, that we are all, very literally, in the same boat. And learning to "think like an ecosystem" can likewise help us to sustain ourselves and maintain our planetary boat as mutually reinforcing missions. Good environmental stewardship begins with leaving the world richer and enhanced as the result of one's actions. When our actions occur within nature's flow boundaries without usury inflows and with benign outputs stimulating the potentiality for self-organization and autocatalysis, this brings us into greater harmony between self and the environment. Another way to simply express this is to extend the Golden Rule to the environment:

> *Do unto others — any other, including the environment — as you would have done to you.*

This is a concise way to express the thought–action needed for human–environment sustainability.

7

ECOLOGICAL FOOTPRINT*

There is no free lunch (a clear consequence of the one of the most basic natural laws, the first law of thermodynamics).

7.1 Growth and ecological footprints

A new vision of the concept of growth is necessary and slowly emerging. There are people that rigidly maintain that economic growth is necessary for everyone to meet his or her needs. It is paradoxical that economic growth is considered compulsory as an initial condition for implementing all projects of importance to society, such as health care, education, pollution control, and energy supply. Therefore, growth has become the final goal of governments and political administrations, and it is the supreme judge of political and economic management. In contrast, others propose alternative concepts to be essential, such as welfare, happiness, well-being, equity, environmental health, prosperous way down (Odum and Odum, 2001), and even degrowth. In sum, it seems that these positions cannot be integrated, especially due to the rigidity of consolidated economic rules and the dominance of economy. Unfortunately, only a few people (or economic subjects such as single consumers, entrepreneurs, investors, multinational firms, or entire states) have the opportunity to take advantage of the economic dynamics of the governing neoliberalism, and this can threaten the possibility of many humans to express their own freedom. Consequently, dangerous phenomena may occur, from large and widespread iniquity to irreversible and progressive environmental disruption.

---

*   This chapter has been written with the fundamental help of Nicoletta Patrizi (Ecodynamics Group, University of Siena).

The fact that some economic rules have been adopted by a wide variety of societies does not mean that these rules are indelible natural laws. On the contrary, the awareness of the existence of natural laws such as the first and second laws of thermodynamics (see Chapter 3) and the properties of ecosystems – which regulate our ability to use energy and ecosystem services, respectively – should orient human behavior toward a sustainable lifestyle that is desirable but also durable. This approach would be in accordance with nature's laws, which, unlike economic rules, cannot be circumvented.

Some authors maintain that greater economic freedom may bring about more economic growth, but we also know that economic growth improves living quality only up to a point, beyond which the quality of life may begin to deteriorate (see Notes 18 and 26). In this sense, we may argue that the freedom to grow has a cost, and this cost grows as well. In more general terms, a number of economic subjects and states probably take advantage of the economic growth, but the direct and indirect consequences are costs paid by a large part of the global population and with environmental degradation as result.

Among the social costs, inequality plays a crucial role. Joseph Stiglitz (see Note 60), Nobel Laureate in Economics, describes the problem of inequality in the United States and defines it as one of the dark sides of the market economy. He states that 1% of the population tends to become richer and richer at the expense of the rest of the population. This current phenomenon of acquisition has been occurring for at least 30 years and, therefore, it does not strictly depend on the economic cycle, namely on economic growth or stagnation, but it is a consequence of our economic system. (See also Section 5.6 and Note 42.)

Environmental problems are often a counterpart of economic growth. The Global Footprint Network (www.footprintnetwork.org) presents annual results for the ecological footprint and overshoot of nations. Cyclically, from year to year, the Earth produces a great quantity of environmental goods and services that humans can use. For example, the water cycle supplies domestic, agricultural, and industrial uses. Food production, by both plants and animals, depends on nature's services. Forest production is an important part of the carbon cycle. The Living Planet Report is released biennially by the World Wildlife Fund (WWF) to divulgate, among other indicators, the most recent Ecological Footprint and biocapacity values for the whole world and countries with populations greater than one million. According to the *Living Planet Report 2012* (WWF, 2012; data referred to the year 2008; see Note 74), the planet has 11.99 billion global hectares of biologically productive space, including 1.1 billion global hectares of ocean, coast, and inland waters. Humans may draw on natural capital, namely the set of elements and mechanisms that, through natural laws, transform primary materials and solar energy into flows of products and services. At the current rates of consumption of resources and production of waste emissions, it has been calculated that this flow of products is insufficient to satisfy annual human needs, or maybe we should call them requirements.

What is overshoot day? Overshoot day is the day in the solar year when humans have used up the year's supply of resources and services provided by nature and begin to eat the capital of the Earth. Greenhouse gases build up in the atmosphere, resources become depleted, and minerals are increasingly expensive to extract. The capacity of

---

Box 7.1 Ecological Footprint is calculated by examining the amount of land required for our (main) activities (WWF, 2012).

1. Cultivating crops – 4.0 billion global hectares.
2. Grazing livestock – 1.4 billion global hectares.
3. Built up land, towns, roads, industries, bridges, and so on – 0.45 billion global hectares.
4. Growing timber and sequestering in trees the carbon dioxide produced by using fossil fuels – 9.9 billion of global hectares. (This is by far the biggest overshoot.)
5. Harvesting fish and other organisms from oceans – 0.7 billion global hectares.
6. Growing timber for forest products – 1.8 global hectares.

Total: 18.2 billion global hectares are utilized, out of 11.99 billion global hectares available. It is an overshoot (we have one planet, but we use 18.2/11.97 = 1.52 planet).

---

the environment to provide the same quantity of goods and services as it did the previous year is also threatened because diminished natural capital can only provide fewer resources. In 2013, the overshoot day was August 20th; this means that humanity has consumed all available flows of resources for that year by the 232nd day. We are using 1.52 times the available area. Therefore, the resource flows that humanity will use in the remaining 133 days to the end of 2013 will come from the stock of resources that should be preserved for the future. Previously, the overshoot day was later: September 22, 2003; October 21, 1993; December 19, 1987. This dangerous escalation is clearly demonstrated by the encroaching time series of the Ecological Footprint. The Ecological Footprint is ever more utilized as an indicator for environmental accounting that considers the area of the planet (in global hectares) as the ultimate limiting factor for material growth of human society. Clearly, endless growth is impossible on a finite planet and *the ecological footprint demonstrates the discrepancy between the available area that the planet offers us* (in terms of lands that could produce all resources we need and absorb wastes we produce) and the unrealistic demand we have.

This situation, known as "ecological deficit," applies also to all industrialized countries, which consume much more than what local ecosystems can offer. This means that they are dependent on the bioproductive space of nations that consume less (e.g., economically "backward" countries) or they are stealing their lack of productive space from the developing countries.

In sum, who gives anyone the permission to maximize economic entities, as stated in economic textbooks? Who is authorized to pursue any economic goal regardless of the consequences? Why is it that these economic rules do not work for everyone? Is there any entity or organism that is able to discriminate between those who can maximize their growth rate and those who are forced to have a more modest lifestyle? Why are the economic benefits for a minority (the industrialized countries have a population of about 1 billion, while the total global population is coming close to 7 billion) determining all the important decisions, while the consequences for the majority and for the future generations are not considered? Why are the full consequences of economic growth resulting in decreasing natural capital of our planet not considered? Who has allowed a few greedy people to steal from our common natural capital of the planet?

Actually, humans are free if they can decide to do as they please but are also free if they can decide NOT to do whatever they want. Nowadays, the world is driven by the prevailing concepts of relative wealth and competitiveness, that induce people to go beyond the limits: not only limits (targets) given by the level of wealth of someone else, but also limits (constraints) determined by laws and regulating principles, human dignity and the crucial role of the environment as life support system. And it is also absolutely necessary to account for limits defined by a fair allocation of resources and possibilities for all present and future humans.

Global warming is one of the most urgent problems that humans are facing. One way to measure it is by using a carbon-based footprint. This is defined as the tons of carbon dioxide per year and often calculated as per capita. Methane, the second most important greenhouse gas, is included as carbon dioxide equivalents by multiplying by methane's GWP100 (global warming potential considering a period of 100 years). Methane has a higher absorption potential than carbon dioxide, but it is oxidized in the atmosphere with a half-life of seven years. Consequently, GWP for methane has been determined to be between 28 and 34 (depending on feedback calculation), or expressed differently, one ton of methane has a greenhouse effect corresponding to 28 to 34 tons of carbon dioxide.

7.2 A biophysics-based vision of sustainability

Every vital system – a single living organism, a city, a production process, a human body, a region – can be interpreted as a system between an energy source and a heat sink and can survive and develop by virtue of its self-organizing properties and vitality. Every system needs a continuous flow of work energy and resources to survive; at the same time, it crucially needs to discharge unusable energy and matter in the form of heat, emissions, wastes, excreta, and so on. A couple of statements from evolutionary thermodynamics can be mentioned to interpret this scheme:

1. A source of usable energy and matter is just as necessary for the system as a sink for dissipating degraded energy and matter.
2. Throughput, not just availability of resources, enables the system to survive, develop, and increase in complexity.

On this basis, the concept of sustainability can be characterized, starting from its biophysical foundations, and some elusive aspects of it can thus be avoided.

In fact, an ultimate definition of sustainability does not exist yet; it has not been well-defined, and it is abundantly misused, embodying in its own meaning all the contradictions of misusing. However, a lot of work has been done by a number of scientists to rigorously clarify the meaning of the concept of sustainability. By virtue of this work, some foundations or pillars can be identified, upon which the concept is based:

Time: The well-known concept of carrying capacity identifies the number of individuals in a population that the local environment can support. It is a dynamic concept; it is not constant but varies with climatic, biogeochemical, meteorological conditions, and other external factors, as well as the pressure exerted by the carried species. Dynamicity, or the fact that carrying capacity varies in time, means that it is a concept close to, but not the same as, sustainability. The verb "to carry" means to hold, contain, or support something, whereas sustain means to maintain in time. To consider time in the ambit of sustainability therefore means considering the dynamics of human activity and of ecosystems, not as a simple sequence of changes of state and modifications but as evolution. This helps us to understand which modifications are positive and which should be avoided and whether or not the future is merely a destiny to accept fatalistically and to which we must adapt. Sustainable, in brief, is something that has the ability to survive or exist in time. This represents the essence of the term, the real meaning of the world "sustainability" or the adjective "sustainable," which is important to avoid misuse. Let us use a piano to give an illustration. Everyone knows how a piano works. A pianist plays a note; his note dies in the silence when he moves his finger from the key. Then the pianist presses a pedal, and, through this mechanism, the note expands and continues even if the finger does not press the key any longer. The pedal is called "sustain," and it maintains the note for a while. Time is thus intrinsic in the meaning of sustainability.

Biophysical Limits: It would be useless to refer to the sustainability of nature. The wonderful, slow, biological evolution occurred through practical application of winning strategies. Nature diversified: biodiversity is a strong general attribute for survival. Nature used the most abundant and certain work energy source, solar energy, learning how to feed primordial vital mechanisms, including photosynthesis, from this source. Nature succeeded in optimizing resource management and in disposing of wastes and excess degraded energy (e.g., by closing cycles or retransmitting heat into space). In brief, nature has been successful in surviving in time. The human species, on the other hand, tends to ignore the winning strategies that nature has demonstrated, behaving, paradoxically, in quite the opposite manner. Modern human's counterpart for biodiversity is homologation (the global consumerism and the erosion of geographic boundaries for stimulating globalization and economic growth). Modern human's counterpart for solar energy is the energy of fossil fuels, the use of which is today limited solely by a technical capacity to extract and refine (and not by the risk of exhaustion or climate change). Modern human's counterpart for nature's capacity to use and reuse all resources and dispose of degraded matter and energy that can no longer be used is irrational use of natural capital and waste of energy and materials (the increase in greenhouse effect is a direct consequence of the complete disregard of the natural absorption capacity of ecosystems). Dealing with sustainable development means to pay particular attention to society and human activities and how they influence the sustainability of natural systems. The human species needs to regulate its own behavior in its thermodynamically closed, finite planet with limited resources.

Relations: Thermodynamics is the science of limits. It sets limits to the total availability and capacity to exploit energy. The first principle of thermodynamics is the principle of energy conservation and defines the very existence of energy. The second principle – energy dissipation – states that in the universe degradation of work energy to heat energy that cannot do work inevitably takes place by all activities. Or expressed differently: all activities cost work energy that is converted to useless heat energy. Biological systems (open systems, i.e., systems that exchange matter and energy with the environment) seem to violate the second principle: they have extremely ordered structures that even evolve in the direction of greater order. These systems have the ability to process the flow of energy and resources they capture from the environment, discharging in the surrounding environment their wastes in forms of degraded energy (heat) and matter, emissions, pollutants, and so on. Living organisms therefore develop and live by virtue of the concurrent presence of a source of resources and work energy (the solar radiation) and a sink for disposing wastes and degraded energy. All this shows the importance of relationships for living systems and the dependence of all such systems on their contexts. The complexity of these structures manifests in the relations that these open systems entertain with their surroundings and in the way they self-organize. Human behavior and its manifestations resemble these kinds of systems: economic systems, social systems, regional systems, and urban systems all develop by exploiting flows of energy and matter, releasing wastes, emission, and heat into their surroundings.

The concept of sustainability therefore rests on three pillars: time, biophysical limits, and relationships. A project cannot be called sustainable without these foundations. The use of the word sustainable would be inappropriate, misleading, illusory, and false (see Note 61).

In general, it is not easy to give an absolute measure of sustainability. Indeed, it is not easy to describe and measure a state of happiness/health in absolute terms. If someone asks you "How well do you feel?" the best answer you can have is "better" or "worse" than in another reference moment. It is basically impossible to measure in absolute terms an ideal state. This is one of the reasons the term "sustainability" is elusive and eventually misused. Nevertheless, sustainability identifies one fundamental concept that tries to alert people of the environmental danger overarching the human race. Assessing sustainability is further discussed in Chapter 8.

A much more familiar approach is to measure the distance from an ideal state. We can think of many health indicators, such as temperature, blood pressure, cholesterol level, and so on, each with optimal ranges and thresholds. Deviations beyond the optimal ranges indicate we have some sort of illness. The gravity of the illness depends on the distance from the threshold. About sustainability, this means that we can invert the problem and try to understand more about unsustainability as the distance from the ideal of sustainability. Unsustainability becomes a relative concept.

In this sense, the Ecological Footprint approach is paradigmatic, comparing the ability of the ecosystems on the biosphere to support human societies (biocapacity) with the actual resource requirement (Ecological Footprint), both expressed in terms of bioproductive land. When the footprint exceeds the biocapacity, there is a deficit, a real measure of unsustainability. Therefore, Ecological Footprint can be seen as a tool able to indicate the *minimum* criteria for sustainable development (see Note 62). Moreover, Ecological Footprint and biocapacity are able to measure the human appropriation of the Earth's regenerative capacity, which is one key aspect of sustainability. The Earth's regenerative capacity is thus seen as a limiting factor for the continuation of socioeconomic systems. If the human demand continues to overuse beyond what the biosphere can renew, then the regenerative capacity is threatened. Ecological Footprint is the ecological load imposed on the Earth by humans in spatial terms (see Note 63). Rockström and coauthors (2009) propose a framework similar to *The Limits to Growth* based on "planetary boundaries"; inside this threshold is the safe operating space for humanity (see Notes 63 and 65).

7.3 The use of resources

One approach to measure whether a system is sustainable consists of investigating the amount and type of resources it uses. A number of approaches exist to aggregate resource use data. Particularly, work energy is an important resource in this context, which will be discussed in the next chapter. The flows of resources feeding a system per unit time, such as material flow accounting and energy accounting, can be used as the basic information. The rationale of the Ecological Footprint analysis and how to use it for assessment of sustainability are presented later.

The ecological footprint

In early 1990s, Mathis Wackernagel and William Rees introduced the Ecological Footprint as a new environmental metric (see Note 64). After the 1992 Earth Summit in Rio, the need to reduce human impact on the Earth became undeniable and widely recognized. Environmental changes such as collapsing fisheries, loss of forest cover, depletion of fresh water systems, and accumulation of CO_2 in the atmosphere are just a few noticeable examples. Environmental changes indicate that humanity is far from sustainable, as human demand is likely to be exceeding the regenerative and absorptive capacity of the biosphere. Moreover, several studies showed that many of Earth's thresholds are being exceeded to the extent to which the biosphere's future ability to provide for humanity is at risk (see Notes 5, 6, and 65). If continued, overshoot will permanently reduce the Earth's ecological capacity and lead to ecological collapse and social misery. Careful management of human interaction with the biosphere is thus essential to ensure future prosperity; systemic accounting tools are needed for tracking the combined effects of the many pressures that humans are placing on the planet.

The footprint methodology is based on six assumptions (see Notes 64 and 66):

1. It is possible to track the annual amounts of resources consumed and wastes generated by countries.
2. The majority of these resource flows can be related to the bioproductive area necessary for their regeneration and the assimilation of their waste.
3. By weighting each area in proportion to its usable biomass productivity (annual production of usable biomass), the different areas can be expressed in terms of a standardized average productive hectare. They are called "global hectares."
4. The overall demand can be aggregated by adding all mutually exclusive resource-providing and waste-assimilating areas.
5. The aggregate Ecological Footprint and biocapacity can be directly compared to each other.
6. Area demanded can exceed area supply.

The ecological footprint accounts for the appropriation of biocapacity across six distinct land use types (namely: cropland, grazing land, forest land, fishing grounds, built-up land, and carbon uptake land). These land types represent the area requested for the production of crop food and other fiber products (cropland), meat and other animal products (grazing land), timber and others forest products (forest land), fish products (fishing grounds), and shelter and other infrastructures (built-up land); the carbon uptake land represents the area requested to neutralize the CO_2 (the only waste the methodology takes into account) and is calculated as the forest area needed to absorb the anthropogenic carbon dioxide emissions. The ecological footprint also relates to six demand categories (namely food and fibers, housing, transport, goods and services, and waste). The final ecological footprint of an individual or a country is the sum of all these different types of land, irrespective of where they are located (for details about the calculations, see Note 41). Average productivity differs between the land use types. As such, for comparability across them, ecological footprint and biocapacity are usually expressed in global hectares (gha; see Note 41). Global hectares are defined as hectares of land or sea area normalized to the world average productivity of all biologically productive land and water area in a given year. Thus, each global hectare represents an equal amount of biological productivity. Yield Factors (YF) and Equivalence Factors (EQF) are the two scaling factors used to "convert" physical hectares to global hectares. The Yield Factors reflect the difference between the national productivity and the world average hectares of a given land use type. Each nation has a set of Yield Factors each year for each land type. The Equivalence Factors account for the difference among ecosystems types. Equivalence Factors are evaluated each year for each land type and are used to convert the areas of different land use types, at their respective world average productivities, into their equivalent areas at global average bioproductivity across all land use types. While the Yield Factor allows a conversion of the actual

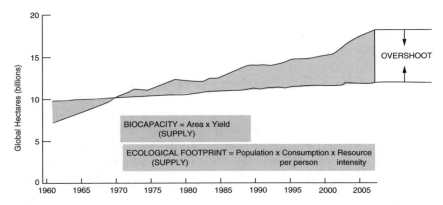

FIGURE 7.1 World's ecological footprint and biocapacity time series (1961, 2008) (Source [Galli et al., 2012] included with the permission of the Global Footprint Network; see Note 62).

area requirement from national to the global level, the Equivalence Factors are used to express results in terms of global hectares. Global hectares provide a useful representation of the ecological demand associated with the use of a product, as they measure how much of global ecological productivity, rather than just the size of a physical area, is required to produce a given flow. In this sense, global hectares contain information about the quality (or productivity) of the hectares instead of the mere quantity.

Borucke et al. (2013) (see Note 66) presented a detailed update for EF calculations. They are shown in Note 67. The time series analysis of the ecological footprint and biocapacity reveals how the human appropriation of natural capital is changing over time (Figure 7.1).

The scientists of the Global Footprint Network also ask the obvious question: "Do we fit on the planet?" The answer is definitely "no." Moderate UN scenarios for future development suggest that if current population and consumption trends continue, we will need the equivalent of two Earths to support us by the 2030s. And, of course, we only have one (for major details, see also www.footprintnetwork.org). The ecological footprint can be used to investigate issues such as the limits of resource consumption, the international distribution of the world's natural resources, and how to address the sustainability of natural resource use across the globe. Assessing current ecological supply and demand as well as historical trends provides a basis for setting goals, identifying options for action, and tracking progress toward stated goals (see Note 68). In fact, it is widely used to demonstrate the unsustainability of resource consumption patterns on individual, local, national, and global scales.

Some analyses have been conducted for identifying the presence of ecological surplus or deficit at the national level and promoting political measures to solve urgent criticalities. More specifically, Niccolucci and coauthors (2012) (see Note 68) identified four major national system typologies that have been called parallel, scissor, wedge, and descent, according to the characteristic profiles of biocapacity and Ecological Footprint trends, that depend on national demand for and supply of natural resources over time, as shown in Figure 7.2.

Parallel systems are rather rare (only 7% of nations fall in this category); they are seen as ecological niches and characterized by low demographic density and increase, large forest area, and generally high human development and industrialized economies. Scissor nations (43%) are industrialized economies in which the growing gap between biocapacity and Ecological Footprint has generally developed since the 1960s; they include emerging economies adopting mass production systems and regions characterized by fossil fuels extraction. Wedge systems (26%) are creditor countries with high demographic increase rates and low consumption life styles, low human development, and rich raw material reservoirs. Most descent countries (24%) are often "underdeveloped" with very low human development and characterized by low income, human weakness (undernourishment, illiteracy, poor health conditions), high demographic rates, and economic and political instability.

Time series analysis enables a geopolitical interpretation of nations to be made, based on the trend of Ecological Footprint, representative of our pressure on local and global ecosystems as well as availability and constraints of biocapacity. In particular, biocapacity may be regarded as a new type of ecological wealth of strategic importance in geopolitics, playing a fundamental role in competitiveness and relationships between nations, as well as in the quality of life of their communities. Biocapacity and ecological footprint may reveal a tangible limit to the expansion

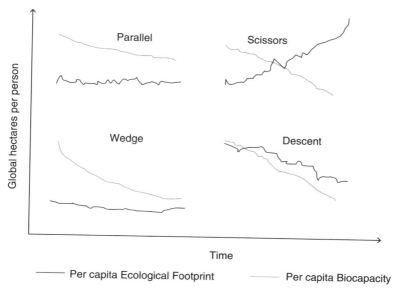

FIGURE 7.2 Major Ecological Footprint and biocapacity trends worldwide (1961–2007) (rearranged after Niccolucci et al., 2012; see Note 68).

of economic growth and help identify environmental excellence, systems at risk, or those vulnerable to be preserved before overcoming those limits. In recent years, the ecological footprint has been also applied to production systems to evaluate natural appropriation, efficiency in natural resource use, and pressure excited on the environment due to production (see the references in Note 66).

In 2004, Meadows and colleagues published an updated version of their book *The Limits to Growth* (see Chapter 2). In this updated version, data produced in the past decades clearly support their suggestion that the world was running in overshoot.

The use of nonrenewable resources

Natural capital supports all human activities. It provides ecosystem goods and services that are useful for human use, survival and well-being, and, ultimately, to feed the economic system. After the industrial revolution, the use of resources was no longer compatible with the environmental biogeochemical cycles; it assumed characteristics more similar to a depredation for power, accumulation, and economic growth. In fact, we have gone from a world relatively rich in natural capital and poor in manmade capital (and humans) to a world poor in natural capital and rich in manmade capital. Our aim is to find compatibility between human activities and the environment and to act in a way that this compatibility is durably maintained. Dealing with the use and management of resources, Herman Daly proposed two "obvious" principles of sustainable development: harvesting renewables consistent with natural regeneration rates and emitting wastes consistent with the natural assimilative capacity. About the nonrenewable resources, Daly says that these "cannot be maintained intact unless they are not used at all. Yet it is possible to exploit non-renewable resources in a *quasi-sustainable* way by limiting their rate of depletion to the rate of creation of renewable substitutes. The quasi-sustainable use of non-renewables requires that any investment in the exploitation of a nonrenewable resource must be paired with a compensating investment in a renewable substitute" (see Note 69). It is, of course, possible to reduce the consumption considerably by using the three Rs: reduce, reuse, and recycle (see Chapter 4).

Both standard and ecological economics pay attention to this kind of problem because the use of nonrenewable resources has to be considered under all circumstances. This became an urgent necessity, especially after the oil shock of 1973–1974, when Arab OPEC countries decreed an oil embargo on countries supporting the military and financial policy of Israel after the Yom Kippur War (October 1973). Between October and January, the price of crude oil quadrupled with respect to prewar prices, triggering a recessive phase that took a long time to overcome for the industrialized countries. This event shook those who, sensitive to economic questions, posed the problem of the survival of our present economic system. With their objective of maintaining positive per capita consumption for an indefinite time, neoclassical economists were faced with the problem of the depletion of resources. However, the presence of nonrenewable resources in the inter-temporal optimization does not imply any great change in the basic principles; the present generation can use limited resources until it is able to increase the stock of reproducible capital (see, among others, the contribution given by Robert Solow and John Hartwick in this field). The intergenerational dilemma can be thus solved because investments can compensate for the rising depletion of natural exhaustible resources and help maintain the total amount of available capital (natural capital + manufactured capital) and, consequently, the productive capacity of the system. However, this growth theory with exhaustible resources only considers the economic implication/advantage of the use of different kinds of resources. It is necessary to fully utilize the three Rs discussed in Chapter 5 to give us time to develop alternatives. Many extremely important resources will be depleted or be close to depletion within this century unless we invest more in the three Rs.

Ecological economists criticize the substitutability between different kinds of capital. In particular, Herman Daly (see Note 69) stated that we have to preserve natural resources that are the less abundant and limiting factor for future development with scarce resources, especially if not renewable. It is necessary to program a compensative investment in renewable resources per used unit of nonrenewable resources. However, it is not always possible to substitute a nonrenewable input with an alternative input able to play the same role, nor it is possible to find a renewable substitute corresponding to the resource that is renounced. Matter inexorably tends to depletion, and the (almost) complete recycling of matter as nature is able to do is probably impossible for us. Several scientists oppose this principle of matter depletion and state that, having at one's disposal a sufficient amount of energy, the recycling of the dispersed matter is physically possible. Odum (1991), for instance, writes (see Note 70): "It is thoroughly demonstrated by ecological and geological systems that all the chemical elements and many organic substances can be accumulated by living systems from background crustal or oceanic concentrations without limit as to concentration so long as there is available solar or other source of potential energy." In practical terms, it is impossible to propose nor it is sustainable, even if it is physically possible, to completely recycle the dispersed matter, but the availability of work energy (that tends to be irreversibly depleted) is crucial. In this context, it should, however, be underlined that recycling will be needed in the future to an extent that is very much higher than today. Complete recycling may be impossible to achieve, but 90% or even more recycling may be possible, which means that the nonrenewable resources will last at least 10 times longer.

Proper management of a combination of renewable and nonrenewable resources is needed, and investments can be designed for determining virtuous solutions. The general consumption of nonrenewables and the creation of new possibilities to use energy from renewable sources can be modulated in order to avoid a "catastrophic" descent. A first step in this direction is the so-called "two source model" by Odum and Odum (2001), who hypothesized a combined use of the two types of resources and stated that in the future, in line with the current trend of exploitation of nonrenewable resources, we should plan a progressive replacement of nonrenewable resources (especially energy) by renewable ones, as discussed in Chapter 4.

Moreover, it can be possible to exploit a portion of nonrenewable resources in order to capture more and more of the free renewable resources that flow on the Earth and, if not withheld, would be lost forever (see Note 70).

7.4 How do we acknowledge the limits to growth? Which indicators should we apply?

Christian Leipert (see Note 71), a German economist, observed that the environmental problems emerging during the 1970s could be defined as co-products of economic growth, with negative side effects on quality of life and well-being. The term "quality of life" was presented with force in the 1970s, and certain politicians – as well as whole movements – began to speak of qualitative growth. Leipert followed Simon Kuznets – the promoter of the system of national accounting – in his conviction that economic activity should aim at satisfying human needs. This led to a criticism of the mechanical assimilation of the economic result (represented by the main index of the economic framework, the GDP) and the level of well-being of people. In the 1970s, various authors expressed the need for a system of indicators that could represent the complex world of economic and social dynamics in their relation to the environment, to replace or at least complete the one-dimensional nature of economic information. Despite much criticism, most economists continue to use GDP and its rate of growth as an objective function. Today, Leipert (see Note 72) writes:

> An obsolete concept of economic growth reigns: it counts the consumption of natural resources and degradation of the environment positively as income. The prevailing concept of growth produces a big illusion of growth and welfare. Under the present conditions of economic development, in which productive as well as destructive forces are at work, it can no longer be taken for granted that economic growth is equated with an increase in welfare. What is needed is a policy of differentiated development focusing on addressing the structural causes of environmentally damaging and costly patterns of production and consumption. Economics has long neglected the difference between wants and needs. Needs are finite, unlike wants which emerge continually in new forms and are therefore insatiable. Economics should address the political-ethical question of balancing the legitimacy of the demands of the living and of future generations for consumption/depletion of natural resources.

An investigation has been recently performed on the behavior and satisfaction of tourists in an area of Tuscany, Italy (Val di Merse, Province of Siena). Patterson and coauthors (2007) (see Note 72) interviewed 220 tourists and 20 lodging providers in that area in order to estimate their consumption level. Respondents declared their country of origin as Italy (62), France (42), Netherlands (31), Germany (20), Great Britain (16), Sweden (11), United States (9), Belgium (9), Denmark (8),

Other (5), Norway (4), Austria (2), and Canada (1). Data on transport, travel distance, accommodation site, daily meal provision, and day-trip destinations as well as energy, water use, and waste production have been collected. A total of 250,115 bednights, corresponding to 685 "equivalent residents" for the Val di Merse, have been estimated, which represents an additional 5% over the registered population. Their resource consumption and waste production have been converted into the Ecological Footprint metrics (namely, global hectare). Authors estimated the Ecological Footprint for the tourist equivalent resident population to be 5.28 gha/year per capita, for a total of 3617 gha/year for all 685 tourist equivalent residents. This compares to 5.47 gha/year per capita for the resident population of 13,624, for a total of 74,523 gha/year.

It must be noticed that the tourism market segment in this area of Tuscany is oriented around agritourism, low energy intensive activity, and locally grown and organic agricultural products; however, the average tourist is often thought to consume more on vacation than at home and often more than local residents. In this case, foreign tourists who spend a week or two here consume fewer resources than when they stay at home, despite the fact that they behave "like tourists." In some cases, the reduction is about 30%, without compromising their satisfaction or good feeling. It seems incredible from an economic viewpoint, but it is possible to live well while consuming less. These unique circumstances allow us to explore culturally determined *wants* versus universal *needs*. Patterson and coauthors went beyond "more is better" and concluded that there is perhaps an infinite number of ways by which we might pursue satisfaction through the consumption of goods; there are a precious few occasions, environments, and situations that encourage us to slow down, consume less, and control wastes. Another example can be the experience of Slow Food, a movement born in Italy in 1989 to preserve food, biodiversity, culture, and the environment against the current homologating tendencies of modern economy.

At the macroeconomic level, the joint use of different diagnostic tools can be of help to acknowledge the economic but also biophysical limits of the growth pattern. In particular, results from pure economic indicators (e.g., gross domestic product – GDP), ecological-economic indicators (e.g., Index of Sustainable Economic Welfare – ISEW), and ecological indicators (e.g., Ecological Footprint – EF, biocapacity – BC) for different countries were compared and analyzed. GDP is the market value of final goods and services produced within a country, and it represents the throughflow activity of an economic system. The ISEW, starting from the main economic aggregates like private consumption, introduces elements of social and environmental performance that positively and negatively influence the level of welfare of the population. The EF, as we have seen before, is a measure how much nature is necessary to provide the resources a population consumes (food, energy, and materials) and to absorb the wastes produced. The BC represents the actual availability of bioproductive hectares and supply of natural resources in a given country. Social pressures and environmental damages reduce ISEW, more than offsetting, beyond a certain point, the benefits derived from economic growth. At this point, ISEW levels off or even decreases as an increasing gap is observed between

GDP and ISEW. This outcome leads to the crucial realization that not all the wealth produced in a nation is translated into welfare. An economic threshold of growth can thus be identified as well as the reasons why a perverse component of growth exists. On the other hand, the comparison between EF and BC may highlight that the finite availability of natural resources is a constraint to economic growth. In most high-income countries, EF overshoots BC, a condition known as ecological deficit. Demand exceeding local supply can be met by importing BC from outside the country (sometimes) and/or by liquidating the stocks intended for future generations. In general, BC is constant or in slow decline everywhere, whereas EFs show increasing trends, showing a general tendency toward deficit conditions. The point of transition from ecological surplus to ecological deficit, when the gap between GDP and ISEW is increasing, represents the biophysical threshold of growth. The comparison among a number of national economies highlighted that modern society, especially in the Western world, is experiencing increasing

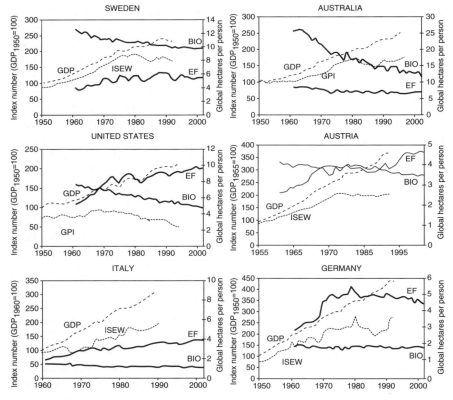

FIGURE 7.3 Time series of EF vs BC and GDP vs ISEW for different countries (see Note 61, included with the permission of WIT Press). Notice that the genuine progress indicator, GPI, used in the cases of the United States and Austria is the same as the ISEW, with small differences in the selection of the items.

environmental pressure (as EF demonstrates) and decreasing environmental sustain-ability (as EF versus BC demonstrates) in the name of economic growth (measured by GDP). The increase in economic wealth often results in worse, not better, con-ditions for people because the welfare related to a given GDP is "polluted" and diminished by environmental stress and social pressures (as ISEW demonstrates).

Figure 7.3 illustrates the trends in economic and environmental performances for six nations. In Sweden and Australia, the increasing gap between GDP and ISEW can be coupled with a decreasing ecological surplus (BC > EF); in Italy and Germany, the difference between GDP and ISEW is accompanied by an increase in the chronic ecological deficit (EF > BC); the case of the United States and Austria is the most interesting one because the ecological overshoot occurred in the same period of the stagnation of the ISEW and the formation of the gap.

From these examples, it emerges clearly that environmental conditions, or in other words the availability of natural capital, is a crucial element of economic systems, even if they are ignored by economic accounting systems. Unsustainable demands for energy, materials, and ecosystem services have catastrophic conse-quences. Demand can be made sustainable by implementing appropriate policies that acknowledge the existence of extra economic factors. A further result of this study is confirmation of the complementary and non-substitutable nature of eco-nomic, ecological-economic, and environmental measures of human behavior. Widening the set of information suitable to describe the context in which we live enables us to transcend the traditional shortsighted, reductionist view of the economic system as a self-sufficient closed system in which households and firms are linked by flows of products and income. New economic scenarios and related policy and legislative measures can be implemented that in turn promote further scientific research in the environmental and social fields, if attention is brought back to the biophysical foundation of all human systems and their sustainability (for details see Notes 68 and 72).

7.5 Estimation of ecological footprint for the scenarios presented in Chapter 5

It is not possible to calculate in detail EF for the scenarios presented in Chapter 5, but it is possible to make an estimation based on the areas required by our main activities and presented in Section 7.1: point 1 (cropland – 4 billion gha) and point 2 (grazing land – 1.4 billion gha) can be considered as the area requested for the food production (5.4 billion gha); point 3 (built-up – 0.45 billion gha) and point 4 (9.9 billion gha) are presumed occupied to cover the neutralization of carbon diox-ide emissions. Points 3, 5, and 6 in Section 7.1 could be lumped to cover the other aspects (2.95 billion gha). These ecological footprints correspond, as we have seen in Section 7.1, to 1.5 planets.

There are relationships between area on the one side and agricultural produc-tion, pollution, resources use, and production/consumption on the other side. It is, of course, not completely correct but could be used for a first estimation of the ecological footprint of the scenarios presented in Chapter 5. (For details of the calculations, see Note 73.) The results of the ecological Footprint calculation are presented in Table 7.1. Notice that it is assumed that the 50% increase of agricultural production is achieved through more effective agricultural practices, particularly in the developing countries (such as improved irrigation; see also the arguments in Note 73). This means that the ecological footprint is found from the *increase* of agricultural production multiplied by 0.5. Furthermore, the 20% increase in production that was qualitative and not requiring resources (a result of the scenarios in Chapter 5) is accounted for by multiplying the production increase by 0.8, implying that only 80% of the production gives an Ecological Footprint. EF has, according to these calculations, increased from year 2000 (about 1.15 planets) to year 2008 (about 1.5 planets). EF was found by model calculations for the following cases:

1. The business–as–usual scenarios will lead to a collapse.
2. The six–point action plan, presuming that the impact from increasing agricultural area is only 50%.
3. 1.5% is used for pollution control instead of 2.5%.
4. 3.5% is used for pollution control instead of 2.5%.
5. A 7% Pigovian tax is applied instead of 8%.
6. A 10% Pigovian tax is applied instead of 8%.
7. Two–tenths of 1% is used as aid to the developing countries instead of 0.8%.
8. Five per cent is used for used for education, research, and innovation instead of 10%.
9. The impact from agricultural production is only 5% (multiplication by 0.05 instead of 0.5 corresponding to 50% impact; see earlier discussion).
10. The production increase is multiplied by 0.5, corresponding to 50% of the production being qualitative and requiring no resources.
11. The production increase is multiplied by 0.25, corresponding to 75% of the production being qualitative and requiring no resources.
12. The impact of the agricultural production is only 5%, and 75% of the production is qualitative.
13. The impact of the agricultural production is only 5%, 75% of the production is qualitative, and 4% is used for pollution control.
14. The contributions from pollution and declining resources are multiplied by 0.25 to account for a possible change of 75% of the fossil fuel to renewable energy. Otherwise, the numbers from scenario 2 based on the six–point action plan have been applied.

In Chapter 5, it was possible to conclude that all six elements of the action plan are needed to achieve positive development and a win–win situation. Aid to developing countries and investment in education, research, and innovation are particularly important for reducing population growth and to kick–start the economy of the developing countries. Increased pollution control implies better health conditions (decreased mortality) and is also a prerequisite for maintaining production.

TABLE 7.1 Estimation of Ecological Footprint for 15 cases. The first case is business as usual (see also Chapter 5), and the second case is the six-point action plan presented in Chapter 5, presuming only 50% impact from agricultural production. All other cases are the indicated changes to the six-point action plan. The initial EF in 2008 for all scenarios is 1.5 planets.

Case number	Case/changes	EF year 2054	EF year 2100
1	Business as usual	1.84	2.32
2	Six-point action plan	1.85	2.25
3	1.5% pollution control	1.97	2.65
4	3.5% pollution control	1.95	1.98
5	7% Pigovian tax	1.93	2.33
6	0.22% aid to developing countries	1.85	2.32
7	9% Pigovian tax	1.91	2.20
8	5% education, research, innovation	1.89	2.64
9	Impact agriculture 5%	1.76	2.06
10	50% of the production is qualitative	1.80	2.07
11	75% of the production is qualitative	1.77	1.92
12	Combination of 9 and 11	1.60	1.88
13	Combination of 9, 11, and 4	1.68	1.70
14	75% renewable energy	1.73	2.22

Continuous production growth is only possible if production becomes more qualitative and less quantitative, which can be intensified through a high Pigovian tax to maintain the resources that are needed for production. A high level of education, research, and innovation is needed to generate new and more effective opportunities that will increase production. Furthermore, this will generate more qualitative development on a long-term basis. Innovation and research can lead to new directions of qualitative development. Investment in education is very important, and it will indeed lead to increased production, but it will be increasingly important that the production growth becomes qualitatively, which can be seen from the results in Table 7.1 – compare the cases 10–13 with cases 1 and 2. Notice that the six-point action plan results in slightly lower EF than business as usual, although poverty has largely been eliminated and the developing countries are offered much better education and much better opportunities.

The Ecological Footprint measures the impact on our planet, and it is therefore not surprising that the pollution control, including the reduction of CO_2 emissions, is a very crucial factor for the Ecological Footprint. The Pigovian tax alone has very little effect on the EF, which is explainable as this tax implies slower declining of the resources and thereby opportunities for increased production. More resources mean decreased EF, but increased production means increased EF. However, together with other factors, it may be important to consider an increased Pigovian tax. Aid to developing countries does not have a major influence on the Ecological Footprint because it will, on the one side, decrease the population growth (EF goes down), but, on the other side, it will also increase the production in the developing countries (EF goes up). The investment in education, research, and innovation has a two-sided effect, too. High investment will imply higher but more effective production and will furthermore decrease the population growth (EF goes down). Ecological Footprint is therefore not very sensitive to investment in education, research, and innovation. The most significant effects on the Ecological Footprint in addition to pollution control are the increase of efficient agricultural production without using more land and chemicals and a shift from quantitative to qualitative production. Case 13 in Table 7.1 shows that this is possible through a combination of improved pollution control, more effective agriculture, and a shift to qualitative production. Ecological Footprint will only increase slightly, although living conditions, particularly for the developing countries, are improving considerably. The six-point action plan scenario is valid for case 14, as discussed in Section 5.4.

Estimations of the Ecological Footprint have told us that the six-point action plan is not sufficient. It is sufficient to avoid a collapse and avoid harsh consequences of an uncontrolled population growth, of shrinking resources, and a lack of pollution control. But it is not sufficient to ensure sustainable development of society. If we want at least to stop the increase in Ecological Footprint, then it is necessary to:

1. invest even more in pollution control
2. not increase the agricultural area but increase the yield on the existing areas by a considerable but still realistic increase of the agricultural efficiency
3. shift to a higher extent than otherwise foreseen from quantitative production to qualitative production.

If we want to reduce EF below the present 1.5 planets, it is necessary to combine the action plan with the aforementioned three steps.

The EF results presented in Table 7.1 should not be taken as predictions but as an examination of which factors could be used semi-quantitatively to control the impacts on our planets. The translation (see Note 73) is reasonable, but they are not exact mathematical relationships, and the results should therefore be taken as first estimations.

Another Ecological Footprint scenario analysis has been carried out by Moore and coauthors (2012; see Note 65) starting from footprint data between 1961 and 2008 as a baseline; the authors estimated the size of each footprint component for 2015, 2030, and 2050. The United Nations Food and Agriculture Organization

(FAO) forecasts that the demand for food, feed, and fiber could grow by 70% by 2050 (FAO, 2009). This has considerable implications for land use and natural eco-systems, as well as for the size of humanity's Ecological Footprint, unless the yield per hectare is increased considerably. The Ecological Footprint Scenario Calculator has been implemented using data and projections from other scenario models for population, land use, land productivity, energy use, diet, and climate change and translates them into corresponding trends in Ecological Footprints and biocapac-ity. In fact, the datasets and parameters used in the business-as-usual scenario are taken from IEA (2008 – projections of the total energy demand), FAO (2006 – data for food consumption), UNDESA (2008 – data for population scenarios), and IPCC (2007 – data for net carbon emissions). The business-as-usual scenario for humanity's Ecological Footprint shows more and more pressure being placed on the planet. Humanity's Ecological Footprint would increase up to 31 billion *gha* by 2050 (3.4 *gha* per capita). Total biocapacity, due to the forecasted increase of land for agriculture as initial effects of climate change, would rise until 2030. Biocapacity would reach its peak at 12.5 billion *gha* and then decrease up to 11.7 billion *gha* in 2050. The main result indicates that by 2050 humanity would require an equivalent of 2.6 planets to support the business-as-usual assumptions (Figure 7.4).

A scenario that projects a reduction of the Ecological Footprint below one planet's biocapacity by 2050 has been found. Data and assumption used in this sce-nario are different from the BAU scenario presented earlier. In particular, the IEA's BLUE map (2008 – stabilization at 50% of the 2005 level of emissions by 2050) data have been considered in accounting for the energy quantity and mix. Con-cerning food, data on the food consumption of Costa Rica in 2005 have been taken

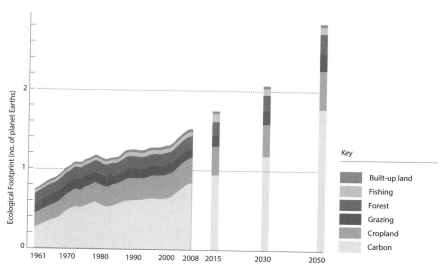

FIGURE 7.4 World Ecological Footprint projection to 2030 and 2050 according to baseline scenario (Source: WWF, 2012; see Note 74, included with the permission of the WWF).

as reference model for the entire world (data are taken from FAO). Population has been set according to the low variant model proposed by the UNDESA (2008). Climate change effects variation has been included as increase of lands suitable for crop productions as consequence of warming.

In conclusion, according to Moore and coauthors (2012): "Meeting aggressive goals on all fronts is just sufficient to bring resource consumption and waste production, as measured by the Ecological Footprint, to within the global capacity to supply it," confirming that the six-point action plan alone is not sufficient to reduce the world's Ecological Footprint in the long run.

Chapters 4 and 5 touched upon the fact that reducing, reusing, and recycling will inevitably result in higher production using less resources, meaning that the production changes partially away from quantitative aspects toward qualitative aspects. There are, however, numerous possibilities for increasing the efficiency of all production in our society. Furthermore, there are many possibilities to make the products more durable and increase maintenance. The Internet is an example of increased quality of communication while using fewer resources because the old "snail mail" is replaced by a fast e-mail. There are signs that we are moving toward the information society in which information and cooperation become increasingly important relative to production of goods. In this context, it is important that we guide society toward a qualitative development based on the three Rs, information, increased efficiency, and maintenance.

It will strongly require that we go from a neoliberalism-based economy to a more equal and democratic society where the goals are not more and more production or more and more money but more and more quality, better living conditions for all, and a far better allocation of all the resources. Economy is overwhelmingly dominant in today's societies. The politicians listen primarily to economists, and only economic indicators are used to direct social development. We need other indicators because life is much more than economics. We need, as we will see in the next chapter, to follow sustainability from different angles, including a number of environmental indicators, and we must use these indicators to direct society. Economic indicators are focused on the short term because most economic models can only look three to five years ahead. Moreover, it is naive and a super-simplification to believe that all activities in a complex society are determined by economics. Conclusively, let us leave the guidance of our societies not only to economic considerations but also consider environmental, sociological, and ecological goals, indicators, and approaches.

8

SUSTAINABILITY

If you always do what you always did you will always get what you always did.
—Albert Einstein

Earth is not ours, it is treasure we hold in trust for our children and their children.
—African proverb

8.1 Introduction

This chapter discusses the concept of sustainability. Many different definitions have been associated with this concept. To understand the concept fully, it is necessary to turn around the various definitions, although they all are more or less rooted in the definition that is presented in the African proverb introducing this chapter. It is consistent with the general concept: we are obliged to give to our children the same freedom of possibilities as we have inherited from our parents. This requires maintaining the Earth's capacity to provide services. Sustainability was also discussed in Chapter 7, where ecological footprint was applied as the measure, that is, our impact on the Earth expressed as area or number of planets.

Section 8.2 will discuss more widely the concept of sustainability, while Section 8.3 will propose to use work energy as an indicator for sustainability and give information about how a sustainability analysis can be performed on this basis. The result of a sustainability analysis based on work energy using a Danish island as a case study is presented in Section 8.4. This example illustrates what such an analysis tells us about how to improve society's organization and activities toward sustainability. Sustainability and sustainable development go hand-in-hand. Our global model in Chapter 5 and the calculation of the ecological footprint in Chapter 7 have this focus, but it is also important to reduce the threat of global climate change associated with an increasing concentration of atmospheric greenhouse gases. Consequently, it is necessary to supplement a sustainability analysis with a carbon cycling model to ensure that the emission of carbon-based greenhouse gases are under control. The results of this model are briefly presented in Section 8.5 to illustrate how this toolbox can be used in addition to the sustainability analysis to ensure that our planning is not worthless due to unexpected surprises from a changing climate. See in this context the discussion in Section 4.3.

It is very useful to comprehend the results of a sustainability analysis for a well-defined area as an island, but it would be more informative, of course, to see the result of a global sustainability analysis based on work energy. This would require many years of effort to provide the information that is needed to set up a global analysis, but it is possible to make a first rough estimation of a global work energy balance. Section 8.6 is devoted to the presentation of such a global estimation. The last section, Section 8.7, will summarize what we have learned from this chapter. Are the results of the global model just confirmed, or are we able to emphasize some additional points and recommendations?

8.2 Different angles on sustainability

Section 2.3 presents an introduction to the concept sustainable development, which is unfortunately used as a political buzzword today more than it is used as a compass for an urgently needed and new direction. Section 2.5 gives a definition of sustainable development, but we propose to apply the definition by Neumayer (2003) (see Note 75). He uses the following summarizing, short, and clear definition of sustainable development: development that maintains the capacity to provide non-declining per capita utility for "infinity."

Sustainable development is strongly dependent on the available resources. For instance, the fast increase in the gross national product per capita and the available technology that has characterized many countries, particularly the industrialized countries, would not have been possible without the relatively cheap sources of fossil fuel energy that humanity has exploited the last few centuries. Resources in general have been utilized at an increasing rate the past 100 years, and continuing resource exploitation at the same acceleration would hinder future generations to have the same standard of living – both qualitatively and quantitatively – as we have enjoyed. The sustainability concept in environmental management is based upon the idea that we ought to maintain nature's diversity, functionality, and service capacity as well as its beauty.

Obviously, our decisions improve if we try to gain as much knowledge about the consequences of our decisions as possible. Using the sustainability concept in environmental management does not exclude applying a cost-benefit analysis to evaluate the consequences from a "here and now" economic point of view, but it is far from sufficient to assess all long-term perspectives. Generally, we should apply *all* the tools in our toolbox to ensure the best possible decisions. This implies that in addition to an economic evaluation, we have to use an environmental evaluation, a socioeconomic evaluation, and a resource evaluation, and so on. A sustainability analysis comprising all the elements – economy, environment, and social conditions in their widest sense – is, however, not easy to perform. This chapter presents how thermodynamics and ecology can be applied to facilitate a sustainability assessment and to plan for sustainable development. Hopefully, this will inspire greater application of sustainability analyses to supplement the standard economic analysis.

We distinguish between weak and strong sustainability (see Note 75). Weak sustainability requires that the sum of all forms of capital (natural capital and manmade capital) is maintained on the same level. Under this definition, human-made capital can replace natural capital as long as the total sum is constant. The proponents of weak sustainability hold that (Neumayer, 2003):

1. Most natural resources are superabundant.
2. The elasticity for substituting human-made capital for resources in the production function is equal or greater than unity, even in the limit of extremely high output-resource ratios.
3. Technical progress can overcome any resource constraint.

Strong sustainability is defined according to a three-point definition presented in Section 2.5:

1. *Renewable resources* are not used at a higher rate than the rate of renewal.
2. *Nonrenewable resources* should not be used at a higher rate than alternatives could be developed in due time before the resources are exhausted.
3. *The rates of pollution emissions* should be adjusted to the rate at which ecosystems can decompose and adsorb the discharged pollutants.

The real issue is therefore to sustain natural capital and not to accept its unlimited substitutability, which is one of the main assumptions of weak sustainability. The proponents of strong sustainability are not against achieving weak sustainability. Rather, they would regard achieving weak sustainability as an important first step, which has to be followed by further steps. Weak sustainability is a move in the right direction, but it is insufficient. It is, of course, better to compensate a loss of natural capital with human-made capital; but, as we are strongly dependent on nature, it is necessary to require that the natural capital is maintained, independent of augmentations in the human-made capital. The point is that settling for weak sustainability will at best only lead to an almost sustainable state, which is insufficient as almost sustainable is not sustainable.

One of the messages of this chapter is that natural systems possess an enormous amount of work energy due to their inconceivably high information content. Natural ecosystems are sustainable on a long-term basis *without* our interference and even able to tolerate certain levels of stress imposed by our activities. This ability to tolerate stress is known under the names buffer capacity, resilience, and elasticity (see Chapter 3). Natural systems are also more effective than most human-made systems with respect to work capacity efficiency (built-up work capacity within the system due to the incoming work energy – solar radiation for natural ecosystems [see Chapter 3]) and resource efficiency. Human-made systems are not able to replace the work capacity or the resource efficiency of natural systems. Therefore, strong sustainability has to be the ultimate goal for our development.

Conservation philosophy can be divided into two schools: resourcism and preservationism. They are understood respectively as seeking maximum sustained yield of renewable resources and excluding human inhabitation and economic exploitation from remaining areas of undeveloped nature. Preservationism has been retooled and adapted to conservation biology. These two philosophies of conservation are mutually incompatible. They are both reductive, ignore non-resources, and seem not to give an answer to the core question: how do we achieve sustainable development?

Lemons et al. (1998) (see Note 76) are able to give a more down-to-earth solution by formulating the following rules that are completely in accordance with the aforementioned definition of sustainability:

A. *Output rule*: waste emission from a project should be within the assimilative capacity of the local environment to absorb without unacceptable degradation of its future waste absorptive capacity or other important services.
B. *Input rule*: harvest rates of renewable resources inputs should be within the regenerative capacity of the natural system that generates them, and depletion rates of nonrenewable resource inputs should be equal to the rate at which renewable substitutes are developed by human invention and investment. The three Rs – reduce, reuse, and recycle – are important tools in this context (see the discussion in Chapters 3 and 4).

Klostermann and Tukker (1998) (see Note 77) discuss sustainability based on product innovation and introduce the concept of eco-efficiency, that is, the reciprocal of the weighted sum of the environmental claims including ecological impacts, and draw on both renewable and nonrenewable resources. We apply the sustainable development concept several times in the next sections with reference to the three-point definition given earlier and with reference to the basic ideas presented in this section.

8.3 Work energy

A very general and holistic sustainability analysis uses the concept of work energy as the basis for assessment. It is important, as presented in Chapter 3, to distinguish between energy that can and cannot do work. Energy is conserved (first law of thermodynamics) – neither gained nor lost – but according to the second law of thermodynamics, all activities reduce the useful capacity for the energy to do

TABLE 8.1 Different forms of energy and their intensive and extensive variables.

Energy form	Extensive variable	Intensive variable
Heat	Entropy (J/K)	Temperature (K)
Expansion	Volume (m³)	Pressure (Pa = kg/s²m)
Chemical	Moles (M)	Chemical potential (J/moles)
Electrical	Charge (Ampere sec)	Voltage (Volt)
Potential	Mass (kg)	(Gravity) (Height) (m²/s²)
Kinetic	Mass (kg)	0.5 (Velocity)² (m²/s²)

further work (see Note 78). We distinguish between different types of energy: electrical energy, potential energy, kinetic energy, and so on. The work energy of each type can be found as the product of a difference in potential and a quantity. For instance, electrical work energy is the product of the difference in voltage times the charge, while potential energy is the difference in altitude (e.g., a waterfall) times the mass of water. Table 8.1 gives an overview of the potentials and the quantities applied for various energy forms. The electrical energy of electricity and the chemical energy of fossil fuels possess practically 100% work energy, which we utilize in many ways in everyday life. Therefore, 1 kWh of electricity has, according to the unit conversion, 3.6 MJ, and 1 g of petroleum contains about 42 kJ of work energy. The efficiency of the specific activities varies greatly depending on the technologies employed whereby less or more work energy is lost. For instance, many cars today travel more than 20 km on one liter of gasoline, which is twice as far as the cars produced 20 years ago – the work energy efficiency has doubled. Nature increases work energy efficiency through network and information development (see Chapter 3).

Fortunately, every day, we receive work energy from the sun in the form of solar radiation, which supports all ecological activity on Earth. Both energy and material flows can be expressed as renewable or nonrenewable work energy and based on energy units. By the method presented in this chapter, it is possible to assess whether the development in a given area is sustainable or not. *Sustainable development, by this definition, occurs when the work energy capacity of the area is maintained or enhanced.* The method also allows us to identify factors needed to make the development sustainable. For example, this can express the extent a particular project proposal – introduction of electrical cars – is able to maintain the work energy. Any complex system is dependent on work energy, and human society uses it for all activities that comprise our living conditions: communication, entertainment, household conveniences, transportation, business, and industry, to name a few. Therefore, it is much more interesting to set up an accounting for society in terms of work energy than the traditional energy accountings, which also includes energies that may not be used for anything – heat energy lost to the environment. In other words, it is important that we get as much work energy as possible out of the energies we use and that as little as possible is lost as waste heat to the surroundings. In this sustainability analysis, we describe all the energy and matter flows that enter our society, circulate (cycle) in it, and eventually leave it as wastes. By accounting for the flows of energy and matter in terms of work energy, we get the advantage of sharing the same energy units, e.g., kJ or kWh. Thereby, we determine how much work energy of a system (the considered area or the entire globe) has changed per unit of time, which is much easier to determine than the absolute work energy of the entire system. Using ecological footprint, we similarly show how much we exceed the Earth's biocapacity, expressed as billions of hectares or number of planets (see Chapter 7).

We can now compare biocapacity and work energy values and may divide the flows according to whether we consider them to be based on renewable and non-renewable resources. Having accounted for energy and matter flows in this manner, we are able to identify areas of activities in which large amounts of work energy are consumed and where work energies are exploited with very low efficiencies. In such areas, it would be logical to take measures with the purpose to improve the work energy exploitation. This is yet another reason why work energy accounting is important.

For practical reasons, we divide an area's activity into six sectors to facilitate the overview of the energy and mass flows (see Figure 8.1):

1. An *energy sector*, which ensures the types of energies needed to maintain our society.
2. A *public sector*, which sees to the implementation of laws and provides a variety of citizen services.
3. A *private household sector*, in which the citizens take care of their own existence in the form of individuals or families.
4. An *agricultural sector*, interpreted as all production activities that are dependent on natural resources and thus includes crop and livestock production, forestry, and fisheries.
5. An *industrial sector*, which comprises all other activities not included in the public or agricultural sectors from industry proper to commerce and trade.
6. *Nature*, viewed as being a sector on its own, which covers the "natural capital," providing ecosystem services for society (see Note 15).

Data from various sources, such as databases, images from geographic information systems, and values quoted in the scientific literature, make it possible to find the work energy of energy flows, of material flows, and of the investment in infrastructure and buildings. A short overview of the literature used is given later. (The methodology that can be used to assess the work energy values needed for the sustainability analysis is presented in more detail in the references mentioned in Note 81.) The references present a sustainability analysis for a Danish island, Samsø. The results of this analysis are summarized in the next section.

The work energy content of energy flows are determinable – such as the work energy in solar radiation, the chemically bound work energy in fuels, the work energy in electricity, and the work energy of thermal inputs. These are the forms of fuels that drive the work energy in society. The work energy calculation is different depending on the different material types. Many of the materials are conglomerates of various chemical compounds and elements – eventually ending up in the final goods produced, which may again be composites of the previous. Analysis of the

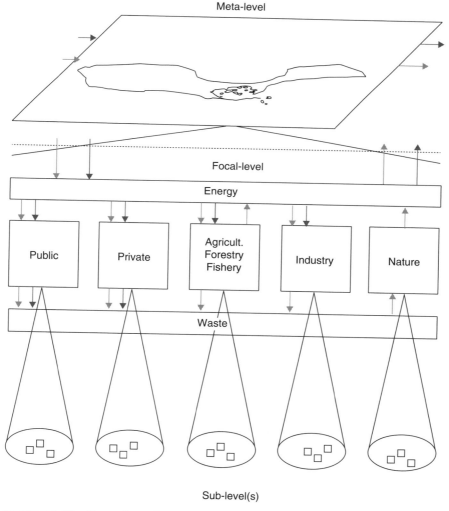

FIGURE 8.1 The figure shows how the considered area is divided into sectors, which together are considered to comprise all societal activities. The sectors contain a number of flows that need to be taken into account in a sustainability analysis. See Note 81.

work energy of chemical elements is often referred to as substance (or material) flow analysis, which is relatively easy to determine. The first type of work energy is well documented in the scientific literature, in particular after the *International Journal of Exergy* was established as well as *Journal of Cleaner Production* and other related engineering journals. For an overview of the concept, please refer to Sciubba and Wall (2007). (See Note 79, where the literature references for calculating work energy for material can be found.)

Work energy values have been published in the aforementioned journals using a mixture of LCA (life cycle analysis) and MFA (material flow analysis) studies (as demonstrated in Note 79). In order to determine work energy values of stocks and flows of material/substances in our society, it is necessary to know the work energy of elemental compositions of a product or subproduct or of chemical compounds. For chemical compounds and elements, values may often be found in the papers of Szargut and coworkers and in the book *Exergy* by Dincer and Rosen (see Note 79) as well as other sources. Work energy of composite materials may also be found in the current literature, but as they are conglomerates of real elements and other compounds, they are often identified as cumulated values. For many complex organic compounds, the work energy content can be calculated by instructions given by these authors. Work energies for various production processes, such as production of energy as well as material goods, may be found in these same references (see Note 79) from which some of the conversion factors used in the work energy analysis presented in Section 8.4 are taken.

We are concerned mostly with the forms of energies that are used to drive our society – the aforementioned energies hitherto mostly derived from nonrenewable resources such as fossil fuels as well as the renewable sources we are developing such as wind turbines and solar photovoltaic energy. In the case of radiant, nuclear, and electrical energy, as well as very energy dense chemical compounds, close to 100% of the energy content is work energy, as we deal with energies with a high work energy potential. For other chemical energies, the values are lower. In the end, during the transformation processes, all energy is dissipated. All work energy potential is broken down and therefore unavailable to do further work because the work energy is converted to heat energy at ambient temperature with 0% work energy content.

In order to calculate the total work energy embodied in infrastructure such as buildings, it is necessary to know two things. First, the relative composition of buildings as fractions of the various types of building materials has to be known. Second, we need to determine the work energy content of the building materials. Having determined this, we are able to estimate the work energy content of a given building infrastructure as the product of the amount of material times the energy density of the specific material. To illustrate this, an assessment of the composition of six types of buildings can be found in Kaysen and Petersen (2010) (see Note 79). The work energy density in MJ per kg for different, commonly used building materials is shown in Table 8.1 (see Note 80).

Box 8.1 Work energies in different fractions of building materials.

Fraction Work energy value [MJ kg-1]. For details, see Note 80.
Stones and sand 1.7
Concrete and mortar 1.7
Tile and clinker 0.75
Metals 200 no distinction possible
Wood 18.7 the same as detritus
Cardboard and linoleum 59.9 quite different materials in origin
Mineral wool and fiber 21.1 as glass
Plastics 91.9
Glass 21.1
Bitumen products 40 oil products approx.
Paint, etc. 1.7

Calculations based on the referred literature values allow us to determine the following four work energy-based sustainability indicators for a given study area:

1. The work energy invested in the six sectors of the area equals the sum of the six sectors, less the internal cycles. The more work energy (kJ) invested in the sectors, the more work energy is available for later use. This additional buffer capacity provides more resistance for the sector in the face of disturbance. This is similar to the situation in ecosystems that have more work energy mentioned in Chapter 3. The indicator is denoted the capacity indicator, CI.
2. The amount of work energy needed to maintain the structures of the six sectors plus the sum of the six sectors is determined. This is the amount of work energy in kJ needed to maintain the work energy capital in kJ (point 1). The ratio between the work energy needed for maintenance and the work energy capacity (unit: kJ/kJ = 1, a ratio) is denoted the structural indicator, SI. Less work energy needed for maintenance implies higher efficiency of the use of work energy.
3. Inputs and outputs of renewable and nonrenewable work energy as energy and as material are determined for all sectors and the sum of the sectors. The ratio between total renewable work energy and total energy applied is calculated, and a higher ratio indicates more sustainable use of work energy. The indicator is denoted renewable ratio, R–ratio.
4. The input work energy has three possible pathways:
    I.   Be accumulated in a sector of the system as work energy representing storage for later use. In ecosystems, solar radiation is stored in biomass growth.
    II. Be exported as work energy. Once it has left the system, it has no bearing on the calculations but likely will be used elsewhere where the work

energy will be utilized and be transformed to heat energy that has no work potential.

III. Be transformed to heat energy and thereby lost in a sector of the entire system. In this case, the work energy is utilized to maintain a complex system far from thermodynamic equilibrium – see point 2.

Solar radiation work energy, which we consider as free, works as the other types of work energy.

Point I is determined as the increase of the CI indicators, for instance, per year, and point III is determined by the SI indicators. The ratio output work energy to input work energy, denoted E/I, is determined additionally to give a picture of the export of work energy in the form of products containing work energy.

Section 8.4 gives a summary of the results of a case study to illustrate how the methodology can be applied to provide an approximate quantification of sustainability.

8.4 The results of a sustainability analysis for the Danish island of Samsø

The analysis results for the Danish island of Samsø are summarized in this section with a particular emphasis on the four sustainability indicators mentioned in Section 8.3. The methodology to account for, evaluate, and monitor a society's sustainability can be used for a region, a country, or an island, as in this case. The method has been developed taking as a starting point the situation on the Danish island of Samsø because it is widely known for its efforts in connection to a project named "Sustainable Energy Island," which started in 1997. The island has an area of 114 km² and about 4,000 inhabitants; tourism brings in about 1,000 additional people. During this project, the inhabitants have succeeded in making the island self-supporting regarding electrical work energy, which is mainly produced by 21 windmills on- and offshore from the island (Figure 8.2). At the same time, part of the heating needed for buildings, which previously stemmed from oil boilers, has been replaced by district heating and plants based on biomass burning (mainly straw; Figure 8.3), photothermal energy (Figure 8.4), and photoelectric energy (Figure 8.5). Meanwhile, the island still has a significant import of fossil fuels necessary to maintain essential functions such as transport by ferry services, transport of goods to and from the island, transport on the island, and heating in areas without access to renewable energy supplies. The details of the analysis are disclosed in the literature presented in Note 81. The calculations of work energy for processes, energy, and material have followed the methodology presented in Section 8.3, including the literature information according to the references in Note 79.

As fossil fuels are finite resources, it is assumed that the island will someday have to replace these energies by other means to sustain the same level of activity. Thus, in spite of the intensive investments in renewable energies, the island still has some way to go before it can be considered fully sustainable in terms of energy supply.

FIGURE 8.2 The island is more than self-supporting with electrical work energy, which is mainly produced by 21 windmills on- and offshore from the island.

FIGURE 8.3 The district heating plants are based on the burning of biomass (mainly straw).

It is the plan to make the island fossil fuel free in the near future, and any changes due to the proposed projects are assessed in the references (see Note 81) and summarized later as an illustration of the possibilities to use sustainability as a powerful management tool.

FIGURE 8.4 Photothermal energy is used for the district heating in addition to biomass.

FIGURE 8.5 The domicile of Samsø Energy Academy. Photoelectric energy is produced to supplement the electricity provided by the 21 windmills.

The consumption and production of various types of energy on Samsø are shown in Table 8.2.

Figure 8.6 shows the work energy balance of the island. The figure distinguishes between renewable and nonrenewable energy and material. This shows that the island lost 193 TJ of work energy in year 2011. This is, however, mainly due to export of work energy in form of electricity and food.

Figure 8.7 presents the work energy in year 2020, presuming that:

1. the cars, trucks, and tractors on the islands use biodiesel or electricity;
2. one-third of the work energy used by the ferries will be covered by electricity or biodiesel;
3. five per cent more renewable energy is produced on the island, mainly by wind turbines; and
4. the remaining houses using fossil fuel will convert to electricity for heating.

Under this scenario, the work energy lost by the island will be reduced 153 TJ from 1,434 to 1,281. But again, this is mainly due to export of electricity and food. We assume that the work energy capacity has not changed from 2011 to 2020 but is still 15,560 TJ. However, this is an approximation because, as will be shown by the carbon balance, a small amount of carbon is annually stored on the island. If it is assumed that organic matter contains 50% carbon and that 1 g of organic matter has 18.7 kJ, then the amount of work energy stored due to the storage of organic matter on the island will be less than 2% both in 2011 and 2020.

The three indicators, structural indicator, SI; renewable work energy ratio, R-ratio; and export-import indicator, E/I ratio (the work energy capacity was presumed unchanged), for the island in years 2011 and 2020 are listed in Table 8.3. The table shows the changes of the three indicators if the projects leading to an (almost) fossil fuel–free island in year 2020 are realized. The E/I ratio could be 1.00 in year 2020, which would require that supplementary crops are produced. This would correspond to an accumulation of organic matter containing work energy on the island. The most ideal situation would be to have a high export of work energy, E/I, that can be utilized elsewhere but also a high accumulation of work

TABLE 8.2 Consumption and production of various energy type (year 2007).

Energy type	Consumption	Production
Electricity	285.7	386.0
Heat	140.4	66.3
Gasoline + diesel	86.3	
Total	512.4	452.3

Plan 2020: fossil fuel–free island

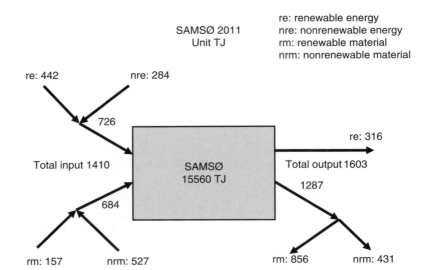

FIGURE 8.6 The figure shows the input and output of renewable and nonrenewable work energy, both in form of energy and materials. The island is losing 1,603–1,410 TJ of work energy per year or 193 TJ, corresponding to about 1.2% of the work energy capital.

energy on the island. The loss of work energy for maintenance is a question about the SI indicator. The long-term goal would be to obtain an R-ratio equal to 1.00. It will, however, be difficult to have all the work energy associated with materials become renewable before the entire global society is shifted to more than 90% recycling. The improvement of the structural indicator, SI, is important because this means that while it costs 9% of the work energy capacity on the island in year 2011 to "drive" the island, it costs only 8.2% to maintain the work energy capacity in year 2020. The 0.8% work energy that is saved can either be used to increase the accumulation of work energy on the island or exported. In both cases, the work energy is not lost.

The energy sector is based on the two laws of thermodynamics (see Note 12), which state that no energy is lost and work energy that is produced relative to the total amount of energy by the sector directly gives the efficiency of the sector. The work energy capacity; the structural indicator, SI; and the renewable energy ratio, R-ratio, for the other five sectors are listed in Table 8.4.

The table shows that the public sector has a high work energy capacity and requires only 5.1% work energy for maintenance, but it has a very low – only 4.7% – use of renewable work energy. It should be possible to increase the R-ratio significantly by using more renewable materials. This is also valid for the industry sector. It is possible to improve the maintenance efficiency as well by using less work energy for maintenance and by increasing the energy and material use efficiency. Notice that nature has a significant work energy capacity, although it is only calculated

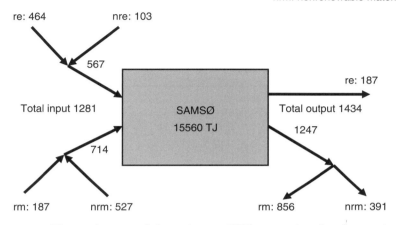

re: renewable energy
nre: nonrenewable energy
rm: renewable material
nrm: nonrenewable material

SAMSØ 2020

Unit TJ

re: 464   nre: 103

567

Total input 1281   SAMSØ   Total output 1434

15560 TJ

re: 187

714   1247

rm: 187   nrm: 527   rm: 856   nrm: 391

FIGURE 8.7 The work energy balance in year 2020, presuming that four projects are realized: all cars, trucks, and tractors use biodiesel or electricity, one-third of the work energy used by the ferries is covered by electricity or biodiesel, 5% more renewable energy is produced on the island, and the last (few) houses using fossil fuel for heating will use electrical heating. Notice that the work energy exported from the island is reduced to 153 TJ in year 2020 compared with 193 TJ in year 2011 as a consequence of increased internal use. The changes of the indicators SI, R–ratio, and E/I ratio are shown in Table 8.3.

TABLE 8.3 The sustainability indicator values in 2011 and 2020.

Indicator	2011	2020	Ideal
SI	0.090	0.082	Low
R–ratio	0.43	0.51	≥ 1.00
E/I ratio	1.14	1.12★	★★

★ Can be reduced to 1.00 by supplementary crops, corresponding to work energy accumulated on the island.

★★ High export of work energy and high accumulation of work energy on the island is most ideal.

as biomass without the information that living organisms have embodied. Living organisms have an enormous amount of information (see Note 16). For many plant species, the information is a couple of hundred times the chemical work energy of the biomass. The work energy on Samsø, including the information, may therefore be in the order of 1.3 million TJ. Consequently, we recommend carrying out a sustainability analysis based on work energy for all the sectors separately and additionally require that the work energy as well as the information of nature independently of the other sectors is maintained.

TABLE 8.4 The work energy capacity, WE; the structural indicator, SI; and the renewable ratio, R-ratio for the five sectors.

Sector	WE*	SI	R-ratio
Public	9,191	0.051	0.047
Private	2,187	0.094	0.62
Agriculture	4,496	0.103	0.828
Industry	754	0.086	0.393
Nature	6,562**	Sun	1.00

* WE = work energy stored in the sector as TJ
** without incl. of information – eco-exergy not applied
SI is reasonable for all five sectors, but R-ratio is much too low for the public sector and too low for the industrial sector.

8.5 The results of a carbon cycle model

Replacing fossil fuel energy with renewables will provide a significant reduction in carbon dioxide emissions. This shift in energy policy is necessary but not sufficient to ensure that the net carbon dioxide emission is zero for a considered area or region. It is necessary to obtain knowledge about *all* the processes involving carbon because significant carbon dioxide emissions result from a number of natural processes, such as decomposition of organic matter in nature, agriculture, and forestry. Fortunately, natural carbon emissions are balanced by carbon uptake through photosynthesis on an annual or decadal timescale. Therefore, a complete carbon balance for the area or region is needed to be able to find the resulting net emission of carbon dioxide. A carbon model for the area or region is the best method to keep track of all the processes and transformations that finally lead to the emission of carbon dioxide or other greenhouse gases. The model should consider all the essential carbon pools and processes that transfer carbon from one pool to another.

A complementary study to the sustainability analysis on Samsø has developed a carbon cycling model for the island:

1. to demonstrate how a carbon cycle model (abbreviated CCM) can be developed for a well-defined area;
2. to show how the carbon cycle model can be applied to find the net carbon dioxide emission; and
3. To illustrate how the CCM can be applied as a powerful environmental management tool to answer such questions as: if a given planned or proposed project is implemented – in this case on Samsø – what would be the consequences for the carbon dioxide emission and the emission of other greenhouse gases? A typical project is illustrated by the following example: all vehicles with a weight below 2,000 kg are changed from gasoline or diesel to electrical vehicles. The CCM can answer this question.

A carbon cycle model of the Siena district in Italy has previously been developed (see Note 82). The experience gained developing this model has been applied in the Samsø model. Generally, it can be concluded from the carbon model projects of Siena and Samsø that a carbon cycle model as a supplement to a sustainability analysis is a useful tool in our effort to control the global climate changes that are resulting from our unrestrained growth policy. It is important to ensure that the recommendations of Chapters 4, 5, and 7 consider the climate changes, too.

The CCM must keep track of the most important carbon sources, sinks, and pools as well as consider all important processes that transfer from one pool to another. Figure 8.8 gives an image of the carbon pools and the processes that we would include in the Samsø CCM after the first considerations of what we should cover in the model. The figure represents what is denoted a conceptual diagram of the CCM. The boxes represent carbon pools and the arrows processes of carbon transfer. The model has 11 more state variables because the agro-production is divided into different products (corn, barley, potatoes, and so on) and nature is divided into wetlands, forest, and other natural areas.

The pools include three fractions of carbon in soil based on decomposition rates: organic matter, fast decomposable organic matter, and soil carbon. The different decomposition rates are realized in a step-wise manner. It is furthermore necessary to distinguish the carbon processes that take place in nature and in industrial and agricultural production. The inputs are the imported feed, food (for the inhabitants and the tourists), and fossil fuel. The domestic garbage (solid waste) is mainly exported in this case. Humans, cattle, and other animals, including domestic animals, respire, which directly yields carbon dioxide. It is necessary to separate cattle and other domestic animals because cattle, as ruminants, produce methane that is oxidized slowly in the atmosphere – the biological half-life in the atmosphere is seven years. (More details about the model are revealed in the references mentioned in Notes 81 and 82.)

A model should always be developed on the basis of the available knowledge about the system – in this case the carbon pools on the island. From the Samsø case, it is clear that knowledge about the external variables and about the initial values of the state variables are needed before applying the model. In other case studies, there may be other external factors and other state variables, but the principles for the data provision are very clear. Most data are provided by the sustainability calculations, although a conversion to tons of carbon is needed for the spreadsheet data used for the sustainability calculations. As much knowledge as possible about the seasonal changes, the harvest time, and about the production of various natural areas should be obtained, as all knowledge can be used in the calibration phase of the model development. The climatic factors, temperature, solar radiation, and precipitation are also considered external variables or forcing functions and should, of course, be known as functions of time or at least as seasonal variations from spring to summer to autumn to winter.

The CCM is able to give two results that are essential for environmental management:

A. What is the net carbon dioxide emission (or uptake) on Samsø Island resulting from the many interacting processes?
B. Is Samsø losing or gaining carbon for the considered time period of one year?

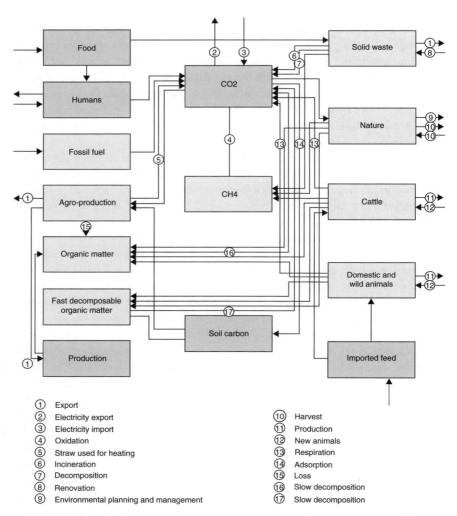

① Export	
② Electricity export	⑩ Harvest
③ Electricity import	⑪ Production
④ Oxidation	⑫ New animals
⑤ Straw used for heating	⑬ Respiration
⑥ Incineration	⑭ Adsorption
⑦ Decomposition	⑮ Loss
⑧ Renovation	⑯ Slow decomposition
⑨ Environmental planning and management	⑰ Slow decomposition

FIGURE 8.8 The conceptual diagram of the model as presented in the project proposal. The boxes represent carbon pools and the arrows processes of carbon transfer. The model used has 11 more state variables because the agro-production is divided into the different products (corn, barley, potatoes, and so on) and nature is divided into wetlands, forest, and other natural areas.

Figure 8.9 illustrates the answer to question 1. The figure summarizes the carbon dioxide uptake by the photosynthesis of agricultural land and of nature. The release of carbon dioxide from fossil fuel use and respiration of humans and domestic animals is also shown. The use of straw and wood energy crops for heating will inevitably release carbon dioxide, although they are almost carbon neutral in the sense that an equal amount of carbon dioxide has been taken up during photosynthesis, but a minor amount of diesel oil is used for transportation. The amount taken up by the photosynthesis is, however, already included in the two sums of photosynthesis of agricultural production and the production of natural areas including bogs and forest. The methane produced by cattle and the wetlands is included in the model equations.

The numbers in Figure 8.9 show that photosynthesis on Samsø removes carbon dioxide from the atmosphere in an amount of 26,460 tC per year. This is able to more than compensate for the soil respiration, the use of fossil fuels, the use of bio-mass fuels, and the respiration of humans and domestic animals. From this, it can be concluded that the island Samsø is a net sink for carbon, capturing already today around 26,500 tC/y. Notice, that the results are based on bogs and forests occupying the same area year after year and that they inevitably will increase the carbon

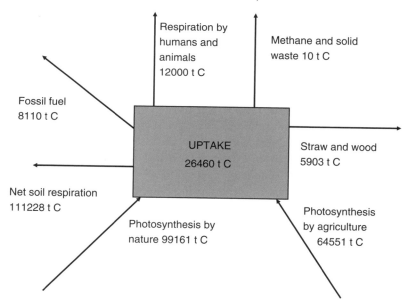

Annual Exchange of Carbon Dioxide with the Atmosphere

Respiration by humans and animals 12000 t C

Methane and solid waste 10 t C

Fossil fuel 8110 t C

UPTAKE 26460 t C

Straw and wood 5903 t C

Net soil respiration 111228 t C

Photosynthesis by nature 99161 t C

Photosynthesis by agriculture 64551 t C

FIGURE 8.9 Results of the CCM show that Samsø sequesters 26,400 tC/year from the atmosphere. The processes leading to this result are summarized on the figure. The processes producing carbon dioxide are: combustion of fossil fuel; combustion of straw and wood; respiration of humans and animals; methane; decomposition of solid waste; and respiration of organic matter in soil, mainly by microorganisms. The processes that take carbon dioxide up from the atmosphere are photosynthesis of agricultural land and of the nature on Samsø.

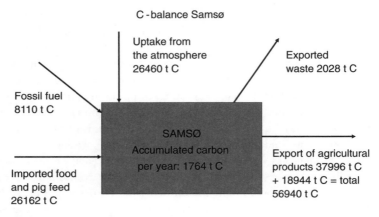

C - balance Samsø

FIGURE 8.10 The export and import of carbon to the island of Samsø are shown. The C on the island is almost in balance, as the difference between import and export is only about 3%. There is an accumulation of carbon on Samsø, according to the figure, of 1,764 tC/year.

pool slightly due to growth. The amount is known from wetland and forest ecology and is in this case estimated to be about totally 5,000 tC/y.

Figure 8.10 shows the import–export balance of carbon for Samsø Island, answering question 2. The island imports carbon from the atmosphere (the net result of Figure 8.9) by using fossil fuels, in the food for humans and the feed for pigs, and it exports carbon through agricultural production and by solid waste exported to Jutland for incineration. Overall, the result of the import–export balance of carbon for the island is an increase of 1,764 tC per year (Figure 8.6). This means, considering the standard deviation of the numbers applied in the model, that the carbon amount on the island is almost constant and the carbon transfer processes are in balance. The difference between export and import is only about 3%.

The CCM can be applied to answer relevant environmental management questions about the influence on the carbon balance of possible changes. Three relevant questions about possible changes will be used as illustrations.

Q1: what will happen with the carbon dioxide uptake/release if Samsø Island becomes fossil fuel free?

A1: The net uptake of carbon dioxide will increase corresponding to the carbon dioxide emission resulting from the fossil fuel use. The other processes are unchanged. The net uptake will therefore increase with the present fossil fuel use, that is, 8,110 tC.

Q2: How will the carbon cycling and the CCM results change if we presume that supplementary crops, such as various types of grass or clover, are increased by 5,000 tC/y?

A2: Both the carbon dioxide uptake and the C-balance will thereby be improved by about 5,000 tC/y.

Q3: How will the carbon dioxide uptake, the CCM results, and the total carbon balance of the island be changed if a fossil fuel-free island is introduced and the supplementary crops are increased by 5,000 tC/y? The answers are shown in Figures 8.11–8.12.

A3: The total carbon dioxide uptake is about 50% higher than in the present situation (see Figure 8.11 and compare with Figure 8.9). The carbon balance of the island (Figure 8.12) is increased almost 5,000 tC/y due to supplementary crop use, and the uptake of carbon is increased also by almost 5,000 tC/y. A small amount of the 5,000 tons of carbon stored in the soil will decompose. The results show that introducing fossil fuel-free measures on the island influences only the carbon dioxide uptake and not the C-balance of the island, while the increase of supplementary crops has influence on both the carbon dioxide uptake and on the C-balance of the island.

The effects of the two examined changes – formulated in the three questions – will be seen as positive under all circumstances. Samsø is, in principle, currently (year 2011) more than carbon dioxide neutral due to the introduction of renewable energy because about 26,000 tC is taken up by the island as carbon dioxide per year. It could, however, be argued that Samsø has an annual net export of 57,000 tC as food + 2,000 tC as solid waste minus the import of food + pig feed of about 26,000 tC = about 33,000 tC per year. This is the amount of carbon dioxide that will be released elsewhere (Samsø-produced food is consumed mainly in the larger towns of Denmark). Carbon dioxide uptake is, however, about 26,000 tC/y today, which

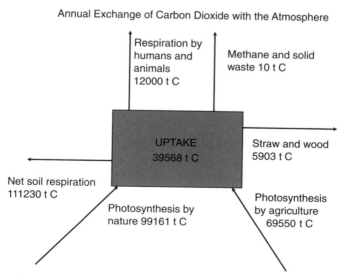

FIGURE 8.11 Results of the CCM by increasing supplementary crops by 5,000 tC/y and eliminating fossil fuels from the island. The uptake is now almost 40,000 tC/y, which is about 13,000 tC greater than the results shown in Figure 8.9.

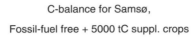

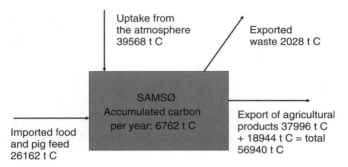

FIGURE 8.12 The carbon balance of the island Samsø when the supplementary crops are increased by 5,000 f/y and a fossil fuel-free island is introduced. Notice that more than 39,500 tC/y is taken up and that the carbon pool on the island is increased by more than 6,700 tC/y.

means that if we include the carbon dioxide release elsewhere by food consumption produced on Samsø, the island causes a *net* emission of carbon dioxide of about 7,000 tC/y. By introducing supplementary crops (5,000 tC per year) and by making the island fossil fuel free, it becomes possible that Samsø takes up more than 39,000 tC per year. This entails that the island removes about 6,000 tC per year as carbon dioxide *more* than the island releases, even with inclusion of the carbon dioxide released elsewhere but originating from the island's food products.

The introduction of renewable energy is urgently needed as soon as possible if we want to limit global warming to 2°C. As the changes of climate mean radically different conditions for humans and all life on Earth, a sustainability analysis should include a CCM to allow us to focus on the processes that are causing the greatest emissions of greenhouse gases. A CCM will furthermore be able to identify processes other than fossil fuel combustion that contribute emissions and even suggest how control of these processes could be used to obtain additional reduction of greenhouse gas emissions.

8.6 Global estimation of sustainability

Figure 8.13 illustrates the annual global work energy balance that results from the various activities indicated. The following nine components should be included in this rough estimation of the global work energy balance:

1.   Nonrenewable mineral resources (non-energy) are reused, recycled, or dispersed. Recycling costs work energy. Dispersion is more or less global. This relates also to the extraction cost of so-called virgin materials, where dispersion

may cause severe environmental problems, in addition to the direct work energy costs to extract the materials; see Table 4.1 in Section 4.3.

2. Fossil fuel consumption directly decreases the global work energy capacity corresponding to the work energy of the fossil fuels.

3. The incorporation of work energy into products increases the work energy capacity, but waste resulting from the production and the depreciation through use of the products entails decreased work energy. Repair may contribute to increased work energy capacity.

4. Renewable resources are used, but they are also continuously formed by the renewal processes.

5. War always costs a considerable amount of work energy.

6. Information contributes positively to the work energy capacity through research, innovation, education, and communication.

7. Nature recovers through natural or human processes, which will contribute positively to the work energy capacity.

8. Nature and ecosystems are deteriorated by a number of human activities, including deforestation.

9. Nature and ecosystems are deteriorated by pollution.

We will attempt to give a first very rough estimation of the seven contributions to higher or lower work energy capacity.

1. *The loss of work energy due to resource dispersion* can be calculated thermody-namically by comparing the concentration of the mining resources and the concentration of global dispersion. (For further details of the calculations, see the references, where the thermodynamic equations that have been applied are displayed, in Note 83.) However, as the amount of material is much less than the amount of fossil fuel, as the material (mainly metals) are mainly recycled, and as a part of the material will contribute positively to work energy in the products, the work energy of nonrenewable resources is insignificant compared with the loss of work energy by use of nonrenewable fossil fuel. The problems of nonrenewable resources are associated with metals that are indispensable. And the question is, can we find alternatives in due time?

2. *A number of statistical sources indicate that global fossil fuel use was about 4×10^{11} GJ in 2013*, which is still increasing 2–3% per year. When using fossil fuels, the chemical work energy of the entire spectrum of carbon compounds in the fuel is lost, which indicates that the global work energy capital decreases by about 4×10^{11} J per year.

3. *Millions of products are produced, but we do not have the data needed to calculate the work energy of these products.* We can estimate the two major contributions, namely construction of new buildings and roads. Buildings require 4 GJ work energy per m^2 and roads about 0.4 GJ per m^2 (see Note 81). It is estimated that 100 billion m^2 of buildings and 5 billion m^2 roads are constructed annu-ally. This means that the work energy capacity due to building constructions will increase 4×10^{11} GJ per year, with the road constructions being 200 times

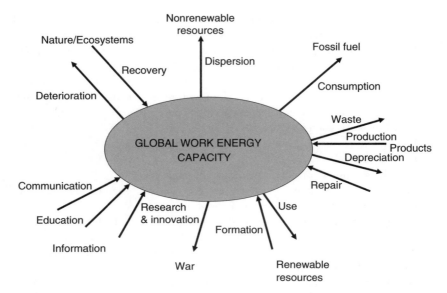

FIGURE 8.13 The diagram shows the processes that are contributing to a higher and lower global work energy capacity. The processes are associated with nonrenewable resources, use of fossil fuels, products, renewable resources, war, information, and nature. We do not have data to calculate all the processes and can therefore only give a very rough estimation, which shows that the global work energy capacity is decreasing.

smaller. By a coincidence, this corresponds to the work energy lost by our consumption of fossil fuel.

4. *The two major renewable resources are fish and wood. The latter will be considered when we estimate the loss of work energy due to deforestation. The global fish stock has decreased at least 300 million tons during the last 50 years, according to a qualified guess by FAO.* (See Note 83.) If we presume that this loss is equally distributed over the 50 years, then we will annually lose six million tons of fish. The work energy of one gram of fish is about 20 kJ. This means that we annually have lost 6,000 billion grams of fish with or 120 million GJ or work energy in the organic matter.

5. *War is a very destructive human activity, which unfortunately not has been abrogated. It is estimated that wars cost in the order of $1,000 billion per year.* The annual work energy costs of wars can therefore be estimated by calculating how much work energy we could purchase for $1,000 billion. As 1 kWh or 3.6 MJ costs about 5 cents, we can buy 72 MJ for $1 and 72 billion GJ for $1,000 billion.

6. *Information contains a great amount of work energy, which we will try to estimate.* A book contains about 12 MJ, which means that if the total printed text including newspapers and commercials corresponds to about one billion books per year, the total eco-exergy increase due to printing would be in the order of $1.2 \cdot 10^7$ GJ/y (see Note 85). The work energy of the paper comes from the harvest of trees and production of cellulose. Some rough estimations:

films produced per year contain about ten times as much information, private photos about 100 times as much information, TV transmissions 1,000 times as much, and private telephone conservations and faxes 10,000 times as much information as the books and newspapers according to Jensen (2004) (see Note 85). This means that books, newspapers, TV transmissions, photos, telephone conversations, and faxes together will contain information corresponding to 1.3×10^{11} GJ/y.

7.   *The energy driving renewable resources is free of charge because the solar radiation is free; but if we use more renewable resources per year than nature can produce, then the work energy capital is decreasing.* We have accounted for the loss of overfishing but have to assess the amount work energy lost by deforestation. When 1 ha of forest with 200 kg of dry biomass per m² (in form of plants, trees, deer, insects, birds, and so on) is cleared, the loss of work energy due to the loss of biomass (about 20 MJ per kg) will be 4 GJ per m² or 40,000 GJ /ha. If we consider the information content, too, then we have to multiply by about 250 (compare with the table in Note 84), which implies that the loss of 1 ha forest means a loss of 107 GJ/ha. Every year, FAO publishes a report called the State of the World's Forests. In accordance to the reports from the last five years, the annual loss of forest is more than 90,000 km² or, with a round figure considering also illegal deforestation, 100,000 km² or 10 million ha. This corresponds to 1014 GJ/y.

We are now able to make a very rough first estimation of the global work energy balance.

The losses are:

Unit 10^{12} GJ per year or 1,000 billion GJ per year (G = 1,000,000,000).

Fossil fuel combustion	0.4
Wars	0.07
Overfishing	0.13
Deforestation (destruction of nature)	100.0★
Total	100.6

The gains are:

Construction work	0.4
Information	0.13
Total	0.53

★ notice that this number is very high because it is an expression for ecosystem services that nature offers us and on which we are very dependent, expressed as work energy including information (see Table 4.3).

This approach to measure the global work energy balance provides a holistic view of all processes and drivers that contribute to gains and losses. The conclusion is that deforestation and other destruction of nature accounts for an enormous loss of work energy due to the high information content in ecosystems. The work energy of the information expresses the loss of ecosystem services, which our generation is depriving from our children and future generations. Nature will be able to offer considerably fewer free ecosystem services than what we have enjoyed. This is not acceptable, and we have to stop continuously robbing nature that rightfully belongs to future generations. We try to increase the work energy capacity by constructing private and public buildings and infrastructure and by enhancing the amount and exchange of information, but it hardly compensates for the work energy that we lose due to our insatiable use of fossil fuel, overfishing, silly warfare, and our destruction of nature. If we shift to renewable energy, make prudent and long-term plans for fisheries, and move beyond wars as a means to settle disputes, then we could positively contribute to sustainability by our activities. Of course, the biggest factor is the loss of nature, which must simultaneously be addressed.

8.7 What can we learn from sustainability analyses?

This chapter has supplemented the global modeling results in Chapter 5 with sustainability analyses. The analysis, performed on Samsø Island, Denmark, shows that work energy is a useful indicator for sustainable development. A complete analysis of sustainability requires generally more than a work energy analysis, but work energy can be used as the most obvious holistic indicator because all activities require work energy. Several other indicators can be used as supplements to the work energy, such as biodiversity and models of the most important elemental cycles, including hydrological. In the case of Samsø, a carbon cycling model was developed.

In this context, it is important to emphasize that nature's work energy should be maintained in order to engender sustainable resource use. The work energy can be calculated as the total work energy including the work energy of information. We determined that the work energy of nature was maintained on Samsø. In other cases, where there may be a change in nature's work energy, it is recommended to use the work energy including information.

The analysis results of the development on Samsø indicate that a shift to renewable energy gives two clear advantages. First, sustainability increases because less work energy is needed to maintain the work energy capital; the renewable fraction of energy and materials increases, and the work energy capital increases or alternatively decreases less. Second, carbon dioxide emissions decrease, and the carbon balance becomes more favorable. All in all, the sustainability analysis and the carbon model are powerful tools to assess how to abate the greenhouse gas emissions. The two tools give approximately the same results from different angles. In conclusion, renewable energy is the key to increase sustainability and reduce the global warming.

While the Samsø investigations gave a reasonably accurate picture of how to measure sustainable development and the island's carbon balance, there are insufficient data available to make a global sustainability analysis. Nonetheless, a considerable number of global warming models have been developed. The global carbon cycling models have all shown what is widely discussed, namely that about a 60–75% reduction in carbon dioxide emissions is urgently needed if we want to ensure that the global average temperature not will increase more than 2°C in this century. In spite of the lack of data for setting up a global sustainability analysis, Section 8.6 attempts to give an estimation of global development in terms of sustainability. While the results should only be considered a first rough estimation, they showed a very clear picture: we lose an enormous amount of work energy due to deforestation. The conclusion is that we must give first priority to conserve nature to be able to hand over to the next generation the Earth as we have received it from our parents. We do increase work energy by our activities, mainly construction work and increase of the total amount of information available for humankind, but at the same time we lose more work energy by using fossil fuels, wars, overfishing, and deforestation.

Therefore, we can turn the development if we shift to renewable energy, stop overfishing and warfare, and launch a serious and rigorous conservation program for nature. This is consistent with the global model results presented in Chapter 5 but gives more specific recommendations concerning pollution and resource maintenance under an expanded paradigm of the three Rs. It is important to shift to renewable energy as fast as possible to avoid global warming being out of control; in this context, it is important that we consider all carbon dioxide sources and reduce their emissions. Furthermore, pollution abatement must be included in a complete conservation of nature. Pollution impacts our health, activities, and production and maintaining intact ecosystem services requires that nature be conserved.

9

CAN WE OVERCOME THE OBSTACLES?

Man cannot discover new oceans unless he has the courage to lose sight of the shore.
—Andre Paul Guillaume Gide

Be the change you wish to see in the world.

—Gandhi

9.1 The obstacles

In this book, we have presented and discussed a course of action that can guide human society closer to ecological balance by learning and adopting how nature flourishes within the imposed biophysical and thermodynamic constraints. The plan calls for increased investment in education and knowledge creation, accounting that realizes the contributions of ecosystem services, a transition from nonrenewable to renewable energy sources, focus on development and quality over growth and quantity, and building community networks within sustainable places, to name a few major aspects. Implementation of this concrete plan has the potential to lead to win–win situations, but what can prevent the plan from being realized? Politicians have almost just to press a button to initiate the strategies presented herein. The proposed changes are based on the results of a global model, ecological footprint calculations, and calculations based on the sustainability of work energy. There are no physical, chemical, or biological barriers, but there are still many very difficult social and political obstacles to overcome. They are rooted in human nature, in political issues, and in the economic structure of our societies.

First of all, political thinking is completely dominated by short-term economic concerns. Our society focuses on money, consumption, and economic growth. Greed is one of the seven deadly sins, but in our society it is almost a virtue because great wealth is viewed as being successful. Gluttony is another of the seven deadly sins, and yet politicians and marketers bombard us with requests to consume ever more – to keep the wheels running, as they say. Again and again politicians and economists use the argument that we need economic growth to have more welfare, to create jobs, and to improve standards of living for everybody. They do not listen to natural scientists that tell us that resource consumption growth cannot continue indefinitely simply because it is against the very basic tenets of nature. As expressed by Kenneth Boulding (an economist): those who believe that economic growth can go on forever are either mad or they are economists. If you, however, question the economic growth philosophy, then politicians will answer that we are obliged to create jobs and therefore we need economic growth. Unfortunately, their conventional wisdom is based on wrong logic because economic growth as it is perceived by the politicians and economists does not, by definition, create new jobs but only more money and more consumption. The jobs are already there – there are millions of tasks that need to be completed by society. Moreover, efficiency increase in our resource use, qualitative development, stronger social cohesion and cooperation, education, and information can create many jobs without increasing resource consumption.

Economic growth during the last decades has only increased inequality, and we have still unemployment. So, something is not working in the economic system or its basic tenets. Why not try to increase the quality and equality and forget about growth? The Nordic countries are the most equal countries in the world, and they are among the richest. So, the experience has not proved that more economic growth delivers greater welfare, on the contrary. In a recent poll in Denmark (see Note 86), 55% of respondents answered that they had no need for increased consumption. Growth is something that is necessary to keep the economic system going, but it not necessarily creating better living conditions for everybody. The Czech economist Tomas Sedlacek, who was President Vaclav Havel's economic adviser (see Note 87), criticizes that we want to solve the economic crisis using the same approach that created the crisis: economic growth and consumption. Economist journalist Thomas Friedman asked: What if the crisis starting in 2008 is rooted in something much more fundamental than just a temporary recession? What if it is telling us that our growth model is wrong and that 2008 was a signal from Mother Nature that we hit the wall: No More (see Note 88)?

Societies are more interested in the economy than ever due to the economic crisis, but we ask the same economists that were responsible for the crisis to tell us how to cure it. Heterodox economists, such as Tomas Sedlacek, say that economists should have courage to tell us: forgive us economists because we do not know what we are doing. The economy is a complex, adaptive system operating under coupled positive and negative feedbacks. We need an understanding of the levers that drive the system dynamics. And while long-term predictions are not possible, we need action and decisions that set us up for long-term management of society, economy, and environment. Therefore, the best approach is to think beyond the scope of simply getting the economy growing again but rather finding an integrated system solution. As Dwight Eisenhower once said, "If you can't solve a problem, enlarge it." Integrated solutions would be based on using the three Rs, investment in education and research, pollution abatement, and greater cooperation among nations. The main obstacle is: how do we convince the people, politicians, and economists that this is the best course of action? We have to use and promote other approaches.

Another major obstacle is rooted in the lack of global considerations in the economy. A great, yet unfortunate, illustration of egoistic, nationally directed economic thinking is the recent round of climate change meetings (Conference of the Parties, better known as COP), where world leaders discussed ways to prevent catastrophic global warming. The wealthiest and largest carbon-emitting countries should take the leadership. But, a country that reduces its carbon dioxide emissions will have practically no short-term benefits for the country. This is a classic, common resource problem, the "tragedy of the commons" mentioned in Chapter 6. A proper solution requires that many (almost all) countries agree and actually reduce emissions: mutual coercion, mutually agreed upon. So, countries hesitate to lead, waiting for others to initiate action. The European Union has started to reduce emissions, but the reduction rate could be much higher. The spatial scale of the problem is global, and the lack of an effective global structure to make and enforce decisions prevents the solution of global problems. All nations are concerned with their inhabitants and are not prepared to invest in problems beyond their borders. At the 15th Conference of the Parties meeting in Copenhagen, the industrial countries agreed to make a fund to support climate change mitigation and adaptation in the developing countries, but until now very few industrial countries have fulfilled what they promised at the meeting. Greediness is indeed also found on the national level.

Similarly, the temporal scale inhibits the necessary actions. These global problems need long-term considerations, in which one could realize win–win solutions, yet they are sacrificed for short-term economic profit. We already mentioned the work of French economist Thomas Piketty's widely debated book, *Capital in the Twenty-First Century* (see Note 89). He claims a fundamental feature in society is that income inequality will increase over the long term given current economic approaches. His scenario is alarming: extreme concentration of wealth by a relatively small group of super-capitalists and super-managers, as well as the increasing inequality particularly in the United States, will inevitably create fierce conflict. At the center of his thesis is that the growing economic inequality during the past two decades is rooted in the growing ratio between capital and work income. A discussion about the inequality statistics is presented in more detail in Section 4.4. This increasing ratio between capital and work income will radically influence the efficiency and competiveness of industrialized countries because work effort is the backbone of modern society. Social cohesion is a prerequisite for an effective and fair-working society, and it requires a society without corruption and equal opportunities for everybody. According to Piketty, the best tools to abate inequality are considerably more investment in education, which is completely in line with our long-term action plan presented in Chapter 5, and the introduction of a global capital tax with simultaneous reduction of the work income tax. He criticizes the unproductive global transfer of money that takes place every day at a higher and higher rate and strongly recommends to introduce the so-called Tobin tax (a low tax on all money transfers) to reduce this transfer and the income on capital. Creative work is much more essential than the virtual transfer of money, which does not create development or progress. We need an economy that recognizes and differentially rewards work and that builds or maintains productive work energy gradients versus activities that exploitatively tap existing gradients. The current situation is that instead of you working for money, money is working for you, which is not creating a healthy and progressive society. Piketty's book has created a stir among the international chattering class; let us hope it also can bring about real changes in our unbalanced and biased societies.

Therefore, we must unfortunately concede that there are enormous obstacles to overcome if we want to implement our win–win plans. Because of the dominance of the economic elite and their failed strategies with very little concern about the real global problems, it is difficult to see how the plan we present can be realized. We probably cannot expect a leader-driven, top-down transformation but must hope for a groundswell, bottom-up approach (see also Chapter 6). Eventually, the people will require that action to address the real global problems should be the main focus, not economic growth and consumption, which only make the problem worse.

9.2 Economic models are often misleading

Mathematical models are widely used in the natural sciences and economics, but there is a significant difference between the applications of models in the two fields. Development of macroeconomic models – for instance, a national economic system – requires modeling human behavior, which is very difficult to express by mathematical equations because individual behaviors vary enormously. Therefore, the influence of human behavior is often covered by a black box approach, where different noncausal approaches are tested. The approaches (and the equations) that best match with data are chosen, but this is not a guarantee for its validity under all circumstances, particularly not for conditions that are outside the range of the conditions valid for the data provision. As the macroeconomic models are widely used to make predictions, they may often fail because the conditions – particularly of human behavior – can change rapidly, dramatically, and unexpectedly (see Note 90). The results of a macroeconomic model themselves may have a recursive effect on human behavior. For example, in 2007, most macroeconomic models predicted strong and steady economic growth, which made people optimistic, contributing to the bubble expansion. As consumption and prices increased more than expected, this added to the conditions for steep economic decline. It is important that we are more critical of economic models and require that they are transparent with a minimum use of black box approaches.

The most distinct example of how an economic model can fail is probably the so-called Black–Scholes model. In the 1970s, Black, Scholes, and Merton developed a model for trading options and other derivatives on the stock exchange. An option is a financial product where a share is bought or sold at a given price before or on a given date. Previously, the market for options was very limited because they were considered very uncertain and perceived as too risky, but the Black-Scholes model claimed to determine the price of an option relatively accurately. The model even eased the restriction on trading derivatives. Today, the trading of derivatives is enormous as a result of using the model. Donald MacKenzie (see Note 91) states that the model has not only influenced today's financial market but also created it. The model is one of the main factors behind the economic crisis that we have experienced from 2008–2013 (see Note 91). The model received the nickname "Black Hole equation" because the model has contributed significantly to the creation of the economic black hole that swallowed the savings of many people. There is no doubt that macroeconomic models have been oversold, which is very unfortunate considering economics so completely dominates society and the political arena.

In the natural sciences, good modelling practices ensure that models are calibrated and validated, but it is often difficult to provide the needed data for economic models. Our model in Chapter 5 is partially based on a calibration from data used for *The Limits to Growth* model. For example, several parameters, such as production, pollution, and population growth, were calibrated for the period 1971–1992. Furthermore, most equations motivating our action plan are based on causality. Of course, it is very important to emphasize that any simulation results *cannot* be considered as exact values and should only be considered approximations or as semi-quantitative results. Nothing is set in stone. Therefore, it is best to interpret the results as developmental directions. As our recommendations are based on understandable and largely causal equations, we have confidence that applying them will have positive outcomes. Simultaneously, we should carefully follow the development and be open to use any additional experience gained from global observations of the plan's implementation. The model should continuously be adjusted to new knowledge and experience.

9.3 Additional considerations

We are proposing a more sustainable society based on what we can learn from nature. The model results give clear, at least semi-quantitative, directions for change, which would lead to a win–win situation. But, is it a utopia? Is it a dream about a paradise on Earth, which is probably not possible? Is it a *fata morgana*? Will it ever be realized? It is always easy to make plans but to realize them is the most difficult part. Experience shows that it is very difficult for humans to cooperate on global plans due to the enormous cultural diversification. Just take the Kyoto Protocol to decrease greenhouse gas emissions as an example. The United States could have met the requirements easily at no or low cost but did not agree because of political failure. Russia had met the requirements before even signing (due to loss in manufacturing post-Soviet breakup and large forest credits), yet took years to negotiate better terms before finally joining. Globally, we have not yet realized that nature sets limits, which cannot be discussed.

In short, the problem is that mankind has so many possibilities and so much power that we can change nature radically. However, we cannot beat nature. Nature will always win in the long term, but our modifications can change (destroy) nature so radically that our own existence is threatened. The most critical period for humans will be within the next 100 years because if the core problems are not solved in this century, then the global population and consumption will inevitably increase beyond the resource limits. If, on the other hand, we manage to stabilize population at a level that would be at most 6 billion and we raise the education level considerably, then the probability for a sustainable future of *Homo sapiens* on the Earth will be much higher.

Unfortunately, there has been a tendency, particularly in the industrialized countries, to give natural sciences a far lower priority than was the case 50 years ago. Newspapers and TV are not very interested in the natural sciences because they are not "selling." Sports and pop music are much more important for them because they are marketable to a wider swath of consumers. Fewer in the young generation are studying natural science, at least in the industrialized countries, because the role models are soccer players, football players, and other entertainers, and so on. However, we need creative ideas by natural scientists and engineers to solve our many urgent problems.

Maybe a first important step to be taken toward global sustainability and bottom-up solutions would be greater dedication and responsibility in the media to showcase natural sciences addressing global problems. The information should be general but may also contain information of direct use in the discussion of global sustainability. The most important point is to motivate a general concern in and knowledge about global problems in the entire population. Furthermore, it is important that the role of natural sciences to address them is emphasized. In a democratic world, we all have to understand the consequences of future development, which is not feasible without a certain educational background. We all do not need to be specialists, but we all need to understand when a specialist is giving an important message in everyday language. Everyday life is full of scientific questions; it is just a matter of formulating them and raising the interest in people to understand why this and that are happening.

Great art and science reflect a deep understanding of fundamental values and worthy objects. There has, however, been an increasing tendency to give commercial activities higher and higher priority, which has had the consequence that the focus has been on commercial values and money, not on cultural and natural values. That has made most people more restless and unhappy because real happiness — when the most elementary needs of food, water, shelter, love, and so on are met — is rooted in culture and nature. Happiness means to live in harmony with people, nature, and the environment, to have skill and knowledge to understand nature, and to be able to appreciate and enjoy the beauty and the wonders of nature. It is therefore important that we support science and art, protect the environment, and resist increasing commercialism.

The start of this century has not brought us closer to an understanding of how fragile our life on Earth is and how many challenges await us in the future. We must nurture our cooperation with nature instead of fighting it and naively thinking that we can control it. Fanaticism and fundamentalism have made progress lately. A growing number maintain that all of what is written in holy books should be taken literally and no interpretation is possible, although we all know that humans have written the holy books and religion should be much more than just words in a book. How far we are from a scientific understanding? It is possible to see in the United States, which is a democratic country with a reasonable good educational system and a high level of investment in research. In spite of these facts, religious fundamentalists have been able to persuade more than 42 million Americans to believe that the Earth is only 7,000 years old! Incredible, but true.

Maybe there is no hope for the human population on the Earth. Maybe we are too shortsighted to understand and appreciate long-term effects and our responsibility to the coming generations. Maybe it is a hopeless task to ask 7–9 billion people to work together on the common goal to save the Earth. It cannot be excluded that the survival strategies we inherited from our ancestors living as hunter-gatherers in small tribes prevent us from thinking in larger spatial and temporal scales. However, evolution brings about changes necessary for survival under the prevailing conditions. Therefore, we can envision and hope for a bottom–up provocation that will precipitate structural development toward sustainable development in which humans are in harmony with themselves and nature. This vision would ensure that future generations can also enjoy the indispensable ecosystem services that nature offers us.

9.4 Flourishing within the limits to growth: a summary action plan

In Chapter 5, the results of a global model are examined to formulate a concrete action plan. Chapters 6–8 and the discussion in this chapter have added a few more details to the plan. In this last section, we integrate these details and ideas as the conclusive results of *The Report of the Club of Siena*.

Chapter 5 proposes a very concrete six-step action plan:

1. All industrialized countries with a gross national product (GNP) per capita greater than $20,000 per year pay 0.8% of GNP, increasing by 0.04% per year, as aid to the developing countries. The model shows that this is beneficial for both the industrialized and developing countries, provided it is a concerted effort.
2. Ten per cent of this support is applied for family planning.
3. Forty per cent of the support is used to improve education, including agricultural education, and with particular emphasis on the education of girls and women.

Under these first three actions, the GNP per year and per capita in the developing countries will increase, which will significantly reduce the birth rate in the developing countries. The reduction is estimated to be 4% per year, starting with a birth rate of 4.4 per 100 inhabitants per year, for every 1,000 dollars the GNP per capita is increased.

4. To sufficiently control pollution, 2.5% of the production value, or maybe more, must be allocated. This investment will have a positive effect on resource maintenance. We assume that pollution is proportional to the production value by a factor of 0.05. Or expressed differently, if the production value increases 100 units, then the pollution increases five units. The ecological footprint calculations in Chapter 7 indicate that it should seriously be considered to increase the investment in pollution control to 4%!

5. A resource-based, revenue-neutral Pigovian tax of 8% on average is implemented. This promotes efficiency and increased reuse and recycling. The effect snowballs because recycling technology is thereby presumed to increase. Pollution abatement has an annual increase, which is slightly dependent on the Pigovian tax.

6. A massive investment, 10% of GNP, is made in education, innovation, and research in the industrialized countries, which has a positive impact on the production and the application of the three Rs and thereby on natural resources maintenance. Innovation and research will inevitably create and realize many new ideas that could direct humanity toward qualitative development based on fewer resources. The UN Secretary-General has denoted education as the best investment any country can undertake. This sixth point in our action plan is maybe the most obvious step to take for politicians. Massive investment in education, innovation, and research will automatically lead to a win–win situation.

Chapter 7 adds three additional recommendations (which become recommendations numbers 7–9):

7. Do not increase overall agricultural area but increase the yield on the existing areas by a considerable, yet still realistic, increase in agricultural efficiency. This would require that the industrialized countries follow points 1 and 3. The support of education must include agricultural education. Chapter 8 strongly supports this conclusion, too, because loss of nature means loss of crucial ecological services. Lately, new possibilities for food supply have emerged through a number of creative uses of the sea, such as cultivation of algae and greater application of aquaculture. These gains can be garnered without increasing harmful pollution by applying necessary precautions.

8. Ensure that nature is kept intact. We recommend assessing the work energy of nature for well-defined focal areas, which must be maintained. When ecological functionality is compromised, management that encourages restoration and recovery along natural succession should be employed.

9. Shift from quantitative to qualitative production as much as possible because this will promote sustainable development and decrease our ecological footprint. The

ongoing development of the information society and a full-scale implementation of the three Rs will inevitably enhance this shift. This is a clear consequence of the action-plan points 4, 5, and 6. There are thousands of possibilities to promote quality of products and processes in society by considering efficiency, resource use, the three Rs in everyday life, and better communication of all improvements. There are numerous other possibilities to shift in the direction of qualitative production by considering reduction of waste. Just to mention two possibilities: 1) the technology exists to build zero energy houses and 2) the benefits of a major shift from meat to vegetables in our diet. Between 1980 and 2007, the energy and material costs of producing one dollar of consumable products decreased by one-third (see Note 92), and this development can easily be enhanced significantly. The reference in Note 92 encompasses several proposals.

Chapter 8 adds one more recommendation, which becomes recommendation number 10:

10. A (fast) shift to renewable energy is compulsory due to disastrous consequences of global warming resulting from the emission of greenhouse gases. The impacts of global warming are dependent on the rate of the shift, so following this recommendation will considerably reduce the impact. The shift will require a major investment, but all calculations show that it is even more expensive not to invest in renewable energy due to the costs of the deteriorated weather conditions. Moreover, in a few decades, renewable energy will likely be cheaper than nonrenewable energy due to technological developments. Investment in education, research, and innovation will reinforce this development. It would be particularly beneficial to phase out the use of coal, which is mainly used for electricity production. Coal emits the most carbon dioxide per joule of work energy that we gain and accounts for 44% of the total global carbon dioxide emissions. Sources claim (see Note 93) that our extensive consumption of coal kills 1 million people every year due to mining and air pollution. In spite of that, China has more than doubled its coal consumption from 2000 to 2011 to 3.4 billion tons. The United States is the second largest consumer, although the use is declining due to a major shift from coal to gas for electricity production. Gas typically emits considerably less carbon dioxide per kJ of work energy than coal.

Finally, the discussion in this chapter shows how the preoccupation with economic priorities interferes with a broader perspective on addressing global problems. This myopic and misplaced focus puts up barriers to the introduction of the 10 recommendations presented earlier. We present an appeal to the politicians and to the entire population to make a bottom-up effort to change:

11. Reprioritize policies toward other more encompassing goals than simply economic growth. *All* major decisions require environmental and social considerations in addition to an economic evaluation. The case study in Chapter 8

shows how a sustainability assessment using work energy and a carbon cycling model can inform ways to adjust the development toward a more environmentally friendly and sustainable direction. The quality of life defined as health, everyday happiness, secure employment, leisure time, stable living conditions, and strong networks of friends and family members can all be determined. The toolboxes for these urgently needed, additional evaluations are ready to be applied: sustainability analysis, environmental indicators (ecosystem services, biodiversity, and so on), GINI indicator for inequality, and various happiness and social indicators (inspired by Bhutan). The population should require all politicians to use these approaches in future planning and stop staring blindly at only economics and the biased GNP per capita.

Bhutan is sometimes perceived as a utopian country, rooted in Buddhist pacifism. There is, however, no doubt that we could learn from the culture in Bhutan. The people are making a concerted effort to prevent the invasion of Western-style consumer culture. Bhutan states that the concept of gross national happiness (GNH) is more important than gross national product. A survey has been launched to collect information from citizens on personal health, well-being, environmental quality, cultural preservation, and use of time. The survey is used to help craft national policies ensuring an increase in happiness and well-being of the citizens. A better world would emerge if this approach to focus more on people's happiness, high-quality life, and well-being rather than on growth of the economy would spread globally.

The inadequacy of GNP was very clearly expressed by Robert F. Kennedy in a 1968 speech at the University of Kansas:

> The gross national product does not allow for the health of our children, the quality of their education or the joy of their play. It does not include the beauty of our poetry or the strength of our marriages, the intelligence of our public debate or the integrity of public officials. It measures neither our wit nor our courage, neither our wisdom nor our learning, neither our compassion nor our devotion to our country, it measures everything, in short, except that which makes life worthwhile.

The problem is that economic thinking has decoupled nature from society such that nature is treated as a capital stock that is open for human exploitation. GNP is a good measure of our consumption of resources but is limited to this one dimension, which does not adequately capture the breadth of factors that contribute to human well-being. For decades, the American economist Herman Daly has criticized economists for their lack of understanding of the total dependency of the economy on the living ecosystems and the amount of natural resources on Earth. This dependence requires an analysis that includes an evaluation of the ecosystems and their available services and resources, which is not considered by the GNP per capita. Note 94 clearly shows that GNP is proportional to demand of resources and waste production, including CO_2 emissions.

12. Change the economic structure such that activities that promote community sustainability are rewarded. Rein in all the unserious gambling and the exorbitant profits on the financial markets. Reduce tax on work and increase tax on financial profits. These rules would be extremely easy to introduce if there would be political will. Understand in this context that equality and fairness regarding the allocation of benefits are important factors for achieving a stable and effective society. Moreover, equality promotes social mobility, which is beneficial for the entire society. It should be easy to make a crystal-clear conclusion: the business-as-usual approach of chasing perpetual economic growth is failing. It is not sustainable on our finite planet, and it is not solving the problems of unemployment, poverty, and inequality – in contrast to what economists and politicians claim.

Introducing these 12 recommendations would make societies fairer and more democratic, enabling pathways for flourishing within the limits to growth.

Follow these 12 Recommendations.

Appeals and Conclusions by
The Club of Siena. December 2014.

APPENDIX

STELLA icons

The model has been developed by use of the software STELLA. It uses the following symbols for the conceptual diagram:

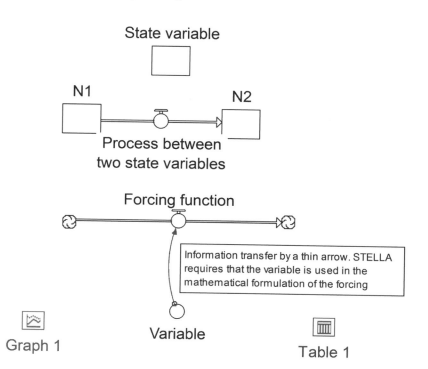

The symbols are applied to erect a conceptual diagram using STELLA. State variables describing the system are boxes for which differential equations are erected as accumulation = inputs − outputs. Notice that the differential equations are just bookkeepers of the state variables. Processes are thick arrows with the symbol of a valve. Forcing functions are thick arrows starting or ending as a cloud. Circles are auxiliary variables or parameters. Graph 1 and Table 1 indicate that the results can be presented as graphs or as tables.

Global model

Below, using the STELLA icons, we present the global system model presented in Chapter 5. The model, inspired by *Limits to Growth*, applies the six steps of the action plan. The model is kept intentionally simple and clear, with only seven state variables. The state variables and forcing functions are discussed in Chapter 5. In total, 12 recommendations are emphasized in Chapter 9. Six are included in the global model, and the remaining six are the results of Chapters 7–9. The global model equations are shown below.

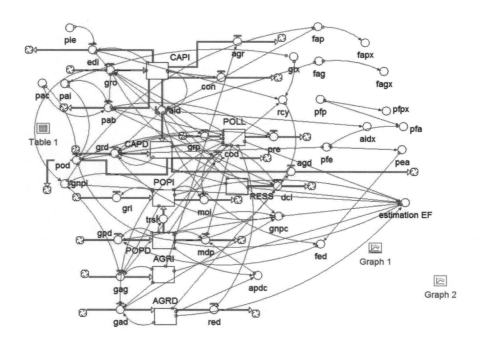

The model equations

Notice that the seven differential equations are formulated as:

Value time $t =$ equal to value at time $t - 1 +$ the input processes − the output processes. The equations for processes giving inputs and outputs are listed after the initial value of the state variable is shown.

All coefficients and parameters are listed at the end of the program.

AGRD(t) = AGRD(t - dt) + (gad - red) ⋆ dt

INIT AGRD = 100

INFLOWS:

gad = 0.03⋆AGRD⋆(1-((AGRD+AGRI)/700)-0.05⋆POLL/200)

OUTFLOWS:

red = (POLL+0.005)/100

AGRI(t) = AGRI(t - dt) + (gag) ⋆ dt

INIT AGRI = 100

INFLOWS:

gag = 0.003⋆(POPI-1300)+0.0001⋆AGRI-0.05⋆POLL/100

CAPD(t) = CAPD(t - dt) + (grd + aid - cod - pod - agd) ⋆ dt

INIT CAPD = 110

INFLOWS:

grd = CAPD⋆0.075+aid⋆(1+4⋆pfe)-(0.01⋆(POLL)+(((20000-RESS)^0.25) ⋆260-30⋆TIME))⋆0.0055

aid = (fap+fag⋆(TIME))⋆0.075⋆CAPI

OUTFLOWS:

cod = ((0.65+0.0001*TIME)*CAPD*0.075)*POPD/4700

pod = (pac+pai*TIME)*grd

agd = (AGRD-100)^0.1*0.075

CAPI(t) = CAPI(t - dt) + (gro - con - pab - agr - aid - edi) * dt

INIT CAPI = 340

INFLOWS:

gro = (edi*1.15+0.075*CAPI-((((20000-RESS)^0.25)*260+0.15*TIME)*0.0055+POLL*0.01))

OUTFLOWS:

con = (0.65-0.0002*(TIME))*0.075*CAPI

pab = (pac+pai*TIME)*gro*POLL/100

agr = (AGRI-100)*0.1*0.075

aid = (fap+fag*(TIME))*0.075*CAPI

edi = pie*0.075*CAPI

POLL(t) = POLL(t - dt) + (grp - pre) * dt

INIT POLL = 100

INFLOWS:

grp = (grd+gro)*0.05

OUTFLOWS:

pre = (pab+pod)

POPD(t) = POPD(t - dt) + (gpd - mdp - trs) $\star$ dt

INIT POPD = 4700

INFLOWS:

gpd = (0.044$\star$(1-gnpc/25)-0.00005$\star$TIME-(fed+0.0075$\star$(TIME-10)$\star$fed)/10)$\star$POPD

OUTFLOWS:

mdp = POPD$\star$((0.02-0.000001$\star$TIME)+0.00005$\star$POLL+0.000008/apdc)

trs = (0.0008+0.0000021$\star$TIME)$\star$POPD

POPI(t) = POPI(t - dt) + (gri + trs - moi) $\star$ dt

INIT POPI = 1300

INFLOWS:

gri = 0.017$\star$POPI

trs = (0.0008+0.0000021$\star$TIME)$\star$POPD

OUTFLOWS:

moi = 0.016$\star$POPI+POPI$\star$0.000005$\star$POLL

RESS(t) = RESS(t - dt) + (- dcl) $\star$ dt

INIT RESS = 20000

OUTFLOWS:

dcl = ((grd+gro)$\star$3-(pab+pod)$\star$15)/(1.33$\star$rcy)

aidx = aid$\star$100

apdc = (AGRD-20)/(POPD)

estimation_EF = IF(TIME<15)THEN(1.15+0.018*TIME) ELSE(1.42+(AGRD+AGRI-200)*5.65*0.5/2240+((POLL-100)/100+ (20000-RESS)/20000)*6.1/11.2+(POPD*gnpc+POPI*gnpi-45260)*0.8*6.1/(11.2*45260))

fag = 0.000055

fagx = fag*1000

fap = IF(gnpi>20) THEN 0.008 ELSE(0)

fapx = fap*1000

fed = aid*pea

gnpc = (grd+gad+aid)*1200/POPD

gnpi = (gro+gag)*1400/POPI

gtx = 8

pac = 0.025

pai = 0.00004*gtx

pea = 0.1+pfe*0.1

pfa = 1-pfe-pfp

pfe = 0.4

pfp = 0.1

pfpx = pfp*100

pie = 0.1

rcy = ((0.5+0.025*TIME)*gtx*0.3+(edi*1400/POPI))

NOTES

Note 1. The book *Enough is Enough* (Rob Dietz and Dan O'Neill, London: Earthscan, 2013) contains this information and gives several proposals (pp. 37–41) on the possibilities to increase the material and energy use efficiency in society.

Note 2. Drake (1992) proposed for intelligence-based organizations the following equation:

$$N = R\star \times f_p \times n_e \times f_l \times f_i \times f_c \times L$$

Here, N is the number of other intelligent civilizations in our galaxy; $R\star$ is a constant of the number of stars born each terrestrial year (20, of which only half would have the right size, therefore $R\star = 10$); f_p is the fraction of stars with planet systems (Drake estimated $f_p = 0.5$; theoretical calculations indicate more like 0.33, see Rasmussen, 2005); n_e is the fraction of planetary systems that could bear life on one planet, which means the temperature is right and the surface is solid or liquid (this excludes gas planets like Jupiter, Saturn, Uranus, and Neptune) – $n_e = 0.15$ according to Drake; f_l is the fraction of planets where life is possible and where life actually can be found ($f_l = 1.0$ where life is possible, it will always emerge); f_i is the fraction of planets where conditions to evolve intelligent life have been favorable for a sufficiently long time ($f_i = 0.1$ as estimated by Drake); f_c is the fraction of planets with intelligent life that can communicate with radio waves (estimated to be 0.5); and L is the time that a highly developed civilization is expected to survive. We can estimate $L = 1,000$ years, 10,000 years, or 100,000 years. For $L = 10,000$ years, we have:

$$N = 10 \times 0.33 \times 0.15 \times 1.0 \times 0.1 \times 0.5 \times 10,000 = 250$$

planets with intelligent life that could communicate with us. If L is reduced to 1,000 years, then $N = 25$. However, if intelligent life is inherently self-destructive, then perhaps $L = 1,000$ years may be too long? Should L rather be 200 years, indicating that we probably soon will destroy human life on the Earth by, for instance, a nuclear global war or lack of environmental concern?

Other factors could, however, be added to the Drake equation (see Jørgensen, 2008). For instance, it may be important that planets with long evolution time have a relatively heavy moon at the right distance to give tidewater that enhances the change of life forms between water and land and stabilizes the inclination of the rotation axis. To reflect this "moon factor," let us multiply Drake's equation by another factor, f_m. Among the three solar-system planets that have the right distance from the sun – Venus, Earth, and Mars – only Earth has a heavy moon. Let us therefore estimate that $f_m = 0.33$, reducing the Drake equation probability for intelligent life by one-third.

As another factor, consider that the Earth has experienced at least five major catastrophes that have all given evolution new directions to evolve toward intelligent life. If the planet had not endured a catastrophe 65 million years ago, giving mammals new possibilities, dinosaurs might still reign supreme. Let us introduce a factor f_k to account for the need for catastrophes to give evolution new chances; f_k could be as high as 0.5 because elsewhere in the universe are probably many possibilities for major catastrophes.

Random climatic changes provide a third factor that could modify Drake's equation. On Earth, the right climatic changes and simultaneous increases in oxygen were prerequisites for the Cambrian biodiversity explosion. Five million years ago, the climate became drier, and rainforests in many parts of Africa changed to savannas. Without these climate changes, anthropogenic apes would not have been forced to walk upright, and *Homo sapiens* would not perhaps have been an outcome. Also, in this case, the climate change coincided with readiness of the anthropogenic apes to undergo further evolution. Different changes in life conditions at other points in cosmic space-time could also lead to an evolution that is completely different from that on Earth. Let us denote this random factor as f_r and estimate that it may be as low as 0.1.

If we introduce the first three additional factors, $f_m = 0.33$, $f_k = 0.5$, and $f_r = 0.1$, we get for 1,000 years, 10,000 years, and 100,000 years of a technological civilization that the number of other civilizations in the galaxy would be $0.33 \times 0.5 \times 0.10 = 0.016$ times Drake's estimate, or respectively 0, 4, and 40 other advanced civilizations in the entire galaxy. Our galaxy has a diameter of 150,000 light years. If we presume there are two more technological civilizations in our galaxy and the distance is a reasonable one-third of the diameter, it becomes impossible to make any contact because the distance may be 50,000 light years.

As the number of galaxies is enormous – probably in the order of 10^{11} – there is of course a very high probability that there are a couple of planets with advanced civilizations in each galaxy, or let us say 2×10^{11} planets with technologically high civilizations. However, the distances are unfortunately so enormous that it will never be possible in the existence time of any life form to make any kind of communication with planets in other galaxies.

Drake, F. and Sobel, D., *Is Anyone Out There? The Scientific Search for Extraterrestrial Intelligence*. New York: Delacorte Press, 1992.

Jørgensen, S.E., *Evolutionary Essays. A Thermodynamic Interpretation of the Evolution*. Amsterdam: Elsevier, 2008.

Rasmussen, I.L., *The Solar System*. Copenhagen: Politikens Forlag, 2005.

Note 3. For further explanation, see S.E. Jorgensen and B.D. Fath, *Fundamentals of Ecological Modelling*, 4th edition. Amsterdam: Elsevier, 2011.

Note 4. Between 1980–1982, a few global warming models were developed, and they can still be found in the literature. The predictions about 30 years ahead based on business as usual have been confirmed with the concentration of carbon dioxide in the atmosphere and the recorded temperature increase the last 100 years of about 0.8°C.

A model developed by the first author of this book represents the type of models developed 30–35 years ago. The model can be seen in S.E. Jørgensen and B.D. Fath, *Fundamentals of Ecological Modelling*, 4th edition. Amsterdam: Elsevier, 2011, or in the original publications:

Jørgensen, S.E and H.F. Mejer, Modelling the Global Cycle of Carbon, Nitrogen and Phosphorus and their Influence on the Global Heat Balance. *Ecological Modelling*, 2: pp. 19–32 (1976).

Jørgensen, S.E and H.F. Mejer, Modelling the Global Heat Balance. *Ecological Modelling*, 2: pp. 273–277 (1977).

The model considers the main processes and factors that may influence the global heat balance. The scenario in Figure 2.1 is based on this model. Recently, models also consider climate changes region-by-region and how these regional changes influence each other and the entire weather systems.

Note 5. James Hoggan, *Climate Cover-Up, the Crusade to Deny Global Warming*. Vancouver: Greystone Books, 2009. It is an important and disturbing book about the lies and corrupt language that government and industry still employ to dismiss the facts about global warming. See especially Chapter 2 ("The Inconvenient Truth: Who says climate change is a scientific certainty?") for a discussion on how the oil industry has influenced scientists.

Note 6. The book *Thinking in Systems, A Primer* (Donella H. Meadows, ed. Diana Wright. London: Earthscan, 2009) illustrates clearly the advantages of using the systems approach to solve multidisciplinary and interdisciplinary global problems.

Note 7. Anders Wijkman and Johan Rockström, *Bankrupting Nature*. London: Earthscan, 2012.

Note 8. United Nations Development of Economics and Social Affairs, Divisions for Sustainable Development (UNDESA) 2012 published two reports: "Review of implementation of Agenda 21 and the Rio Principles: Synthesis" and "Back to our common Future: Sustainable Development in the 21st Century." These reports conclude that approximately only twenty out of one hundred statements from these international conferences have actually resulted in actions and corresponding changes.

Note 9. E. Neumayer discusses various definitions of sustainability and their implications in his book *Weak and Strong Sustainability*, 2nd edition. Cheltenham: Elgar, 2003.

Note 10. Heather M. Farley and Zachary A. Smith, *Sustainability – It Is Everything, Is It Nothing?* London: Routledge, 2014. The book reviews the concept of sustainability from many different angles.

Note 11. Further readings: A good overview of a modern ecosystem theory is provided in the following three books (the 14 proportions can be found in the two last books):

Jørgensen, S.E., *Integration of Ecosystem Theories: A Pattern*, 3rd edition. Dordrecht: Kluwer Academic, 2002. (First edition 1992, second edition 1997.)

Jørgensen, S.E., Fath, B., Bastianoni, S., Marques, M., Müller, F., Nielsen, S.N., Patten, B.C., Tiezzi, E. and Ulanowicz, R.E., *A New Ecology. Systems Perspectives*. Amsterdam: Elsevier, 2007.

Jørgensen, S.E., *Introduction to Systems Ecology*. Boca Raton: CRC, 2012 (Chinese edition 2013).

The application of modelling to understand ecosystems can be found in S.E. Jørgensen and B.D. Fath, *Introduction to Ecological Modelling*, 4th edition. Amsterdam: Elsevier, 2011.

Note 12. Chapter 4 in S.E. Jørgensen, *Introduction to Systems Ecology*. Boca Raton: CRC, 2012.

Note 13. Chapter 12 in S.E. Jørgensen, *Introduction to Systems Ecology*. Boca Raton: CRC, 2012 (Chinese edition 2013) gives a comprehensive presentation of network theory, which is very important in systems ecology. Software in various platforms is available online to perform ecological network analysis.

Network Environ Analysis: www.mathworks.at/matlabcentral/fileexchange/5261-nea-m; EcoNet: eco.engr.uga.edu/; enaR: cran.r-project.org/web/packages/enaR/index.html

Note 14. See Chapters 6 and 7 in S.E. Jørgensen, *Introduction to Systems Ecology*. Boca Raton: CRC, 2012 (Chinese edition 2013).

Note 15. For a theoretical presentation of the characteristics of properties of ecological hierarchies and the accompanying high diversity, see the following publications:

Jørgensen, S.E. and Nielsen, S.N., The Properties of the Ecological Hierarchy and Their Application as Ecological Indicators. *Ecological Indicators*, 28: pp. 48–53 (2012).

Straskraba, M., Jørgensen, S.E. and Patten, B.C., Ecosystems Emerging: 6. Differentiation. *Ecological Modelling*, 278: pp. 29–51 (2014).

Note 16. Boltzmann, L., *The Second Law of Thermodynamics* (Populare Schriften. Essay No.3 [Address to Imperial Academy of Science in 1886], 1905). Reprinted in English in *Theoretical Physics and Philosophical Problems, Selected Writings of L. Boltzmann*. Dordrecht: D. Riedel.

Note 17. Jørgensen, S.E., Ecosystem Services, Sustainability and Thermodynamic Indicators. *Ecological Complexity*, 7: pp. 311–313 (2010).

Note 18. World Watch Institute. 2008. The data and graph are discussed in T. Jackson, *Prosperity without Growth, Economics for a Finite Planet*. London: Earthscan, 2009, 2011.

The same issue is discussed detailed in M. Max-Neef, Economic Growth and Quality of Life: A Threshold Hypothesis. *Ecological Economics*, 15: pp. 115–118 (1995).

Note 19. The report Recycling Rates of Metals published by UNEP 2011 gives the statistics of recycling metals.

Note 20. See the discussion in Mason Inman, The True Cost of Fossil Fuels. *Scientific American*, pp. 40–43 (April 2013). The values in Table 4.1 and the definition of EROI are taken from this reference.

Note 21. *Transformation to Green Economy*. (Omstilling til grøn økonomi). Published by DIA, Danish Engineering Association, Summer 2013.

Note 22. Table 4.2 is based on the cost of producing electricity by various technologies, based on the experience gained by the Danish Energy Ministry (Energistyrelsen). The values were published in *Berlingske Tidende*, 2nd section, Berlingske Business, Friday, July 18, 2014.

Note 23. The information about the costs is presented in a special issue of *Scientific American* entitled "Energy's Future Beyond Carbon," September 2006, and in K. Zeibel, J. Mason and V. Fithenakis, A Solar Grand Plan. *Scientific American*, pp. 48–57 (January 2009).

Note 24. Peter Ward, *The Medea Hypothesis – Is Life on Earth Ultimately Self-Destructive?* Princeton: Princeton University Press, 2009. The book reviews the self-destructive property of life and is consistent with the discussion in Note 1.

Note 25. Climate Change. Species on the Move. *Nature*, 2 no. 9 (September 2012). This special issue of *Nature* includes the presentation of Opinion and Comments, Review Article, Letters, and Articles on the influence of climate changes on species' composition and emigration. The conclusion is that many species are expected to move to meet the challenges of climate changes.

Note 26. The book *Enough is Enough* (Rob Dietz and Dan O'Neill, London: Earthscan, 2013) contains this information (pp. 27–28), as well as a graph showing life satisfaction versus GNP per year and capita that is consistent with Figure 4.1. An income of $25,000 per year and per capita seems to be the income where adding more income fails to buy more happiness. It is the saturation income.

The gap in income in various countries and health index versus inequality are shown on pp. 89–90.

Note 27. Thomas Piketty, *Capital of the Twenty-First Century*. Cambridge: Belknap Press, 2014. The book contains a comprehensive analysis of the last two hundred years' economic development but has a particularly critical analysis of the present economic policy in the industrialized countries and the change in the ratio capital/work income. He gives statistics about the inequality in various countries and states that the current system in the United States will inevitably lead toward higher inequality. He uses an equation to describe the ratio capital to income: $R = s/g$, where s is the percentage of saving of the total national income and g is the growth rate in percentage of the total national income. He concludes, therefore, when g is decreasing, R will increase.

Note 28. The information about LHL, the sustainability principles applied, Figure 4.6, and the results in Table 4.3 can be found in:

Schweisfurth, K.L., Gottwald, F.T. and Dierkes, M., *Wege zu einer Nachhaltigen Agrar- und Ernährungskultur*. Munich: Schweifurth-Stiftung, 2002.

Vestergaard, B., *Sensitivitets Modellen* (master's thesis, Roskilde University Center, 2005).

Note 29. For further explanation and conceptual diagrams of nitrogen, carbon, and phosphorus cycling, see S.E. Jorgensen and B.D. Fath, *Fundamentals of Ecological Modelling*, 4th edition. Amsterdam: Elsevier, 2011.

Note 30. The weed control and the model in Figure 4.7 are presented in J.L. Hatfield and D.L. Karlen, *Sustainable Agriculture*. Boca Raton: Lewis, CRC, 1994.

Note 31. The value of ecosystem services has been estimated by Costanza et al., The Value of the World's Ecosystem Services and Natural Capital. *Nature*, 387: pp. 252–260 (1997).

Note 32. The global management problems of agriculture and how to solve these problems are the result of an in-integration of the following references:

Brown, L.R., *Full Planet, Empty Plates: The New Geopolitics of Food Scarcity*. New York: W.W. Norton, 2012.

Falkenmark, M. and Rockström. J., *Balancing Water for Humans and Nature: The New Approach in Ecohydrology*. London: Earthscan, 2004.

Breman, H., Groot, J.J.R. and van Keulen, H., Resource Limitation in Sahelian Agriculture. *Global Environment Change*, 11: pp. 59–68 (2001).

Pandey, R.K., Maraville, J.W. and Admou, A., Deficit Irrigation and Nitrogen Effects on Maize in Sahelian Environment. *Agricultural Water Management*, 46: pp. 1–13 (2000).

Note 33. Applying ecological indicators has shown that while integrated agriculture and organic farming may be sustainable, industrialized agriculture is not sustainable. The references showing these results are:

Jørgensen, S.E. and Nielsen, S.N., Application of Ecological Engineering Principles in Agriculture. *Ecological Engineering*, 7: pp. 373–381 (1996).

Jørgensen, S.E., *Eco-Exergy as Sustainability*. Southampton: WIT Press, 2006.

Note 34. Jonathan Foley, Five Steps to Meet the Global Food Demand. *National Geographic*, 5: pp. 22–47 (2014, May). The article underlines that the environmental problems of agricultural production require that we do not need to expand the agricultural land area but increase the efficiency. Today the agricultural area is 50.2 million km² (38.6%), while nature occupies 60.6 million km² (46.5%), and towns, roads, parks, gardens, mines, reservoirs, railways, and fallowed land correspond to 19.4 million km² (14.9%). This allocation should be maintained to avoid increasing environmental problems and reduction of the ecosystem services. The article proposes five steps to produce the increasing demand of agricultural products without increasing the environmental problems: 1) maintain the total agricultural area unchanged, 2) increase the yield of the existing agriculture, 3) utilize the resources more effectively – water and other resources, 4) shift from animal to vegetable dietary habits, and 5) reduce the waste of food in all production steps.

Note 35. The crude but useful model using the three factors: population, consumption, and technology as decisive for environmental impact was proposed by Ehrlich; see also P.R.

Ehrlich and P.H. Raven, Differentiation of Population. *Science*, 165: pp. 1228–1232 (1969). The model has been widely applied; see for instance S.E. Jørgensen, *Principles of Pollution Abatement*. Amsterdam: Elsevier, 2000. This book discusses how it is possible to compensate for the population and resource consumption increases by increasing technological efficiency of the use of the resources, denoted the eco-efficiency. Recirculation, reuse, and reduction will all increase the eco-efficiency.

Note 36. Current statistics published by the United Nations regarding the relationship between the GNP/ capita and population growth. S.E. Jørgensen, The Application of Global Models for Comparison of Different Strategies on Sustainable Living. *Ecological Economics*, 11 no. 1: pp. 1–8 (1994). These statistical results were applied in a global model, similar to the *Limits to Growth* model. This publication also examined the estimated effect of using 10% of the aid for family planning.

There are no statistics that can be used directly to set up an equation for the effect of investment in education and the population growth. However, UNESCO recently published a global monitoring report in 2013–2014 discussing the effect of the education level of women on the number of children in the African countries south of the Sahara. The results are mentioned in the text and were published in the Danish newspaper *Politiken* on April 9, 2014.

Note 37. The information in Table 5.1, see Foreign Aid for Development Assistance, www.globalissues.org/article/35http://www.bing.com/search?q=foreign+aid&form=MS NH60&mkt=da-dk&x=151&y=11.

Note 38. The average interest rate of money invested in production capacity is 7.5% in accordance with D. Begg, S. Fischer, and R. Dornbusch, *Economics*, 3rd edition. London: McGraw-Hill, 1991.

Note 39. The book *2052* (J. Randers, White River Junction: Chelsea Green, 2012) is a global forecast for the next 40 years. The content of the book was mentioned in Chapter 2.

Note 40. Moyo Dambisa is an adviser for the G20 countries. She is known from her controversial books *Dead Aid* (*New York Times* Bestseller, 2009, 188 pp.) and *Winner Take All* (*New York Times* Bestseller, 2013, 258 pp.). In a recent interview in *Financial Times*, Ms. Dambusa claimed that the advantages of a market economy, democracy, and globalization are oversold and that they have several questionable consequences, including that the politicians in democracies inevitably become too shortsighted because they want to be reelected. William Wallis, Lunch with FT: Moyo Dambisa, *Financial Times*, 30 January 2009.

Note 41. The data and a graph (income inequality versus index of health and social problems) are discussed in T. Jackson, *Prosperity without Growth, Economics for a Finite Planet*. London: Earthscan, 2009, 2011.

Joseph E. Stiglitz, who is professor at Columbia University and Nobel Laureate, notes that in 2007, one year before the explosion of the crisis, the first 0.1% of American families were gaining an income level 220 times larger than the average level of the 90% of the rest of the population. For further details, see J.E. Stiglitz, *The Price of Inequality: How Today's Divided Society Endangers Our Future*. New York: W.W. Norton, 2012.

Note 42. Joseph E. Stiglitz wrote recently in *Project Syndicate 2013* (29 October 2013) about the inequality, which is the result of neoliberalism and the strong market economy in the United States.

Note 43. Earlier work on win–win ecological relationships: Fiscus, D., Fath, B.D. and Goerner, S., A Tri-Modal Nature of Life Applied for Actualizing a Win-Win Human-Environmental Relation and Sustainability. *Emergence: Complexity & Organization*, 14 no. 3:

pp. 44–88 (2012); Fiscus, D., Life, Money, and the Deep Tangled Roots of Systemic Change for Sustainability. *World Futures*, 69 no. 7–8: pp. 555–571 (2013).

Note 44. Keller, E.A., and Botkin, D.B., *Essential Environmental Science*. Hoboken, NJ: Wiley, 2008.

Note 45. Examples of the sustained life perspective in:

Ecological network analysis: Patten, B.C., Environs: The Superniches of Ecosystems. *American Zoologist*, 21: pp. 845–852 (1981); Patten, B.C., Bosserman, R.W., Finn, J.T. and Cale, W.G., Propagation of Cause in Ecosystems. In B.C. Patten (ed.), *Systems Analysis and Simulation in Ecology*, Vol. 4, pp. 457–579. New York: Academic Press, 1976; Patten, B.C., Systems Ecology and Environmentalism: Getting the Science Right. Part I. Facets for a More Holistic Nature Book of Ecology. *Ecological Modelling*, 293: pp. 4–21 (2014); Ulanowicz, R.E., *A Third Window: Natural Life beyond Newton*. West Conshohocken, PA: Templeton Foundation Press, 2009; Fath, B.D. and Patten, B.C., Network Synergism: Emergence of Positive Relations in Ecological Systems. *Ecological Modelling*, 107: pp. 127–143 (1998); Fath, B.D., Jørgensen, S.E., Patten, B.C. and Straškraba, M., Ecosystem Growth and Development. *Biosystems*, 77: pp. 213–228 (2004); Fath, B.D., Sustainable Systems Promote Wholeness-Extending Transformations: The Contributions of Systems Thinking. *Ecological Modelling*, article in press (2014).

Systems sciences and systems ecology: Ulanowicz, R.E., Process Ecology: A Transactional Worldview. *Journal of Ecodynamics*, 1: pp. 103–114 (2006); Jørgensen, S.E., Fath, B.D., Bastianoni, S., Marques, J.C., Müller, F., Nielsen, S.N., Patten, B.C., Tiezzi, E. and Ulanowicz, R.E., *Systems Ecology: A New Perspective*. Amsterdam: Elsevier, 2007.

Energy network science: Goerner, S.J., *After the Clockwork Universe: The Emerging Science and Culture of Integral Society*. London: Floris Press, 1999; Goerner, S.J., Corrective Lenses: How the Laws of Energy Networks Improve Our Economic Vision. *World Futures*, 69 no. 7–8: pp. 402–449 (2013).

Relational systems theory: Kercel based on work of Rosen and Rosen's mentor Rashevsky. Rosen, R., A Relational Theory of Biological Systems. *Bulletin of Mathematical Biophysics*, 20: pp. 245–260 (1958); Rosen, R., *Life Itself: A Comprehensive Inquiry into the Nature, Origin, and Fabrication of Life*. New York: Columbia University Press, 1991; Kercel, S.W., *Endogeny and Impredicativity*, IEEE conference publication, 2003. Obtained from the author via electronic mail; Kercel, S.W., Entailment of Ambiguity. *Chemistry & Biodiversity*, 4 no. 10: pp. 2369–2385 (2007).

Note 46. Examples from environ theory: Patten, B.C., Environs: The Superniches of Ecosystems. *American Zoologist*, 21: pp. 845–852 (1981).

Dialectical thinking: Elbow, P., *Embracing Contraries: Explorations in Learning and Teaching*. New York: Oxford University Press, 1986.

Note 47. The full world and empty world aspects are presented in R. Goodland and H. Daly, Environmental Sustainability: Universal and Non-Negotiable. *Ecological Applications*, 6 no. 4: pp. 1002–1017 (1996).

Note 48. Watts, Alan, *Beat Zen, Square Zen, and Zen*. San Francisco: City Lights Books, 1959.

Note 49. Leopold, A., *A Sand County Almanac*. New York: Oxford University Press, 1949.

Note 50. van Breemen, N., Soils as Biotic Constructs Favouring Net Primary Productivity. *Geoderma*, 57: pp. 183–211 (1993).

Note 51. Jacobs, Jane, *The Nature of Economies*. New York: Vintage Books, 2000, p. 45.

Note 52. Ulanowicz, R.E., *A Third Window: Natural Life beyond Newton*. West Conshohocken, PA: Templeton Foundation Press, 2009.

Note 53. The example of forests in Nepal is in the framework of E. Ostrom, A General Framework for Analyzing Sustainability of Social-Ecological Systems. *Science*, 325 no. 5939: pp. 419–422 (2009), and applied to a particular case described by H. Nagendra, S. Pareeth, B. Sharma, C.M. Schweik and K.R. Adhikari, Forest Fragmentation and Regrowth in an Institutional Mosaic of Community, Government and Private Ownership in Nepal. *Landscape Ecology*, 23 no. 1: pp. 41–54 (2007).

Note 54. Mann, C.C., *1491: New Revelations of the Americas before Columbus*. New York: Knopf, 2005.

Note 55. Cunha, T.J.F., Madari, B.E., Canellas, L.P., Ribeiro, L.P., Benites, V.D.M. and Santos, G.D.A., Soil Organic Matter and Fertility of Anthropogenic Dark Earths (Terra Preta de Indio) in the Brazilian Amazon Basin. *Revista Brasileira de Ciência do Solo*, 33 no. 1: pp. 85–93 (2009).

Note 56. Bakshi, B.R. and Fiksel, J., The Quest for Sustainability: Challenges for Process Systems Engineering. *American Institute of Chemical Engineers (AIChE) Journal*, 49 no. 6: pp. 1350–1358 (2003).

Note 57. Ostrom, E., A General Framework for Analyzing Sustainability of Social-Ecological Systems. *Science*, 325 no. 5939: pp. 419–422 (2009).

Note 58. Arne Naess, developer of Deep Ecology: Drengson, A. and Devall, B., eds., *Ecology of Wisdom: Writings by Arne Naess*. Berkeley: Counterpoint, 2008.

Note 59. Patten, B.C., Bosserman, R.W., Finn, J.T. and Cale, W.G., Propagation of Cause in Ecosystems. In B.C. Patten (ed.), *Systems Analysis and Simulation in Ecology*, Vol. 4, pp. 457–579. New York: Academic Press, 1976; Higashi, M. and Patten, B.C., Dominance of Indirect Causality in Ecosystems. *American Naturalist*, 133: pp. 288–302 (1989).

Note 60. The data and a graph (income inequality versus index of health and social problems) are discussed in T. Jackson, *Prosperity without Growth, Economics for a Finite Planet*. London: Earthscan, 2009, 2011.

Stiglitz (Nobel Prize Laureate) notes that in 2007, one year before the explosion of the crisis, the first 0.1% of American families were gaining an income level 220 times larger than the average level of the 90% of the rest of the population. For further details, see J.E. Stiglitz, *The Price of Inequality. How Today's Divided Society Endangers Our Future*. New York: W.W. Norton, 2012.

Note 61. Pulselli, F.M., Bastianoni, S., Marchettini, N. and Tiezzi, E., *The Road to Sustainability*. Southampton: WIT Press, 2008.

The book is a result of a workshop on sustainability. The book discusses the criticism of GNP as an economic sustainability index and presents an alternative Index of Sustainable Economic Welfare (ISEW). The core chapters of the book discuss the use of thermodynamics and transdisciplinary approaches to determine sustainability.

Note 62. Ecological footprint as a minimum requirement for a sustainable development is discussed in the following two publications:

Bastianoni, S., Niccolucci, V., Neri, E., Cranston, G., Galli A. and Wackernagel, M., Sustainable Development: Ecological Footprint in Accounting. *Encyclopedia of Environmental Management*: pp. 2467–2481 (2013).

Galli, A., Wiedmann, T., Ercin, E., Knoblauch, D., Ewing, B., and Giljum, S. Integrating Ecological, Carbon, and Water Footprint into a "Footprint Family" of Indicators: Definition and Role in Tracking Human Pressure on the Planet. *Ecological Indicators*, 16: pp. 100–112 (2012).

Note 63. For the role of spatial distribution for ecological footprint, see the following paper:

Rees, W.E., Concept of Ecological Footprint. *Encyclopedia of Biodiversity*, 2: pp. 701–713 (2013).

Note 64. For details about footprint analysis, how the concept was introduced and the interpretation of the results of an analysis, see the following publications:

Rees, W.E., Ecological Footprints and Appropriated Carrying Capacity: What Urban Economics Leaves Out. *Environment and Urbanization*, 4: pp. 121–130 (1992).

Wackernagel, M. and Rees, W.E., *Our Ecological Footprint: Reducing Human Impact on the Earth*. Gabriola Island: New Society, 1996.

Wackernagel, M. and Galli, A., An Overview on Ecological Footprint and Sustainable Development: A Chat with Mathis Wackernagel. *International Journal of Ecodynamics*, 2 no. 1: pp. 1–9 (2007).

Note 65. See the details of the results in:

Haberl, H., Erb, K.H., Krausmann, F., Gaube, V., Bondeau, A., Plutzar, C., Gingrich, S., Lucht, W. and Fischer-Kowalski, M., Quantifying and Mapping the Human Appropriation of Net Primary Production in Earth's Terrestrial Ecosystems. *Proceedings of the National Academy of Sciences*, 104: pp. 12942–12947 (2007).

Meadows, D.H., Randers, J. and Meadows, D.L., *Limits to Growth – The 30-Year Update*. White River Junction: Chelsea Green, 2004.

Moore, D., Galli, A., Cranston, G.R. and Reed, A., Projecting Future Human Demand on the Earth's Regenerative Capacity. *Ecological Indicators*, 16: pp. 3–10 (2012).

Nelson, G.C., Bennett, E., Berhe, A.A., Cassman, K., DeFries, R., Dietz, T., Dobermann, A., Dobson, A., Janetos, A., Levy, M., Marco, D., Nakicenovic, N., O'Neill, B., Norgaard, R., Petschel-Held, G., Ojima, D., Pingali, P., Watson, R. and Zurek, M., Anthropogenic Drivers of Ecosystem Change: An Overview. *Ecology and Society*, 11 no. 2: p. 29 (2006).

Rockström, R., Steffen, W., Noone, K., Persson, A., Chapin, F.S., Lambin, E.F., Lenton, T.M., Scheffer, M., Folke, C., Schellnhuber, H.J., Nykvist, B., de Wit, C.A., Hughes, T., van der Leeuw, S., Rodhe, H., Sörlin, S., Snyder, P.K., Costanza, R., Svedin, U., Falkenmark, M., Karlberg, L., Corell, R.W., Fabry, V.J., Hansen, J., Walker, B., Liverman, D., Richardson, K., Crutzen, P. and Foley, J.A., A Safe Operating Space for Humanity. *Science*, 46: pp. 472–475 (2009).

Scheffer, M., Carpenter, S., Foley, J.A., Folke, C. and Walker, B., Catastrophic Shifts in Ecosystems. *Nature*, 413: pp. 591–596 (2001).

Stern, N., *The Economics of Climate Change: The Stern Review*. Cambridge: Cambridge University Press, 2006.

Note 66. The methods of calculation of the ecological footprint are presented in detail in the following four publications. The method presented by the first publication is shown in Note 67.

Borucke, M., Moore, D., Cranston, G., Gracey, K., Katsunori, I., Larson, J., Lazarus, E., Morales, J.C.M., Wackernagel, M. and Galli, A., Accounting for Demand and Supply of the Biosphere's Regenerative Capacity: The National Footprint Accounts' Underlying Methodology and Framework. *Ecological Indicators*, 24: pp. 518–533 (2013).

Galli, A., Kitzes, J., Wermer, P., Wackernagel, M., Niccolucci, V. and Tiezzi, E., An Exploration of the Mathematics behind the Ecological Footprint. *International Journal of Ecodynamics*, 2 no. 4: pp. 250–257 (2007).

Bastianoni, S., Niccolucci, V., Neri, E., Cranston, G., Galli, A. and Wackernagel, M., Sustainable Development: Ecological Footprint in Accounting. *Encyclopedia of Environmental Management*: pp. 2467–2481 (2013).

Monfreda, C., Wackernagel, M. and Deumling D., Establishing National Natural Capital Accounts based on Detailed Ecological Footprint and Biological Capacity Assessments. *Land Use Policy*, 21: pp. 231–246 (2004).

Note 67. Borucke, M., Moore, D., Cranston, G., Gracey, K., Katsunori, I., Larson, J., Lazarus, E., Morales, J.C.M., Wackernagel, M. and Galli, A., Accounting for Demand and Supply of the Biosphere's Regenerative Capacity: The National Footprint Accounts' Underlying Methodology and Framework. *Ecological Indicators*, 24: pp. 518–533 (2013).

For a given nation, the ecological footprint of any given product P (EF_P) is calculated as:

$$EF_P = \sum_i \frac{P_i}{Y_{N,i}} \times YF_{N,i} \times EQF_i = \sum_i \frac{P_i}{Y_{W,i}} \times EQF_i \qquad (1)$$

where:

P is the amount of each primary product i that is harvested (or carbon dioxide emitted) in the nation (in tonnes);

$Y_{N,i}$ is the annual national average yield for the production of commodity i (or its carbon uptake capacity in cases where P is CO_2) (in t ha_N^{-1} yr^{-1});

$YF_{N,i}$ is the country specific yield factor for the production of each product i (in t ha_N^{-1} yr^{-1}/ t ha_W^{-1} yr^{-1});

$Y_{W,i}$ is the average world yield for commodity i (in t ha_W^{-1} yr^{-1});

EQF_i is the equivalence factor for the land use type producing products i.

The definition of $YF_{N,i}$ as the ratio between $Y_{N,i}$ and $Y_{W,i}$ and leads to the equivalence of the second and third terms in Equation 1 (for further details, we recommend Galli et al., 2007 and Borucke et al., 2013).

The ecological footprint is calculated for each product separately and then everything is added up. However, the ecological footprint of a nation is also a function of the number of its inhabitants and their lifestyle (the ecological footprint of consumption, EF_C). In fact, for accuracy, a consumer-based approach is used in the evaluation of the ecological footprint of a nation. In practical terms, this means that consumption data are trade corrected, resulting that the ecological footprint of consumption for each land-use type is calculated as:

$$EF_C = EF_P + EF_I - EF_E \qquad (2)$$

In other words the ecological footprint of consumption (EF_C) is the sum of the ecological footprint of production (EF_P) and imports (EF_I) minus the ecological footprint of export (EF_E). For each traded product, EF_I and EF_E, is calculated as equation 1 where production P is the amount of product I imported or E exported, respectively (Borucke et al., 2013).

The biocapacity, on the other hand, represents the land available within a nation. The biocapacity represents the natural capital that provides the basic life-support services, expressed as the available regenerative capacity of the biosphere. The biocapacity represents the ability of the biosphere to produce crops, timber, and livestock as well as to absorb carbon dioxide. The total biocapacity of a nation (or planet) is calculated as the sum of the biocapacity supplied by each land type (Galli et al., 2007; Borucke et al., 2013):

$$BC = \sum_i A_{N,i} \times YF_{N,i} \times EQF_i \qquad (3)$$

where $A_{N,i}$ represents the bioproductive area expressed in nation-specific hectares that is available for the production of each product i at the national level; $YF_{N,i}$ and $EQF_{N,i}$ are the yield factor and the equivalence factor, respectively, used as in the equation of the ecological footprint to convert nation specific hectares to global hectares.

Note 68. For an interpretation of the ecological footprint calculations, see:

Borucke, M., Moore, D., Cranston, G., Gracey, K., Katsunori, I., Larson, J., Lazarus, E., Morales, J.C.M., Wackernagel, M. and Galli, A., Accounting for Demand and Supply of the Biosphere's Regenerative Capacity: The National Footprint Accounts' Underlying Methodology and Framework. *Ecological Indicators*, 24: pp. 518–533 (2013).

Niccolucci, V., Tiezzi, E., Pulselli, F.M. and Capineri, C., Biocapacity vs. Ecological Footprint of World Regions: A Geopolitical Interpretation. *Ecological Indicators*, 16: pp. 23–30 (2012).

Note 69. Daly, H.E., Toward Some Operational Principles of Sustainable Development. *Ecological Economics*, 2: pp. 1–6 (1990).

Note 70. See the following references:

Odum, H.T., Energy and Biogeochemical Cycles. In C. Rossi and E. Tiezzi (eds.), *Ecological Physical Chemistry*. Amsterdam: Elsevier Science, 1991.

Odum, H.T. and Odum, E.C. *A Prosperous Way Down: Principles and Policies*. Boulder: University Press of Colorado, 2001.

Bastianoni, S., Pulselli, R.M., Pulselli, F.M., Models of Withdrawing Renewable and Nonrenewable Resources based on Odum's Energy Systems theory and Daly's Quasi-sustainability Principle. *Ecological Modelling*, 220: pp. 1926–1930 (2009).

Note 71. Leipert's ideas about the environmental costs are presented in C. Leipert and F.M. Pulselli, The Origins of Research on Defensive Expenditures: A Dialogue with Christian Leipert. *International Journal of Design & Nature and Ecodynamics*, 3 no. 2: pp. 150–161 (2008).

Note 72. For details about the result of the investigation, see T. Patterson, V. Niccolucci and S. Bastianoni, Beyond "More Is Better": Ecological Footprint Accounting for Tourism and Consumption in Val di Merse, Italy. *Ecological Economics*, 62: pp. 747–756 (2007).

Pulselli, F.M., Bastianoni, S., Marchettini, N., and Tiezzi, E. *The Road to Sustainability*. Southampton: WIT Press, 2008.

Note 73. Calculations/estimations of ecological footprint of the scenarios in Chapter 5. EF is calculated in 2054 and 2100 with the starting point of 2008, where we use 1.5 planets. All increases from year 2008 are found by the model presented in Chapter 5. We calculate EF in number of planets, and 11.99 billion hectares correspond to one planet unit. In 2008, agriculture occupies $5.4/11.99 = 0.45$ planet units (see the numbers in Section 7.1). The agricultural production is calculated in the model in Chapter 5 with a start of 200 at year 2000, which has increased to 208 by the action plan in 2008. This means that the increase in EF due to growing production can be calculated in planet units as:

$$(\text{Agricultural production at year 2054 resp. } 2100 - 208)$$
$$\times 0.45 \times 0.5 / (208) \text{ planet units}$$

For the other scenarios, it is necessary to use the value for the agricultural production in year 2008.

It is, however, possible to increase agricultural production without occupying more land, as it was discussed in Section 4.10. A higher yield is possible through more effective use of irrigation. It is therefore presumed that it is possible to obtain just as much increased agricultural production from improved irrigation as by increased agricultural area. Therefore, multiplication by 0.5 has been introduced in the equation. In case 9, it has been presumed that it is even possible to reduce the impact from agriculture production increase to 10%. This would require a significant increase of the yield in the developing countries. It has recently been shown that the yield in Africa can be increased considerably by organic farming, which is beneficial for the developing countries because they can often not afford to buy sufficient fertilizers. Generally, the possibilities to obtain more agricultural yield by better irrigation, new innovative developments, and gen-technology are many.

In the estimation of EF development due to the increased pollution (relative level in year 2000 is 100) and the shrinking resources (resources in year 2000 is indicated as a relative number, 20,000), it is presumed that the area point 4 in Section 7.1 – 9.9 billion ha for growing timber and sequestering in trees the carbon dioxide produced by the use of fossil fuel is changed according (proportional) to the development of these two factors: pollution and loss of resources. The 9.9 billion ha correspond to 9.9/11.99 planets = 0.83 planets.

The contribution to the change of EF due to the pollution and the shrinking resources can be calculated according to the following equation for the six-point action plan:

$$\big((\text{pollution level at year 2054 or } 2100 - 106)/106 + (19920 - \text{ resources})/19920\big) \\ \times 0.83 \text{ planet units}$$

For the other scenarios, 107 and 19,840 will be replaced by the corresponding numbers for the scenarios – the pollution level and the resource level at year 2008. Scenario 15 calculates the EF contribution according to the equation but multiplies by 0.25 as a major part of the 0.83 planets in 2008 due to the use of fossil fuels and the fact that scenario 15 shows that 75% of the use of fossil fuel is replaced by renewable energy. The same factor – 0.25 – is used for year 2054 and year 2100 in Table 7.1.

The built-up land and the harvesting of fish and forest area, totaling 2.95 billion ha, is presumed to be increasing according to the growth of GNP. The higher the production as a result of the growing population and the growth of the GNP/capita, the more built-up area is needed, and the more area is needed for harvesting fish or producing fish by aquaculture, and the more nature is needed to provide ecosystem services. The 2.95 billion has corresponded to 2.95/11.99 = 0.25 planets. It has, however, been found that 20% of the production growth is due to qualitative growth, which means that a multiplication by 0.8 would be able to account for this shift from quantitative to qualitative growth. The global production value in billions of dollars in year 2008 is 46,154.

It implies that the following equation has been used to estimate EF for the production growth:

$$\big((\text{POPD} \times \text{gnpc} + \text{POPI} \times \text{gnpi} - 46154) \times 0.8 \times 0.25/46154\big) \text{ planet units}$$

POPD is the population in the developing countries in millions of inhabitants, and POPI is the number of inhabitants in the industrialized countries + the middle class population in the BRIC countries. The variables *gnpc* and *gnpi* are the gross national product per capita in the developing respectively industrialized countries. These four-time variables are based on the model results determined for year 2054 and year 2100.

Business as usual was applied using the same equations except without the multiplication by 0.8 for the production/consumption. Scenarios 10 and 11 have presumed a higher ratio qualitative to total growth, namely 0.5 and 0.75, respectively.

Notice that the six-point action plan is based on the use of an initial value in year 2000 for the aid to developing countries on 0.8%; a Pigovian tax of 8%; 2.5% used for pollution control; and 10% for education, research, and innovation. Estimations are made for other scenarios, and the conditions used for these scenarios are indicated in the text and in Table 7.1

Note 74. WWF. 2012. *Living Planet Report 2012*. Gland, Switzerland:WWF International.

Note 75. Neumayer, E., *Weak versus Strong Sustainability*, 2nd edition. Cheltenham: Edward Elgar, 2003.

Note 76. Lemons, J., Westra, L. and Goodland, R., *Ecological Sustainability and Integrity: Concepts and Approaches*. Dordrecht: Kluwer Academic, 1998.

Note 77. Klostermann, J.E.M. and Tukker, A., *Product Innovation and Eco-Efficiency*. Dordrecht: Kluwer Academic, 1998.

Note 78. Jørgensen, S.E., *Introduction to Systems Ecology*. Boca Raton: CRC, 2012 (Chinese edition 2013).

Note 79. The work energy for processes and materials needed for the sustainability analysis can be found in the literature. The following six publications cover almost completely the information needed. Note 80 illustrates typical information (work energy density for commonly used building materials) used for the analysis.

Baccini, P. and Brunner, P.H., *Metabolism of the Anthroposphere. Analysis, Evaluation, Design*. Cambridge: MIT Press, 2012.

Szargut, J., Morris, D.R. and Steward, F.R., *Exergy Analysis of Thermal, Chemical and Metallurgical Processes*. New York: Hemisphere, 1988.

Szargut, J., *Exergy Method. Technical and Ecological Applications*. Southampton: WIT Press, 2005.

Dincer, I. and Rosen, M.A., *Exergy*, 2nd edition. Amsterdam: Elsevier, 2007 (2nd edition 2013).

Kaysen, O. and Petersen, C. (Econet AS), *Vurdering af genanvendelsesmålsætninger iaffaldsdirektivet*. Miljøprojekt, Nr. 1328. Miljøministeriet, Publication number 1328 by the Danish Environmental Ministry. Miljøstyrelsen, 2010.

Note 80. The following references present the details of a sustainability analysis based on work energy:

Nielsen, S.N. and Jørgensen, S.E., *Evaluation of Local Sustainability. The Case Study of Samsø (DK) 2011*. Scientific and Technical Report, 2013.

A summary of this report and the development of a carbon model are available; see the webpage of Energy Academy Samsø (www.energiakademiet.dk).

For papers in international peer-reviewed scientific journals, see Note 81.

Note 81. Nielsen, S.N. and Jørgensen, S.E., A Sustainability Analysis of a Society Based on Exergy Studies, A Case Study of the Island of Samsø (Denmark). Submitted to *Cleaner Production*.

Jørgensen, S.E. and Nielsen, S.N., A Carbon Cycling Model Developed for the Renewable Energy Danish Island, Samsø. Submitted to *Ecological Modelling*.

Note 82. Marchi, M., Jørgensen, S.E., Pulselli, F.M., Marchettini, N. and Bastianoni, S., Modelling the Carbon Cycle of Siena Province (Tuscany, central Italy). *Ecological Modelling*, 225: pp. 40–60 (2012).

Note 83. Jørgensen, S.E., *Eco-Exergy as Sustainability*. Southampton:WIT Press, 2006.

Note 84. Multiplication factors account for the work energy of the information carried by different organisms: the factors are determined on basis of the genomes of the organisms. See Jørgensen, S.E., *Introduction to Systems Ecology*. Boca Raton: CRC, 2012 (Chinese edition 2013).

Table Multiplication Factors

Detritus, dead organic matter	1.00
Virus	1.01
Bacteria	8.5
Yeast	16
Algae	20
Amoeba	43
Spongy	61
Jellyfish	91
Worm	120
Leach	133
Insects (several species, ant, bee, wasp)	167
Squid	191
Most plants and trees	200–300
Butterfly	221
Crayfish	232
Mussel	310
Fish	499
Frog	688
Reptile	833
Bird	980
Mammal	2,127
Monkey	2,138
Chimpanzee	2,145
Human	2,173

Note 85. Susani, L., Pulselli, F.M., Jørgensen, S.E. and Bastianoni, S., Comparison between Technological and Ecological Exergy. *Ecological Modelling*, 193: pp. 447–456 (2006).

Jensen P.K.A., *When the Man became Human* (In Danish: *Da mennesket blev menneske*). Copenhagen: Gyldendal, 2004.

Note 86. The result of a poll about the consumption in Denmark was published in the Danish Newspaper *Berlingske Tidende* on April 6, 2014 in the Business Section of the newspaper. Some of the results are quoted below:

- 55% expressed no need for increased consumption, while 17% told that they did not have possibilities to increase the consumption
- 61% could not feel the economic crisis in 2008–2013, and 86% did not want to finance increased consumption through loans. Only 26% had the same opinion as the economists that more consumption would promote growth.

Note 87. Sedlacek, T., *Economics of Good and Evil*. Oxford: Oxford University Press, 2011.
Note 88. In the book *Enough is Enough* (Rob Dietz and Dan O'Neill, London: Earthscan, 2013), several analyses of the crisis are presented, all with a clear indication that growth

does not solve anything and has to stop to cease the continuous development in the wrong direction.

Note 89. Piketty, T., *Capital of the Twenty-First Century*. Cambridge: Belknap Press, 2014. The book contains a comprehensive analysis of the last two hundred years of economic development but has a particularly critical analysis of the present economic policy in the industrialized countries and the dominance of useless mathematical models in economics.

Note 90. Lucas, R.E., Econometric Policy Evaluation: A Critique. *Carnegie-Rochester Conference Series on Public Policy*, 1: pp. 19–46 (1976).

Note 91. The Black-Scholes Model. The enormous influence the equation has had is uncovered in D. MacKenzie, An Equation and Its Worlds: Bricolage, Exemplars, Disunity and Performativity in Financial Economics. *Social Studies of Science*, 33 no. 6: pp. 831–868 (2003).

It is claimed that the equation is the main factor of the economic crisis starting in 2008; see I. Stewart, The Mathematical Equations that Caused the Banks to Crash. *Observer*, February 11, 2012.

Note 92. The book *Enough is Enough* (Rob Dietz and Dan O'Neill, London: Earthscan, 2013) contains this information and gives several proposals (pp. 37–41) on the possibilities to increase efficiency of using materials and energy in society.

Note 93. Statistics about the global coal consumption can be found in:

Nijhuis, M., Coal. *National Geographic*, 4: pp. 66–91 (2014).

Note 94. *Bankrupting Nature* (Anders Wijkman and Johan Rockström (Note 7), London: Earthscan, 2012) shows how the demand for metals and the amount of waste increase in accordance with the GNP. The carbon dioxide emissions per dollar of production value has decreased from 1980 to 2008, but in the same period the total CO_2 emissions has increased 60% due to the corresponding higher GNP/capita.

SUBJECT INDEX

AUTHOR INDEX

INDEX OF THE MOST IMPORTANT TOPICS AND CONCEPTS

These core topics and concepts are used and discussed throughout the book. The text on the pages shown in this index provides the most detailed description of these topics and concepts.